Jon Silverman is BBC Radio's Home Affairs Correspondent. He has done extensive research on the issue of police drugs raids for a Fellowship of the Cambridge Institute of Criminology. He has contributed to the *Independent*, the *New Statesman*, the *Police Review* and the *British Journalism Review*. He also wrote and presented the documentary, 'The Yardies', on BBC2. *Crack of Doom* is his first book.

Crack of Doom

Jon Silverman

HEADLINE

First published in 1994
by HEADLINE BOOK PUBLISHING

First published in paperback in 1995
by HEADLINE BOOK PUBLISHING

10 9 8 7 6 5 4 3 2 1

ISBN 0 7472 4255 0

Typeset by
Avon Dataset Ltd., Bidford-on-Avon, B50 4JH

Printed and bound in Great Britain by
Cox & Wyman Ltd, Reading, Berks.

HEADLINE BOOK PUBLISHING
A division of Hodder Headline PLC
338 Euston Road
London NW1 3BH

To Alex and Daniel, without whom this book would have been written in half the time. And Jackie, without whom it would not have been written at all.

Contents

Acknowledgements

I owe thanks to a number of people on both sides of the Atlantic for helping my research for this book, but above all, to John Brennan, now of the South-East Regional Crime Squad, for sharing his unrivalled expertise on 'Yardie' crime and for allowing me to read his MA thesis on the subject.

Through John Brennan, I was introduced to the 'brotherhood' of Jamaican crime specialists in the United States, who have been most generous with their time and help – Walter Arsenault, Jimmy Killen, Billy Fredericks and Bob Powell in New York, Jim Harter in Florida – and especially, J.J. Watterson. I am also grateful to Bob Stutman, formerly of the DEA, and to the late Don Thompson, of the Metro Dade Police, for permission to make use of his account of an eventful night with a marine drugs patrol.

In Britain, many thanks are due to a small number of Customs and Immigration officers whose confidential information has been invaluable – again, I respect their anonymity. And at a higher level, I am indebted to the former Customs Chief Investigation Officer, Douglas Tweddle, his ACIO, Dick Browne, and Hughie Donagher, for their time and co-operation.

The list of police officers whose brains I picked would fill several pages and some would not thank me for naming them. There are three in particular who deserve a special mention – Chris Flint, first head of the Crack Intelligence Co-Ordinating Unit, Superintendent John Jones, who headed Operation Dalehouse, and Commander Roy Penrose, for opening doors for me.

It goes without saying that I am grateful to all those involved in Operation Howitzer, who re-lived the experience for me – above all, Yozzer Hughes.

The chapter on couriers could not have been written without the help of Olga Heaven, of Hibiscus. Thanks also to John Sussex.

Finally, thanks are due to my agent, John Pawsey, for his initiative, and my editor at Headline, Anna Powell, for her support. And to Glynn Jones and Phil Rees, from the BBC *Assignment* programme, who gave me the opportunity to make a 45-minute documentary in Jamaica and the US, which was not only a stimulating experience but also provided invaluable material for this book.

Chapter One

Ambush

In the visiting room at Long Lartin top-security jail, amidst the whorls of cigarette smoke which the antique air conditioning has failed to dispel, a lithe black man in a lime-green tee-shirt is talking animatedly. His close-shaved head bobs up and down as he makes a point. A tiny gold stud glints from his left ear. He is a bundle of concentrated energy, which has somehow withstood the torpor of two years of prison life. Even in this setting, it is not difficult to imagine this man jumping out of his Five Series BMW and talking tycoon numbers into a Vodafone. A man used to pulling in so much money every week that he really doesn't know what to do with it all.

As far as the prison system is concerned, Sam Lewis is PN 1679, a Category A inmate serving twelve years for attempted murder and five years for supply and possession of a Class A controlled drug. Under the rules which applied when he was sentenced, he will be eligible for consideration of parole on 12 November 1996. But Sam Lewis is not holding his breath. When you shoot a police officer through the heart, you don't expect any favours from the parole board.

Paul Hughes works in a set of modern office buildings between Vauxhall and Lambeth bridges on the south side of the Thames.

Even on the days when he feels fit enough to go in, he finds it hard to summon up a fraction of that enthusiasm which used to sustain him through shifts of ten, twelve or sixteen hours. He suffers from asthma and a range of allergies, and if he has to run for the tube, his breathing comes in staccato gasps for several minutes while he recovers from the exertion.

Paul Hughes is a detective constable, though he knows he could, and should, have been a sergeant by now. If fate, and a man called Sam Lewis, had not intervened, he probably would have been. Like Sam, Paul also wears an ear stud. And he carries a more permanent reminder of their relationship. Encased in the fatty tissue surrounding his kidney is a .32 bullet.

Paul Hughes and Sam Lewis have never spoken to each other. Indeed, they have met only twice – once, on a street in north-west London and the second time, in a court room at the Old Bailey. But their lives are inextricably linked by a drug which has come to symbolise crime and violence – crack cocaine.

The date is 14 March 1991. At 10 a.m., Paul Hughes is riding the lift to the fourteenth floor of Scotland Yard. It is one of two floors occupied by the Central Drugs Squad. The squad has six teams, with twelve officers in each. Under the direction of a capable Scot, Chief Superintendent Derek Todd, it is the police strike force against drug dealing.

Hughes is twenty-eight, a stocky, fair-haired man of medium height. He has nine years service with the Metropolitan police behind him. Two months earlier, he had been switched from C to A team and he is in a buoyant mood about the job. Drugs policing, despite the need for patient nurturing of informants, and the inevitable tide of paperwork, can be fast-moving at times. Paul Hughes is adept at living on his nerves and reacting swiftly. After eighteen months in the squad, he is acknowledged as a ferociously dedicated officer with a number of good 'collars' to his credit. In the office, as outside, he is known as Yozzer. The nickname has stuck with him since his boyhood in Liverpool. The Scouse inheritance has also left its mark in a passion for football. He plays three times a week for different teams, including a midfield role for the Territorial Support Group (TSG) in number three area of the Met. Number three area embraces a swathe of south-east London, including Dartford, where he lives.

The TSG emerged from the ashes of the Special Patrol Group, which was sacrificed to quell public anxiety about its over-zealous use of force during street disturbances. The TSG, too, cultivates an image of hardness – and in this macho company, Yozzer Hughes knows how to take care of himself. He is almost fanatical about fitness and, as if the thrice-weekly soccer is not enough, he swims and does weight training.

At noon, Yozzer is in a coffee bar near Highbury trying to tease some nuggets from an informant, but it is heavy going and he is quite grateful for the bleep which tells him that something has come up and he is to be back in the office by mid-afternoon for a briefing. He duly returns to the Yard at three o'clock. Yozzer's friend and partner, DC Jason Squibb, is already in the office. The two men are the same age, with the same length of service, but physically poles apart. Jason is the son of Spanish-Irish immigrants who had come to Deptford in south-east London to work in the docks. He is lean as a whip and habitually sports two days' stubble. With lank, jet-black hair flapping at his collar, he is able to pass convincingly as a southern European or even Middle-Eastern drugs dealer. He is a natural for undercover work.

The three o'clock summons is brief and businesslike. The team is wanted for a job later in the day in north-west London. They are to report to Kingsbury police station at six o'clock.

Time to catch up on some more paperwork before then. And sink a mug of tea or two.

17.00 hours. Kingsbury police station. The headquarters of number seven area of the Metropolitan police. It is in the Mall, in Kenton, a genteel-sounding address in a 1930s suburb, but that shouldn't fool anyone. In the 1990s, crime in number seven area is more Mad Max than Miss Marple. If, in 1991, you had asked people which area of London they thought produced the highest number of arrests related to crack cocaine, nine out of ten would have opted for Brixton or perhaps Stoke Newington. But with the estates of Camden and Brent within its boundaries, number seven area is actually way out ahead at the top of the league.

On this day, a big, very big, crack operation is being planned, and area HQ is filling up with bodies. For some time, Metropolitan police vans have been pulling into the car park and disgorging teams of officers. Dog handlers and their alsatians. The heavy mob who specialise in busting open fortified doors with their hydraulic jacks and thermic lances. The area Territorial Support Group. There is also a surveillance unit from Scotland Yard's SO11 Intelligence branch. Officers from the Central Drugs Squad and from the Crack Intelligence Co-ordinating Unit (known as the crack squad). Community relations is represented, in case the arrests provoke a racial backlash from local residents. And there are the uniformed lads from Harlesden, just down the road. It's quite a party.

Yozzer and Jason join in the usual joshing as old police acquaintances – including a few enemies and rivals – meet. But like most of the others, they can feel the undercurrent of nervous tension which precedes any major operation. Clearly, something heavy is going down – and they will feel a hell of a lot better when they have an idea what it is. With about a

4

hundred other officers, they squeeze into the largest briefing room available to hear The Word from the 'governors'. It must be a sensitive job because there are three bosses. The commander designated 'Gold', which means in overall strategic control, is Chief Superintendent Peter Hampson. But the deployment of forces is handled by Superintendent David Jarvis, who's in charge of the Harlesden sub-division, and by Detective Chief Inspector Roy Daisley, who heads the Crack Intelligence Unit at Scotland Yard.

Daisley, despite a receding hairline, looks younger than his forty-two years. He is ex-Flying Squad, a CID man to his fingertips who has graduated through some tough stamping grounds in East and Central London. In his time, he has done a lot of drugs policing. It is Daisley's specialist squad which has the intelligence on the chief target of the operation, and he takes the floor.

'Ladies and gentlemen, I know you are all anxious to hear why you've been gathered here, so let's get straight down to it. Welcome to Operation Howitzer. We're aiming to sweep up a crack-dealing network tonight. This man' – pointing to a large slide – 'is the main target, India One. His name is Sammy da Costa Lewis, and some of the local people here will undoubtedly know him already. He is only twenty-three but my squad rate him as one of the biggest crack suppliers in London.

'We've had him under surveillance for some time and our intelligence is that he is planning to leave the country pretty soon. Hence the need to take him out of circulation.

'He lives in Kilburn and he has dealers working for him all over north London but his manor is Stonebridge Park and the Church End estate. We are intending to pick him up at Church End. One of our team, working undercover, has established a business relationship with Lewis and he has arranged to buy a large amount of crack from him tonight.

'We will have "eyeballs" watching the spot where the buy is going down. When our man signals that India One has the crack on him, the arrest plan will be put into action. And I stress that we will not activate the arrest until we are satisfied that he is in possession of the crack. Assuming he comes to the wicket, the first priority is to take out Lewis and anyone with him. After that, there will be co-ordinated knocks on five separate addresses. We expect to recover a certain amount of cocaine, either in powder or rock form, from those addresses. But I emphasise that our overriding priority is to take Lewis out of circulation.

'Now, there is a lot more detail that you need to know but it makes more sense for your own governors to do the briefings. After that, there will be time to eat before we begin deploying. Any general questions before we split up?'

Daisley fields a volley of brief queries. It is pointed out that Church End has a high proportion of Afro-Caribbean tenants. Isn't there a danger of a riot if things go wrong? It is agreed that the 'wheels could come off' in a spectacular way if Lewis or any of the other targets are injured. The sensitivity of the operation has to be taken into account at all times. But in view of what is to happen later, the last question of all is the most pertinent. 'Just a quick one, guv. Is India One likely to be tooled up?'

Daisley replies that the best available intelligence says 'no'. The undercover man making the buy has dealt with Lewis twice over the last six days and he reports no evidence of a gun. That is reinforced by an informant who knows the dealer well. The word is that Lewis will not be carrying a weapon.

The dense throng in the hall splinters into small knots of officers. Jason Squibb and his mate, Paul Hughes, are part of a tight group gathered around Detective Inspector Denis Devereux of the Central Drugs Squad, their boss. He keeps his

6

briefing short: 'We have been tasked with arresting India One, lads. The reason being that none of our faces are known on this manor.

'The RVP (rendezvous point) is Taylors Lane, NW10. The buy will be outside, hopefully in the undercover man's car. As soon as the eyeballs (surveillance officers) are satisfied that Lewis has the stuff on him, we move in. Our man has placed an order for four ounces of crack. Obviously, it is a bloody large order, and Lewis may well have protection with him. Our job ends with the arrest. The crack squad will take over after that. There will be back-up if we need it. But we will have surprise on our side so we should get a result.'

They talk in detail about Lewis's modus operandi, then they study a street map of the estate and discuss timings. Devereux says they won't be away much before eight thirty, so they have the best part of ninety minutes to wait.

Most of the team trek upstairs to the canteen for a fry-up, but Yozzer and Jason prefer to get some fresh air. There is a McDonald's along the road and they wash down their Big Macs with a pint of lager in the pub. As they sit over their drinks, they reflect that it is going to be an unusual job. They feel like gatecrashers at someone's party. They have not been involved at any stage of the operation. They do not know the area. And most disturbing of all, they have no real idea who they are going up against and how much of a threat he represents. To say they are hardly in a comfortable position is the understatement of the month.

In 1991, Sammy Lewis might well be the richest black twenty-three-year-old in the whole of London. He is in the big time and things are going so well, he is looking to expand. Forget the old crap about boxing being the only route out of the ghetto. A brother who stands five feet eight and weighs no more than one hundred and forty pounds dripping wet, can still wrap himself in gold if he knows where to lay hands on a bag of cocaine powder. But success on the scale he craves depends on something more. There are plenty of wannabe coke stars and if Sammy is to keep ahead, he has to give himself an edge over his rivals. He calls it cryptically, a 'little trick I've learned from a guy in Trinidad'.

The trick is two-fold. He buys two kilos of cocaine hydrochloride every fortnight from a white guy, who gets it in twenty-five or fifty kilo consignments from God knows who, most probably someone whose real home is Bogota or Caracas and who can't resist the overpowering temptation to exploit the only collateral South America has, apart from coffee. Sammy pays his supplier slightly over the odds, £30,000 per kilo. He can afford to be generous because he 'steps on' or adulterates the powder with other substances so that each kilo stretches a long, long way. So far, in fact, that for every thirty grand he shells out, he gets back at least £65,000, more than doubling his investment. But unlike most of the competition, Sammy converts the powder into washed crack himself rather than selling it on as hydrochloride. He knows that it is crack which brings the heavy duty return and he supplies slabs of the magnolia-coloured rock, in two gramme parcels, to each of the three dealers who buy regularly from him.

Sammy is the first big wholesaler in London to sell crack in this fashion and he can offer his 'crew', as he calls them, a tempting deal. They buy a parcel for £175 and they can guarantee to double that amount when they sell it on to the street dealer. The crew are happy. They are each making £1500 a week, and the street sellers aren't complaining either. They recoup their stake from the punters, who will keep buying rocks, even if they are only 75 per cent pure, until there is nothing in their wallets but fluff – and then start stealing to get some more.

At the apex of the triangle, Sammy Lewis can't spend his income fast enough. When asked how much he is making, he calls for a pen and spends minutes scribbling on the table top trying to put a figure on it. Eventually, when you grow impatient and agree to settle for a rough estimate, he reckons that between £9,000 and £12,000 a week may not be too wide of the mark. 'And that's because I am selling good will as well as a product. I'm a one-man John Lewis. Never knowingly undersold!'

Sammy Lewis had grown rich not only through business acumen but by being careful. He knew the police had him marked down as a drug dealer. Indeed, in 1989 they thought they had him implicated in a deal with a Dutch heroin trafficker but he pulled his fingers from the fire before he got burned. The law did not relax its pressure though. Once, as he was walking along Church Road, a Territorial Support Group unit spotted him. 'One minute, it was nice and peaceful, the next I was surrounded by cops. They had my trousers down – but I was clean as a whistle. Didn't even have a fart to give them.'

But after that he began to take more care of his security arrangements. Police observation reports noted the two-storey flat where he converted the cocaine into rocks. The process was always carried out on the upper level so that if the front door was penetrated, the incriminating evidence could be flushed down the loo before the feet of the first intruder had reached the top step of the stairs.

Sammy also liked to play tricks with his police watchers. He would let one of his 'crew' drive his distinctive red BMW around during the day while he conducted his business at four o'clock in the morning. As the cops were chasing his tail, Sammy Lewis successfully panhandled for gold. Sammy also gave himself extra insurance cover by dealing with very few people other than those he trusted implicitly. Not for him the risky exposure of street dealing. He was a commodity broker attending to a few favourable clients with open-ended accounts. But no-one is impregnable, and like others before and since, Sammy Lewis was brought down by an informant.

When he was told by an intimate that Ricky was trying to contact him, his business brain began turning over numbers.

'Ricky used to live in London. He was an old mate of mine. Now, he had moved to Nottingham, and when he made contact, it seemed like good PR to talk. Nottingham is a strong crack market and even if the start was small, I was seeing big possibilities. I reckoned I could push half a kilo of crack a month his way eventually. I didn't know that the cops had got to Ricky, did I?'

Ricky also held out the tantalising prospect of tapping into the Birmingham market. He had a friend from Handsworth who wanted to deal with Sammy. Would he see him? His name was Andy Morris. Andy Morris is the assumed name of a black police undercover officer who was brought into Operation Howitzer only six days before its climax. On Friday, 8 March, the policeman – referred to at the trial as Officer X – was instructed to go to Tintagel House on the Embankment – headquarters of the crack squad. He was told to ask for Chief Inspector Roy Daisley.

Daisley motioned him to a chair and asked for his police notebook. On the first page was a set of guidelines headed 'Instructions to Undercover Officers'. Daisley read them aloud, asked whether he fully understood them and then told him that for the purposes of a special mission, he was to be given the identity of a drug dealer called Andrew Morris. He was told to sign his notebook under his new name. At 7.30 p.m. the same day, Andrew Morris reported to the high security Paddington Green police station where IRA suspects are held. Roy Daisley gave him £400 in £20 notes. It was bait to catch a big fish.

Ninety minutes after picking up the £400 from Roy Daisley, Andy Morris and Ricky are in Bishop's Way on the Church End estate. A young, slim black man holding a portable phone shouts over to them: 'Yoa.' It is Sammy Lewis.

Ricky makes the introduction. Sam and Andy shake hands. Before any conversation begins, the cellphone rings and Sam wanders away to take the call. At the same time, a car pulls up and two black guys get out and join Sam. The three of them and the unseen caller engage in a series of transactions which swallow up twenty minutes. Eventually, Sam saunters back to Andy and Ricky.

Andy: 'Can we go somewhere private?'

Sam: 'This will do. I live here. It's safe.'

Andy: 'OK. How much crack can you do me?'

Sam: 'As much as you want. If you want one-eighth, that's £160.'

Andy: 'Give me two of them.'

Sam then summons another man over and speaks briefly to him. The man disappears and Sam says: 'It will soon come.' After another spate of calls on the cellphone, he says abruptly: 'Come,' and walks off through the estate to a children's play area, where he sits down underneath the slides. The sound of soft footfalls on wood shavings signals the return of the gofer. He is carrying two magnolia-coloured slabs wrapped in clingfilm. Sam says: 'You got the money?' Andy replies: 'Of course,' and hands over £320. The bait has been taken.

In between more phone calls, Sam establishes that Andy is in the market for more crack, at least a few ounces a week, and they arrange to meet again on Monday, after Andy has returned from a 'business' trip to Cardiff. Andy begins to walk away and then remembers something.

Andy: 'How can I contact you?'

Sam: 'By Ricky.'

11

Andy: 'I don't want to use Ricky, it's costing me money. Give me your number.'

Sam: 'Give me your phone. I'll store my number for you.'

Andy walks away satisfied. Later, he recalls the number from the memory. It is 0831 210903.

On Monday, 11 March at 7.30 p.m., Andy Morris is again at Paddington Green police station, where he is given £450 in £20 notes. Once again, he heads for Bishops Way, NW10. Sammy Lewis is wearing a blue shell suit and carrying a money bag and a large bunch of keys.

Andy: 'Yoa, Sammy. Everything all right?'

Sam: 'Yeah, cool, man, you want more stuff?'

Andy: 'If you got some.'

Sam: 'I'm the main man on this estate for crack. If anybody wants crack round here, they come to me. How much do you want?'

Andy tells him two one-eighths and the same procedure is followed as before, with the crack being brought out in two film-wrapped slabs. Andy hands over £320. Sam is anxious this time to make the next deal.

Sam: 'How much crack can you shift in a week?'

Andy: 'I told you last time, about four or five ounces.'

Sam: 'Do you want me to give you a price for four ounces? I can do you an ounce for eighteen.'

Andy: 'Do me four for seven then. At those prices, four works out at £7200 but you can give me for seven at least.'

Sam: 'OK, that's cool.'

Andy leaves, promising to return later in the week, either Thursday or Friday. Sam tells him to ring, there will be no problem. It is just cool.

On Thursday, 14 March at 6 p.m., Andy Morris calls 0831 210903 and the phone is answered on the first ring.

Sam: 'Yeah, who is it?'

Andy: 'It's me, Andy. Is everything all right for later?'

Sam: 'No problem, ring me when you get here.'

Andy: 'I am only just leaving so it will be a couple of hours. But I'll tell you this. I'm not bringing that much money onto the estate.'

Sam: 'Don't worry. Just ring me when you get near and we will sort something out. No problem.'

20.30 hours. An unmarked transit van slides out of the car park of Kingsbury nick and edges into the A4140 traffic flow, heading in the direction of Harlesden. Inside, as well as the driver, are DI Denis Devereux, and four Detective Constables – Yozzer Hughes, Jason Squibb, Gordon Heyes and Dave Porter. Despite earlier misgivings, the adrenalin is starting to pump now and they are confident that within two hours, they will have this one sorted and be on their way home.

To Yozzer Hughes, a cocaine operation is nothing new. He has done many in his time on the drugs squad. 'You get the information, you get a warrant, and bang, you're through the door feet first. Danger, sure. But I can handle that if I know the odds.' Jason Squibb is acutely aware that it is his first crack raid. He may be a drugs cop but crack hasn't been around too long, and it has already got a reputation for inducing violent and unpredictable behaviour.

'Four ounces of crack is one hell of an amount. You can make four hundred and fifty rocks from that. So I am figuring it like this. If someone is selling, say, five rocks, they would probably risk losing it without too much of a fight – unless they are a nutter. But four hundred and fifty. That is worth protecting. A guy carrying that amount has got to be crazy if he hasn't got some insurance, maybe a knife.'

The conversation inside the transit van begins to dry up as

13

each cop carries on his own interior monologue. The man who has sent them on the mission, DCI Roy Daisley, is going through the same process. A few hundred yards from the Church End estate, he is ensconced in the control room of Harlesden police station. He tests the communications contact with his teams, and strives to make sure that nothing has been left to chance.

21.20 hours. Taylors Lane snakes into the heart of the Church End estate from Church Road, a wide dual carriageway. A series of three- and four-storey blocks, in poor repair, sit morosely behind strips of couch-grass. Even the trees look despondent. The transit van approaches, not from the illuminated main road but from the more secluded Bridge Lane. It skirts a deserted basketball court, its headlights picking out the cream pebble-dashing of the Willesden Progressive Club thirty yards ahead. At that point, the road curves round to the left and the van pulls slowly into the side, coasting just beyond the orange arc cast by a sodium lamp. The driver cuts the engine and douses his own lights. He gets out casually, shuts his door without locking it and saunters off in the direction of the main road. It's a dry night, with a crescent moon silvering up the cooling towers of Taylors Lane power station.

The van has two doors at the back, each with a window. There's a sliding door on the pavement side. The five men left inside are lying down just in case anyone peers in through the windows. They are wearing dark clothes and would be difficult to pick out from the shadows. With people walking by occasionally, it is not safe to talk. Whispers must suffice. The staccato communications traffic filtering from DI Devereux's radio earpiece is their only contact with the outside world. They have already decided which of the four DCs is going to make the arrest and who will be the back-up. Jason Squibb and his partner, Yozzer Hughes, are considerably younger than DCs Heyes and Porter. They also look more street-wise. It has been agreed with little discussion that the two younger men will seize Lewis.

This is the plan. Hughes and Squibb will walk towards their prey making a lot of noise, a drink-cocky pair of jack-the-lads, oblivious to anyone else around. It is an act they have used successfully before to still any suspicion that they might be the law. Heyes and Porter will be the back-up. Gordon Heyes, by far the oldest at forty-six, and looking even older, will slip into his usual routine. Wearing a flat cap, and with a practised arthritic limp, he is the harmless old boy shuffling home after a stout at the pub. At face value, he looks no more like a cop than the bemedalled amputee in *The Day of the Jackal* resembled an assassin.

Jason Squibb: 'Once you have sorted out how you are going to play it, all you can do is sit tight, waiting for the off. It seems like hours just lying there. You know you have got to be patient – but all the while, you're fighting down the excitement and fear which keep trying to take charge. And you are turning over all the options in your mind. If he goes for a knife, I will do this. If he tries to get help, I will do such and such. It is the great unknown you are up against. You are putting yourself on offer. And you just don't know how it is going to turn out.'

Yozzer Hughes: 'It's funny looking back at it. The adrenalin was going, yes. But I had no fear. I had done this sort of thing before – drugs raids, I mean – and I'd come through all right. In fact, in my entire police career, I'd only had one serious injury, apart from scrapes playing football. And that was when I arrested a gipsy for burglary. He butted me straight in the face. Broke my nose. It's still crooked.

'But don't get the impression that I was complacent. Whoever you are, there's always someone bigger and stronger. And, believe me, I wouldn't have tackled Lewis if I'd thought he was armed. I am not stupid.'

* * *

21.25 hours. A grey Daimler Jaguar saloon cruises slowly down Taylors Lane, passing the parked transit van. Out of sight, one of the plain clothes surveillance team watches as it turns right into Denbigh Close which runs parallel with Church Road. By her watch, another minute passes before the car reappears and swings lazily back into Taylors Lane before drawing to a halt on the left. The driver is Andy Morris. In the drugs world, image is everything. A brand-new, four-door Daimler Jag makes a strong enough statement of affluence. But if a more brazen display should be needed, then the crack squad will whistle up a Porsche, maybe even a Jensen.

As the Jag's engine cools, a woman heading for the public phone box near the corner with Church Road glances incuriously at the driver. She sees a black man, apparently in his early thirties, clean-shaven with short hair and wearing a dark jacket. If she could look into his mind, she would confront a level of nervous concentration entirely beyond her experience. A man living a lie in a world of crack dealers knows he is putting his life at risk. In the boot of the car is a carrier bag containing wads of used notes, held by elastic bands. In all, there is £7000. The next few moments will be the pivot of the whole operation.

21.36. Andy's Daimler Jag is parked in Taylors Lane between the public phone boxes and a small flight of steps leading into the estate. Andy calls 0831 210903 once more. Sam tells him to sit tight. For ten minutes, the undercover officer waits, tapping his signet ring against the dashboard sporadically to drain the tension. Then, in his wing mirror, he sees two black men on the opposite side of the road walking in the direction of the car. They glance casually at the Jag but say nothing and both sit down on a wooden bench on the corner of Taylors Lane and Holly Close. He recognises one as the man

who went off to fetch the crack the first time he met Sammy
Lewis. Suddenly, another black figure looms in front of the
windscreen without warning. It is Sammy. Andy operates the
nearside electric window.

Andy: 'Everything all right?'

Sam: 'Yeah, yeah.'

Andy: 'Have you got the stuff?'

Without replying, Sammy walks away from the car towards
Church Road. He stands for a few moments at the phone boxes,
looking around him, and then turns right, down a service road
which runs parallel with the dual carriageway. A minute or so
later, he is on his way back. The hiss of the Jag's electric window
is heard again.

Andy: 'What's the matter, man?'

Sam: 'Nothing, nothing.'

Andy: 'What are they doing here?', indicating the two men
sitting motionless on the bench opposite.

Sam: 'It's all right. They're with me.'

Andy: 'Well, I don't like it. I don't want any funny business.'

Sammy's response is to unzip his black leather jacket and
slide out a manila envelope. He rips off the top and produces
several slabs of magnolia-coloured rock, each measuring about
six inches by four. The biggest crack deal on a British street is
about to go down.

21.52. Inside the transit van, the four DCs are flexing their
legs to ward off cramp. They're beginning to wonder if
something has gone wrong when DI Devereux's earpiece
crackles with urgency. The 'eyeballs' can see everything that
is happening. India One is out in the open where they want
him. Devereux shouts two words: 'Go, go' and the side doors
of the van slide back.

17

Chapter Two

Firefight

Yozzer Hughes and Jason Squibb bounce out through the side doors of the transit van, the soles of their trainers recoiling from the tarmac. They have swallowed up eight yards of pavement before Porter and Heyes emerge from the back. Hughes is on the left-hand side of the road, Squibb on the right. The two younger men slip straight into their prepared routine.

Squibb bawls: 'I'm gonna bell Jimmy. The bugger must be back by now.' Hughes: 'Yeah. Tell him he owes me a twenty.' Hughes turns off down a short path leading into the estate. The phone boxes are diagonally opposite, on the other pavement. His partner heads for them. He pulls a phone card from his jacket pocket while his eyes freeze-frame the scene.

The difference between success and failure in a police operation can hinge on many things – an intelligence blunder in the planning, the wrong decision made on the ground, or the random whimsy of chance. In this case, the slow-motion tableau is hot-wired into life by something banal – a car coming down the road at speed.

Sammy is standing by the window of the Daimler Jag holding the crack.

Andy: 'How much is there?'

Sam: 'You asked for four ounces. Have you got the scales?'

Andy: 'It's all right. There looks enough there.'

Sam: 'Where's the money?'

Andy: 'It's in the boot. Hold on, I'll get it.'

Suddenly, they are both aware of a car flashing past them, trying to beat the lights onto the dual carriageway. Sammy is rattled and shouts out: 'Don't open the boot, don't open the boot.' He backs away from the Jag and sits down as casually as he can on the flight of steps, trying to recover his sang-froid.

Jason Squibb: 'I clock the Daimler Jag parked there and our man in the driver's seat, with the window down. On my right is a small flight of steps leading towards the flats. Sammy is sitting on the fifth step, with his left arm leaning against a wall about four feet high. By now, I am parallel with the steps and I can almost smell Sammy's leather jacket. He's got the statutory jogging bottoms on, a light colour I remember, and he's wearing black leather gloves. He's sitting quite still but I can see that his fists are on the alert. He's a skinny guy, pretty insignificant sitting down really.

'One of the guys who had been sitting on the bench opposite – a fairly light-skinned black man – has crossed the road and is standing doggo near the Jag, presumably acting as lookout.

'I'm thinking about the odds and they are fairly acceptable. But suddenly I become aware of the light in the stairwell behind Sammy. And there's a large shadow there. So, he has got someone watching his back too. Now there are three of them around the steps and just me. I knew I couldn't handle that so I had to do something to even it out.

'I've got the phone card in my hand and I start peering at it as though I've realised that it has already expired or something. And I shout out: "Fuck." They are all staring at me as though I am a raving loon. Then, instead of continuing towards the phone box, I head up the steps, past Sammy, towards the stairwell. There is only one thought in my mind now – to scare off the guy covering the rear. If it doesn't work, I am in serious doo-dah.'

Eight yards away, on the opposite pavement, Yozzer Hughes has retraced his steps and is stepping off the kerb. The plan is that he will approach the target head-on while Jason attacks from behind. To Hughes's right, much further down the road, Heyes and Porter are strolling into view.

Jason Squibb: 'When I had got to the top of the steps, past Sammy Lewis, I headed straight for the guy in the stairwell, keeping my head down at first. But at the last minute, we made eye contact and he must have decided it was all getting on top of him, because without a word, he just took off. Turned and disappeared into the stairwell.

'I spun round, facing Sammy and screamed "Police". Then I ran at him full tilt and flung myself on top of him. I grabbed him round the neck with my left arm and tried to lock his right arm with my right. But his leather jacket made it bloody difficult to get a grip on him. And though he was only the same build as me, he was wriggling like an eel. Fighting for his life.

'I am trained in judo. I represent the police at county level and I was going for a neck-hold to choke him out so that if he had a gun or knife he would not be able to use it. But his movements were too frenzied. And before I could stop him, he reached inside his waistband and pulled out a pistol.'

From the statement of DC Jason Squibb, given in evidence at the Old Bailey trial of Sammy da Costa Lewis: 'I struggled to pull the arm holding the gun down towards the ground. I was aware of DC Hughes immediately in front of us on the steps. Lewis broke my grip momentarily – he raised his arm up at DC Hughes and deliberately took aim at him. I heard the gun go off.'

Yozzer Hughes: 'I don't know whether I can describe what it is like. It was just one shot and the bullet hit me in the chest two inches above the left nipple. I thought he had got me with a stun gun because the breath was just punched out of me. You know that feeling you get when a football hits you in the nuts at top speed? You can't breathe and you think you are going to die. It was the same as that – except that in football, your breathing returns to normal after thirty or forty seconds. This just went on and on. Struggling desperately to breathe.

'I can remember hitting the ground and then trying to prop myself up against the brick wall. And then just a blur of faces above me.'

Jason: 'When Lewis fired, it was like a dream. It was so unexpected. All I could think was "you cheeky bastard, I can't believe you've done that." I saw Yozzer reel back and I knew he wasn't the sort of guy to bottle out so I realised he must have been badly hurt. But there was no time to think – I was fighting for my own life.'

From the statement of DC Jason Squibb: 'After the gunshot, almost immediately, I managed to throw both of us off the wall to the left. We landed on the ground a few feet below. We had turned over during the fall and I ended up on top of him with my left arm still around his throat. My right arm was holding his right. We wrestled violently and I felt him bring the gun across my body under my chin to the left side of my neck. I heard the gun go off about four times in quick succession.'

If any of the bullets had hit their target from that range, Jason Squibb's head would have been, quite literally, blown off. The bluish-yellow afterburn scorched his neck but fortunately for him, the Colt discharged its payload into the night air. As it was, the tumble over the brick wall had cracked two ribs and inflicted a welter of cuts and bruises to his arms and legs. And still he was struggling, with every last fibre of strength, to stay alive.

From the statement of DC Jason Squibb: 'We continued to

wrestle. I held him in a handlock and tried to hold the arm with the gun above my head. We flipped over. He was now lying on my chest, he broke my grip and brought the gun down hard, striking me on the right-hand side of my head. I was dazed and lost my grip on him. I felt him scrambling off me.'

With two of the four police officers down, it was time for the back-up pair, Dave Porter and Gordon Heyes, to move centre stage.

Gordon Heyes: 'When Yozzer was shot, I was about eight yards away, Dave Porter was just ahead of me. People ask you how you react to something like that. The answer is that there is no time for reaction. You are on automatic pilot. Dave and I broke into a run and we pounded full-tilt for Lewis. But we were still three or four yards from him, when he struggled free of Jason.

'He stood up, pointed the gun at us and fired – four or five shots in rapid succession. Rat-a-tat, like a machine gun magazine. There was no time to duck or do any belly-dancing. It was all too quick for that. We survived because Lewis, thank God, was not trained in the use of firearms. I am. And I have been instructed in what's called "shooting instinctively". The crucial thing is to bring the gun to eye level to get a fix on your target. If you don't, the slightest movement will make you miss. Lewis was pointing the gun at us – but he did not have it at eye level.

'The last shot was fired as he began to turn and run. He hared through the archway and across the grass. He was running for his life. We just kept on after him. God, I was angry. I was boiling with rage. There we were in the middle of bandit territory – remember, this was a mainly black estate and of course, the shooting had brought lots of people out of their flats to see what was happening – and I was screaming: "you black bastard" and other racist abuse. I could not control myself.

'Lewis got to the end of the grass and legged it into the little cul-de-sac at the back of the flats. Dave shouted to me: "He's dropped something," but we had no idea what it was. There was no time to search (it turned out to be the gun). I suppose we were twenty-five yards behind him when he got to the road and that was the point that he just disappeared.'

Jason Squibb: 'After Lewis had got away from me, I lay on the ground for some time, dazed. I was really in no shape to get moving again but it is funny how your mind works at a time like that. It is a sacrilege to lose your prisoner and that is all I could think of. So, I got up and started running after Heyes and Porter. I was running for the sake of running because I was really buzzing. But, to be truthful, I didn't know where the hell I was going.

'I know I had my personal radio with me and I was getting updates on what was happening. And then I heard that someone had been shot and the call for an ambulance. By this stage, I was three hundred yards from where Yozzer had been shot and I realised that there was no point in going forward so I retraced my steps.

'Yozzer was lying on the steps where I had fought with Lewis. He was propped up against the wall. We got his leather jacket off – it was his best jacket and I remember later that he was as sore as hell that it was ruined. He was wearing a grey tee-shirt underneath and there was only a small patch of blood showing through. But it was slap bang over his heart and you knew it was serious.

'He was moaning and he didn't say a word but I could tell from his expression that he recognised me. I remember turning him over to see if the bullet had exited. That probably didn't do him much good but it was a reflex action. By this time, a paramedic, Colin Chandler, had arrived but he could not do much except help comfort him. It was all pretty dreadful.'

And for the men in charge of the operation, it was nothing

short of a nightmare. The last thing they could have expected was a murderous attack on one of their own officers. DCI Roy Daisley was listening over the radio at Harlesden nick when the message 'Shots being fired' leapt from the static. Followed instantly by: 'Officer down officer down.'

'Then the worst words I have ever heard as a policeman: "Suspect has got away." That put twenty years on me, I can tell you. I was out of the door in a flash and heading for the scene. When I got there, it was pandemonium. Uniforms everywhere, blue lights flashing. Paul Hughes lying there bleeding, looking close to death – and no prisoners. I have never felt so stressed in my entire life.'

Sammy Lewis's nerve ends were also scraped raw. 'I felt as though I was losing control of the situation from the moment that Andy Morris arrived. I wanted to do the deal at the playground where we had done it before. The road was far too public. But he insisted on staying by the car.

'That made me nervous and I began to get suspicious – not that he was a cop but that he was working for another dealer and trying to rip me off. But what set the alarm ringing was when I showed him the envelope with the crack. He didn't want to weigh it. He was quite happy to hand over the cash. That ain't normal behaviour – especially because there was nowhere near four ounces there. It was more like two and a half. And yet he was still prepared to give me the seven thou. I was sure at this point that he was going to produce a gun and just grab the crack and run.

'As I sat down on the steps, Andy was just staring at me from the car – making me even more jumpy. I began to feel for my gun just in case. And then, I was attacked – from the side rather than behind. And as a matter of interest, there was no shout of "Stop, Police". That's utter bollocks.

'From then on, everything happened at double speed. I was so scared, I wasn't even aware of my finger squeezing the trigger. And I didn't know that Hughes had been shot until I was arrested. As I was fighting with Squibb, all I could think of was: "I've got to get the fuck out of here."

'Once I had struggled free, I just legged it as fast as I could. I knew that bordering the service road at the back of the flats was a wall leading to the railway line. That's where I was heading. And if it hadn't been for some bad luck, I might have made it. I was running so fast that my shoe skidded on the road and I slipped over. That cost me a couple of precious seconds – after that, it was just survival time.'

Gaining ground on him fast were DCs Porter and Heyes. *Gordon Heyes*: 'We were certain that Lewis could not have got away because the road was a cul-de-sac and ahead of him was a fence, maybe eight feet high. It didn't seem possible for him to have climbed that in the time it took us to reach the corner. So we decided he must have gone to ground.

'Our problem was that we were out of communication with anyone. We didn't have our radios and it would not have been safe for one of us to have gone for help leaving the other with no back-up. So we stayed together and began searching the road.

'There were four black guys standing around a BMW and we asked if they had seen anyone running. They must have seen him but, of course, they sure as hell were not going to tell us. There were a number of cars and vans parked there and I got out my pocket torch and began flashing it on the doors and trying them to see if any were unlocked. They weren't.

'Dave Porter looked under the white van and saw nothing. We searched the area as well as we could considering it was badly lit. But there was nothing to see.'

On the contrary, however, there was. The white transit van

was Sammy Lewis's last desperate throw. He was clinging to the prop shaft, with every ounce of his strength, and holding his breath.

'The first thing that alerted me to the cops coming was the sound of their radios. Then I could see their legs walking around. I couldn't believe it when they both looked under the van and didn't see me. I thought: "Fucking hell, Christmas has come, I must be invisible." I really thought I was going to get away.'

Gordon Heyes: 'By this time, about ten minutes had gone by. We were still convinced he was around somewhere when one of the surveillance cars turned up. We told the driver to get help quickly so that we could make a thorough search and he began doing a three-point turn. As he did so, the headlights were full on the transit van for a few seconds and the driver suddenly put his brakes on and motioned us over. "I think there is someone under there," he whispered.

'Dave and I walked casually over to the van. I went to the back, bent down and saw a pair of feet. I just yanked at them as hard as I could and dragged him out into the open. And then it became clear why we hadn't spotted him with the torch. He was covered in oil from head to foot. He had been clinging to the prop shaft of the van the whole time we had been there, until, finally, his strength gave out and he had fallen to the ground.

'The effort had knocked all the life out of him and he offered no resistance. He just said: "Don't hit me, don't hit me." I admit I was terribly angry, and I did shout racial abuse at him but I was too long in the tooth to rough him up. We hauled him to his feet, handcuffed him and then searched him in case he was carrying another gun or a knife. He wasn't – nor did he have any crack on him, so we reckoned he must have chucked that as he was running (it was recovered later).

Sammy Lewis: 'When they yanked me out of the van, I played sick because I thought they were going to beat the hell out of me. I clutched my stomach and pretended I had terrible pains. The truth is that physically I was all right, mentally I was in a shambles. I just kept thinking. "Christ, I am in deep shit." '

His captors started to lead him back to the scene of the shooting but by now, the cavalry had arrived. Uniformed officers took over and relieved Heyes and Porter of their prisoner to avoid any cross-contamination.

Gordon Heyes: 'I can tell you, I felt great, over the moon. We'd got him. And Roy Daisley was just cock-a-hoop. He looked absolutely shattered when he got to Taylors Lane. The wheels had come off in a spectacular way and we'd saved the day.'

Roy Daisley: 'The ten or fifteen minutes after I arrived at the scene were the longest of my life. And when I saw the guys coming back with Lewis in handcuffs – well, the relief was indescribable.'

But for Yozzer Hughes, the nightmare was only just beginning.

Yozzer: 'I can remember them trying to bung up the hole in my chest with handkerchiefs and seeing my sweat shirt covered in blood. But I did not feel any pain. It was a complete void – like being wrapped in cotton wool.'

Jason: 'The ambulance seemed to take ages to come. Everything was chaotic while we waited. There were uniforms everywhere, sirens going, radio traffic – absolute bedlam. And finally, thank God, the ambulance showed up.'

They carried Yozzer inside, and clamped an oxygen mask over his face. Jason got in beside him and held his hand, murmuring over and over again like an incantation 'You'll be all right, you'll be all right.' As they sped along the North Circular towards the North Middlesex hospital in Edmonton, Jason recalls an ambulanceman tapping Yozzer on the shoulder and asking: 'Does it hurt?' Yozzer motioned for the mask to be removed and said: 'You are having a fucking laugh, aren't you?'

The North Middlesex is a well-equipped suburban hospital but it took the medical staff no more than a few minutes to decide that the patient would surely die if he did not receive specialist attention immediately.

Jason: 'By the time we got there, Yozzer's face was yellow. The nurses kept saying: "You'll be OK, the bullet has not hit any vital organs." But that was just to keep his spirits up. I don't think they gave him much of a chance.'

In fact, the bullet could not have done any more damage without killing Yozzer outright. Sammy had fired from the steps above him and the angle of the shot determined the nature of the injury. The entry point was the right chamber of the heart but the velocity of the impact caused the lump of lead to behave like a pinball, ricocheting off his ribs, and splintering bone and nerves on its demented progress. It chopped off a piece of liver and finally came to rest against the right kidney. In the antiseptic under-statement of medical bulletins, it was a 'life-threatening' injury.

It is more than likely that if Paul Hughes had been shot anywhere else in the country – even in another area of London – he would not have survived. But the world-famous Harefield heart hospital is in Uxbridge, and in the early, traffic-free hours of the morning, the journey can be made from the North Middlesex in under half an hour.

Yozzer: 'I was still fully conscious when they put me in another ambulance to take me to Harefield. I could feel the blood gurgling around my stomach and that was the first time that I seriously thought I was going to die. I can recall them rushing me into the theatre and a nurse clutching my hand saying: "keep going, keep going". And then I was out cold for a day and a half.'

Yozzer Hughes was given no more than a 15 to 20 per cent chance of survival when he arrived at Harefield. The surgeon who examined him was a member of Dr Magdi Yacoub's team. He had no certainty that the battered heart and internal organs would be able to withstand the rigours of such a major operation. But Hughes was a sportsman and superbly fit and they gambled that his constitution would be robust enough to see him through. *Yozzer*: 'They had to cut me open from neck to waist and break the sternum (the breast bone) in half to be able to repair the entry and exit wounds in my heart. Then they turned me over, cut me open down the back and patched up the wounds in my lungs. They decided that they might cause irreparable damage to my kidney if they tried to remove the bullet so they left it where it was.

'The operation lasted for hours and I needed twenty-six pints of blood. They tell me that that is very nearly a record for a transfusion at Harefield.'

On Sunday morning, after forty-eight hours, Hughes came round briefly but was on such heavy shots of morphine that he was only hovering on the frontiers of reality. He had five tubes draining the blood out of his system, two drips pumping in drugs and was connected to a respirator. An electrocardiogram tracked every palpitation of the heart muscles.

He was in a private room under an assumed name, with an armed guard sitting outside. Ostensibly, that was to protect him against any attempt by Sammy Lewis's associates to finish the job. But it was also an effective means of shielding him from the intrusive attentions of journalists whose appetites had been whetted by the story.

Paul's mother Dawn sat with him for three days and nights, holding his hand and willing him to survive. 'She was never in any doubt that I would pull through – a mother's instinct, I reckon.' Finally, on the Wednesday, the doctors agreed with her, and Yozzer was moved out of intensive care.

Over the next fortnight, they took the tubes and the catheter out – 'God, the agony – like pulling chunks of glass out of you' – and, with little more than willpower, he attempted to fight the waves of pain which accompanied the reduction in morphine injections. He also had to come to terms with the growing realisation that the body which he had fashioned into a temple of fitness had been struck by a hurricane.

'I had pins stapled down my chest where they had clamped the sternum together. And every time I turned over, I could hear them clicking. I would be hit by terrible shooting pains in different parts of my body or my arm would suddenly go dead with no warning because the bullet had struck so many major nerves. This included the main nerve which controls your diaphragm, so for nine months afterwards, when I breathed, only half of my diaphragm responded. As a result, I was breathless all the time.'

The multiple blood transfusions also caused problems. 'They said: "The good news is that you are not HIV positive. The bad news is that the fresh blood has left you with a host of allergies, including asthma." ' Indeed, that has proved to be a permanent legacy. 'But let's face it, I am a bloody medical miracle. No-one who gets shot in the heart has a right to survive, so how can I complain?'

At 22.20 on the night of Friday, 14 March, while the fate of Yozzer Hughes still hung in the balance, there was a policing job to complete. The arrest of Sammy Lewis was the signal for co-ordinated raids on five addresses in Harlesden and Kilburn, which had been under surveillance for several weeks. Sixty police officers, some wearing flame-proof overalls and carrying sledgehammers, battered down doors and handcuffed thirteen people – seven men and six women. The raids yielded one and a half kilos of cocaine powder, which would have earned Sammy Lewis more than half a million pounds when converted into crack.

The blood was still warm on the roadway in Taylors Lane when his chief lieutenant – a man called Martin Greenidge – was picked up in a flat just a hundred yards away from the shooting. There was some cocaine and pounds of baking powder in the flat. At a house in Woodcock Hill, Kenton, on which Greenidge paid the mortgage, the police found a record 678 grammes of crack, as well as forty-three rounds of ammunition of the type used by Sammy Lewis in his .32 Colt. Greenidge's girlfriend, who lived in a comfortable detached house in Wembley Park was also amongst those arrested that night. Unlike the earlier part of the operation, the co-ordinated 'knocks' went entirely to plan.

In Taylors Lane, a local superintendent had arrived to take charge of the scene of crime investigation. Working under 'dragon' lights, the SOCO team found the spent cartridges from Lewis's gun and the .45 which his minder had dropped in his headlong escape. Jason Squibb was especially thankful that he had: 'Thank God, the guy legged it. If he had kept his nerve, he could have killed me and the rest of the lads with that.' (The minder was never caught.)

Meanwhile, the members of the Lewis arrest team were taken to Harlesden police station.

Gordon Heyes: 'I needed to calm myself down. I had a cup of coffee, then I rang my wife to say I was all right because I knew the shooting might have been on the news by then. And while the sequence of events was still fresh in my mind, I tried to make a note of the order in which things had happened. I know from bitter experience that the battle is not over with the arrest. If the evidence does not stand up, you might as well not have bothered.'

It was a long and dismal night. Some time around four thirty in the morning, the head of the Central Drugs Squad, Chief Superintendent Derek Todd, booked the team into a hotel and they were finally able to get a few hours' sleep.

Gordon Heyes: 'I was up by about seven. I knocked Jason up because we had had the closest relationship with Yozzer and we were anxious to find out how he was. Jason had not shown any particular reaction until then but as we walked towards the public phone box, he began to cry. I was still feeling relatively stable inside and I comforted him. The phone call to the hospital did not reassure us much. They gave Yozzer no more than a fifty-fifty chance.'

That brief spasm of emotion was a grim augury – though, as it turned out, more so for Gordon than his colleague. Jason Squibb saw the police surgeon later that day and was signed off for a fortnight. He had cracked ribs, a badly lacerated scalp and a mass of bruises. He also needed time to handle the explosive anger he felt inside him and to work his way through the delayed shock and remorse.

Jason: 'I must have been over the events of that night a thousand times. I was the one who decided in the transit van how we would tackle Lewis. I had him in my hands and I let him get the gun out and fire it. I blamed myself for that and I felt terrible that, maybe because of me, Yozzer might die. OK, so I had escaped being killed by a fraction – but the point was that I had survived and it looked as though Yozzer wouldn't't.'

Gordon Heyes, unhurt physically, went back to his flat, never thinking that he would not work as a policeman again.

'Bearing in mind that I had been fine after the shooting and all day on Friday, I was totally unprepared for what happened on the Saturday morning. I woke up tearful and shaky. I could not concentrate on anything for more than a few moments and I knew even then that there was no way that I could return to work on the Monday.

'Over the next week, I would wake up every night at about one o'clock in a cold sweat. I did not have more than six hours' sleep during the whole week. I saw the doctor and then the force psychiatrist, and on his recommendation, I was booked into the Met nursing home in Hendon. I was diagnosed as suffering from post-traumatic stress disorder.

'It wasn't just the shooting of Yozzer but the culmination of twenty years or more as a front-line copper. I had been at all of the big IRA bombings in the seventies. I had done train crashes. I had actually been shot once before, during an armed robbery in 1977, and been off work for seven weeks.

'I had been in the Special Patrol Group during riots and disorders – in fact, I had very nearly been killed in the Brixton riots in '81 when I was struck by a rock. Luckily, I was one of the first officers to have been issued with the NATO-style helmet and that saved my life. I had taken all that strain and stress and none of it had affected me at the time. But it was clearly building up inside me over the years, and when Yozzer got shot, something just snapped.'

At Christmas 1991, after a spell in a convalescent home at Goring-on-Thames, Gordon Heyes was advised by the Chief Medical Officer for the Met to consider early retirement. It was a painful decision to take. Ironically, after three years on the Central Drugs Squad, he had been due to join the Crack Intelligence Unit. At his age, he had thought his application would probably be rejected. But they had been keen to get someone with his experience.

'I had twenty-eight years under my belt including a lot of drugs work. So the crack squad would have been the ideal way to bow out. But it wasn't to be. I had to accept it was all over for me.

'And it wasn't just the end of the job. My personality had

changed overnight. I used to be carefree, almost happy-go-lucky. Now, I am a worrier. Sometimes, I am aggressive for no reason and I still find it difficult to concentrate. It is ironic that with all this time on my hands, I have not read a book since I retired. I just can't get past the first few pages.'

The shooting of Yozzer Hughes marked a watershed in the law enforcement response to crack trafficking. Never again would the police attempt an arrest in such circumstances without armed back-up. 'Up to that point,' says DCI Roy Daisley, 'we had been aware that crack generated violence but the police had not been confronted by firearms. Now we knew what the dealers were capable of.'

Inevitably, there was an inquest into what went wrong. And private misgivings about the way the operation had been planned quickly became public. Some of the harshest criticism appeared in an article in the *London Evening Standard*, which was later sued successfully for libel by Roy Daisley and the two local officers in operational charge, Chief Superintendent Hampson and Superintendent Jarvis. But nothing stills the canteen talk. There were claims that it had been suspected that Sammy Lewis would be armed though there was no evidence to back up such allegations. Indeed, even three years on, attacks on police officers by crack dealers are thankfully very rare. It was said that the operation had been conceived and executed in haste because Sammy Lewis had been on the point of taking his drugs gains back to Jamaica.

The police version of how their target came to be armed is at sharp variance with Sammy's. The Met said that both guns, the .32 Colt Automatic fired by Sammy, and the .45 Webley carried by his minder, were stolen about a week before the raid from a house in Southall in West London. It is certainly true that Sammy Lewis told his trial that the pistol had been given to him for his own protection during the deal. And that it was the first time he had carried a gun. But this was part of his attempt to sanitise his past to woo the jury. He now admits frankly that he had sometimes gone about his business armed – and that his associates, and those he dealt with, knew it.

'I had never used the gun before – but I came close to it at least once. A guy I was dealing with kept mouthing off on the Vodafone, so when I met him, I showed him the gun – that quietened him down straight away. The fact is that I had both the .32 and the .45 a long time before the police said I did.'

But this might be considered typical crack dealer's bravado. Roy Daisley is determined to set the record straight. 'The day before the raid I attended a meeting at Harlesden police station which considered all the key issues including the question of whether Lewis would be armed. The intelligence supplied by local officers, who after all knew Lewis, was that he did not carry a gun. That was what guided our actions. If we had had information to the contrary, we would have arranged for the arrest team to be armed.'

Gordon Heyes takes the view that they might have been armed, had it not been for fears of inflaming community relations. And it is certainly the case that racial sensitivities were a factor in the planning of the raids. It explains why a Trojan armed response unit was held in reserve, equipped with CS gas and baton rounds.

'That was a decision taken at a high level,' says Roy Daisley, 'in case of civil disorder or in case a siege developed at any of the addresses we were raiding. But there was a mistaken impression in some quarters that because we had firepower in reserve, we were expecting Lewis to be carrying a gun. That is not so.

'As for the planning, it is true that our informant had indicated that Lewis was about to head back to Kingston. In fact we were told that he had already had his BMW shipped out there and that he was preparing to buy his "yard" – in other words, a nice house in the hills overlooking the city. But for all the sense of urgency, we had adequate time to plan the operation.'

Gordon Heyes, though, remains bitter about what happened. 'I had been on many drugs jobs and arrested far bigger hoodlums than Sammy Lewis – drugs importers handling gear worth much more than the rocks he was carrying. So I ask myself, "Why did things go wrong on this occasion?"

'I have been a trained firearms officer since 1969 and it might have made a difference if I had been armed. This was the first crack raid I had done but I knew that drug dealers can be dangerous and volatile people. Not just because they are naturally scared of being arrested but also because they are terrified of being ripped off by other gangs.'

It was a full two years before Yozzer Hughes was passed fit enough to return to work. But only to a desk job. He knows that he will never be on the streets again. 'People say: "You look all right." But if a car backfires fifty yards away, I jump ten feet in the air. I would be a danger to myself if I was at the sharp end.

'And physically, I really fit the label "walking wounded". The doctor won't allow me to drive. I can't run. I can't play football. I can only swim with difficulty because of my bad breathing. Fortunately, the bullet hasn't moved since the shooting. But if it does, they will have to take it out and I have been warned that that could threaten my kidneys or even the spine.

'But the worst thing of all is what it has done to my career. I lived for the job. I was dedicated. With the service I have got, I would have been promoted by now but there is no way I could take my sergeant's exams. I can't study, I can't concentrate for any period of time.'

It must be all the more galling then to accept the progress made by his old partner, Jason Squibb, who has become a sergeant, running his own CID team in Southwark. In contrast, his horizons have expanded since the events of that night.
Jason: 'I have thought about it a lot. I was doing very little with my life before the shooting. But coming so close to getting killed turned me around. I started going out night clubbing at every opportunity. I was determined to make the most of what I had. Not to let it get me down.

'Mind you, I am a hell of a lot more wary now in certain situations. I never used to think about the danger. Now, I watch people's hands like a hawk. I'm always ready to react. There is no doubt that, for me, some of the old pleasure has gone out of the job for ever.'

None of the arrest team had ever done a job in Harlesden before 14 March 1991. And all, to a greater or lesser degree, reflect constantly on the way in which their lives were flipped upside down by a crack dealer they had never met and knew nothing about until the fateful encounter. They must also wonder whether it was worth it.
Jason Squibb: 'I didn't want to hear any mention of Harlesden or crack again after what happened. But by chance, some time later, I found myself over that way. So, I thought: "Sod it, I'll go and exorcise my ghosts." I drove over to Church End and parked by the steps where I had fought Sammy Lewis and where Yozzer had been shot. And do you know what? When I looked up at the stairwell, there was a geezer trading crack. And I thought: "That says it all – life goes on." '

Chapter Three

The Scourge of Society

There is an intimate relationship between a victim and his attacker. Bound by ties of hatred, terror, guilt and humiliation, neither can escape the other's shadow, try as they might. For almost a year after the shooting, Yozzer Hughes underwent surgery and physiotherapy to rebuild his body – but no amount of expert attention could prevent his mind dwelling on the brutal separation from the job he loved and the knowledge that even if the trauma receded, it would be brought surging back by the forthcoming trial.

Meanwhile, Sammy Lewis spent the time wondering how his boundless ambition had been corralled into a remand cell at the absurdly young age of twenty-three. He saw the trial not so much as a reawakening of the past but as a chance to influence his future by making the right moves.

Lewis faced a shopping list of charges. The first three counts related to the possession and supply of a Class A controlled drug – crack cocaine. Given the circumstances of his arrest, Lewis knew that he had little option but to plead guilty to these lesser charges and duly did so. That left attempted murder; possession of a firearm with intent to endanger life; possession of a firearm with intent to resist arrest; and a number of conspiracy charges. To all these, Sammy Lewis pleaded not guilty.

He recognised that he was on a hiding to nothing. Despite recent miscarriages of justice, few juries would fail to convict a defendant charged with the near-fatal shooting of a police officer, and a ferocious attack on several others. The only slender hope lay in a plea of mitigation.

On Lewis's instructions, counsel argued that the gun went off by mistake. None of the police officers had been in uniform and Lewis had understandably believed himself to be the victim of a rip-off by another drug dealer. 'I said I was sorry for the situation. But when you have guys running at you, and half a second to respond, you ain't got no time to think. You just act.'

To underpin the plea, Lewis appeared in a suit and wearing spectacles. He looked even younger than twenty-three, less like the indictment sheet's demonic Mr Big of crack-dealing than a skinny black kid way out of his depth. Yozzer Hughes had difficulty reconciling the demure figure with the man who had almost killed him. 'I have given evidence in court hundreds of times. But this was different. This was personal. For that reason, I decided to stay away from the court apart from when I delivered my own testimony.'

It was personal, too, for Sammy Lewis. 'Hughes put on a real act when he gave his evidence, clutching his chest, coughing. It was a great performance.' An outrageous suggestion given the extent of Yozzer's injuries.

Yozzer: 'The only time that I looked directly into his eyes was when I demonstrated to the judge and jury how he had pointed the gun straight at me and pulled the trigger. I saw no emotion, no feeling there whatsoever. I think the court recognised that.'

The jury heard four days of evidence – including that of the undercover officer, Andrew Morris, who gave his testimony from behind a screen. The judge summed up on the afternoon of Thursday, 5 March – 'it came down so hard on me that even

I began to think I had no case at all' (Sammy Lewis) – and then the jury was sent out to reach their verdict. They returned after eighty minutes. Guilty on all counts.

Yozzer Hughes had been tipped off that the jury were out and arrived in court in time to hear the verdict. As a professional policeman he admits to no special feelings other than relief, but even after all this time, he can recall verbatim most of the comments made by Judge Kenneth Richardson before sentencing.

'Sammy da Costa Lewis, you are the scourge of society. Your dealing in crack cocaine has brought misery to hundreds of people on the streets of London. But that pales into insignificance compared to what happened on the night of March 14th, 1991. You carried a gun knowing that if you were caught, you would use it.

'You knew full well that your victim was a police officer and you shot him in cold blood. You could have been standing here on a murder charge. The fact that you are not is a tribute to the resilience of this officer and the skill of his surgeons.

'It is my duty to protect people on the streets of London from the likes of you – and especially, police officers. I must make an example of you – though I take into account your youth and your previous good record. You will go to prison for twelve years on the charge of attempted murder. For possessing a firearm, I sentence you to ten years – the term to run concurrently. And for supplying crack cocaine, you will serve five years.'

Sammy Lewis waved to his family and friends in the public gallery and was led down by police officers. 'When I heard the judge say: "twelve years for attempted murder" I smiled. I was expecting to get life. I must admit it was a bit of a downer when I realised that I had been given another five years on top of that for the crack. But, all in all, it could have been worse.'

As the courtroom cleared, Yozzer Hughes sat for a few minutes trying to collect his thoughts. Seventeen years in all – but five of those were for the crack dealing. Which left only twelve years as society's retribution for the terrible injuries inflicted on him.

'Lewis will still be a young man when he gets out, not much more than thirty, probably. Meanwhile, I bet he is having a fine time in nick. He is a hero. He shot the Old Bill.'

Sammy Lewis might argue about whether he is having a fine time in Long Lartin but there is no doubt that in a jail with a fair proportion of big city hard men, where one inmate killed another in 1994 in a brawl over a televised rugby match, it is more than useful to have a reputation for violence.

The struggle to modernise and reform the police over the last decade has not just been fought over working practices. It has also attempted to wrench the service away from glib assumptions which can slide unchecked into prejudice. And, all too often, they concern race.

In the case of Operation Howitzer, the crack squad was certainly guilty of one assumption which turned out to be utterly wrong. Whatever the beliefs of Roy Daisley and some of those serving under him, Sammy Lewis is not a Jamaican. Sitting in his cell at Long Lartin, he is highly amused that they should think he is.

'The idea that I was going to buy or build a house in Kingston is laughable. I don't come from Jamaica. I got no family there. Why would I want to go there? It is crazy. And all this stuff about me preparing to leave the country. I was going to take a holiday in New York, that's all. Do some shopping, maybe make a few contacts. I was certainly counting on coming back here. I had too many deals going.

'It sure looks like the cops spun a story and a half around

41

me. Mind you, I ain't surprised. People always say to me: "Where you from – Jamaica?" They ask the question and answer it in the same breath. Seems like Jamaica is the only Caribbean island in the world for most folks.'

Sammy Lewis was actually born in Reading, England (though, coincidentally, there is a Reading in Jamaica too). But his parents came from Barbados and Sammy was taken back to live there at an early age. He stayed until he was fifteen, his principal claim to fame being his prowess at the game of table tennis. In fact, he was so good that he represented the island in inter-Caribbean competitions.

He continued playing, even after he had moved back to the UK in 1983 but by then, ways of making money were preoccupying him to the exclusion of virtually all else. A job working the oven in a Pizza Hut in Willesden lasted three months but clearly wasn't going to be the passport to the kind of life he wanted to lead. Drug dealing – first ganja (marijuana), then cocaine – was.

'The cops seemed to think I was bringing the coke in by courier. I did get one shipment that way but it is too uncertain unless you're running a lot of girls. Mind you, if things had worked out different, I might have got more of my stuff from the Caribbean.

'I had a partner in Trinidad who was getting coke at very competitive prices from South America. Two thousand five hundred US per kilo in Venezuela. Doubles in price when it reaches Trinidad. Goes up tenfold when it gets to Britain. Big, big money.

'We were going to start bringing it over in steady amounts but, unfortunately, he got killed in Trinidad. It was probably a Venezuelan supplier who took him out. I suppose he hadn't paid up on time. Anyway, that was bad news for me because he owed me five kilos of coke when he died.'

For a moment, his face clouds with concern, then the thought of buying a house in Kingston, Jamaica, sets him cackling again.

'Sounds like real good intelligence Roy Daisley had. Wonder who told him that. If I had survived on the street, I suppose I would have gone back to Barbados eventually when I had made enough. Put my money into nightclubs, music promotions – it is a good way of laundering cash. But Jamaica? Never.

'They are the most disorganised people in the world, the Jamaicans. And most of these so-called Yardies are thick. They blow folks away for the sake of it. That's what makes them dangerous – very dangerous.'

The violence is self-evident. Shootings, attacks with machetes, kidnap, rape and torture – a litany of human abuses have become the sordid currency of drug transactions. A Home Office immigration officer says it is the 'killing fields out there'. A detective investigating yet another murder in South London talks of 'Gunfight at the OK Corral'. Increasingly, law enforcers find the language of traditional policing inadequate to describe what they are dealing with. Crack has come to be seen as the embodiment of this onslaught. A drug for those who crave instant gratification. A drug which rewards the dispossessed with swanky cars and gold-plated jewellery. A drug which makes the maladjusted feel invincible. Truly, a drug for our times.

But this is much more than a story about cocaine. Addictions come and go. The only constant narcotic is money – though for some, violence runs a close second. When a society is forced to acknowledge that some of its citizens regard their dress as incomplete without a semi-automatic, and openly proclaim the philosophy that 'life is sweet but short' it is pertinent to ask why.

Chapter Four

The Posse Rides Out

'PNP Rule' proclaims the message scrawled in orange lettering across a smoke-blackened wall in Stoke Newington, North London. It is a February late afternoon. In the incessant drizzle, sallow-faced Chasidic Jews shrink inside their sombre gaberdines to keep dry. Two elderly Pakistanis push a supermarket trolley against the stubborn headwind, their ear-muffs shiny with rain.

Even the natural rulers of these streets, the black kids in their anoraks and baseball caps, have had some of their habitual jauntiness chipped away by the morose English weather. But that slogan, 'PNP Rule' is an emblem of another place, another climate – and another form of politics, conducted with Uzi sub-machine guns rather than election leaflets. PNP stands for the People's National Party of Jamaica. It is the governing party, under Prime Minister, P.J. Patterson. And in March 1993, it won an overwhelming victory in the general election. With only a dozen or so people killed during the short campaign, this was a relatively peaceful poll by the standards of recent Jamaican history.

But the election thirteen years earlier, in 1980, was a veritable bloodbath. And from the carnage emerged the diaspora of Jamaican gangsters who are now equally at home in Miami,

New York, Toronto or London as long as there's a crack deal to be made or a sucker to be ripped off. In 1980, the PNP was ousted from power by its bitter rival, the JLP – the Jamaica Labour Party. By 1980, the domineering presence of the JLP leader, Edward Seaga, had already cast a shadow over the island for more than a decade. Brilliant, cynical – by turns, charming and menacing – Seaga knew instinctively how to ride the tiger of Jamaican politics.

Between elections, there is an uneasy co-existence between the PNP and the JLP but when polling day is set, they are transformed into warring tribes. Even the discourse of their rivalry bristles with menace. And invective, Jamaica-style, has a piquancy all of its own.

'The government is like a woman lying on her back with her legs open, waiting for the "big man" ', is one of Seaga's more memorable insults – uttered when he was opposition leader. In truth, though, it's the island itself which has been violated repeatedly over the years – in colonial times, by the slave masters, and in recent years, by the gunmen. Perhaps politicians should be added to the list.

Edward Seaga's power base is an extraordinary housing project in West Kingston called Tivoli Gardens. So complete is his authority here that in the 1993 election, he got more than 99 per cent of the vote. In Tivoli, Seaga is not merely the leader of the Opposition, he is a living god. And it is easy to understand why. Before Tivoli was built, in the early 1970s, the area was a wasteland of zinc squatter shacks with all the homeliness of an open sewer. This benighted slum was called Back-a-Wall and when, at Seaga's behest, the bulldozers moved in, few mourned its passing.

In its place, there emerged concrete apartment buildings, mains water and electricity, tarmac roads, a school, a maternity clinic, a community centre – in short, for the first time in their lives, the inhabitants of West Kingston felt that someone had invested in their welfare. In return, they were prepared to give Seaga and the Jamaica Labour Party their undying loyalty.

In a political system which locks its two protagonists together like Siamese twins, it was inevitable that the People's National Party would respond in kind to the challenge set by Tivoli. Within a couple of years, the charismatic leader of the PNP, Michael Manley, had set about constructing his own municipal fiefdom in an area called Arnett Gardens. It is known colloquially as the Concrete Jungle. These ghettoes of Kingston, and others, like Southside and Tel Aviv, have become the crucible of Jamaican politics – rancidly partisan and hostile to any reason other than that which emerges from the barrel of a gun. On any street corner, you will find young men bearing bullet wounds or machete scars, as the consequence of the last bout of electioneering. Curiously, few object to spilling their own blood in the cause of the party.

The relationship between the politicians and the street toughs was a devil's contract. The JLP and PNP could rely on a number of safe seats. The chieftains of Tivoli and Arnett Gardens, who channelled the weapons to their henchmen, had a new and persuasive badge of authority. And one which they had no intention of relinquishing. Guns conferred status. Access to firepower – and the reputation for using it without mercy – was the only assured means of retaining 'respect'. Sure, the street dons were happy to come to the aid of the party at elections, but for the rest of the time, their hardware could be put to other uses – straightforward street crime, settling personal feuds, protection for drug dealing.

When it became apparent that replacing the machete with the .38 was beginning to poison Jamaican society, some of the very politicians who had quietly connived at the distribution of weapons to the ghettoes were amongst those squawking loudest in alarm. But there was no putting the genie back in the bottle. By the late 1970s, many of the political enforcers had a lot of blood on their hands. And some had already carved out legends for themselves. One such was Rankin Dread, who controlled the Rema district of Kingston under the streetname, Bowyark. He fought his way up to become a 'don' – which carries the same sort of connotation in the Jamaican ghettoes as it does in Sicily.

'I was outspoken, a firebrand recruiter for the JLP. I was involved in many outbursts of violence – sure I was a hit man. But I was a political hit man in the sense that I was particularly good at getting votes and bringing new people into the party. It was war in those days. Hundreds of people were murdered.'

It was the ideal preparation for the 1980 election. The so-called 'garrison towns' belonging to the PNP and the JLP were awash with guns and stoked to an incendiary pitch by the rhetoric of their leaders. With the PNP having fallen under the sway of Castro-led Cuba, and the JLP clinging to US coat-tails, the ideological divide between the two parties had never been sharper. Setting a polling date was akin to lighting the blue touchpaper. In the explosion of raw violence, no-one knows exactly how many died. But the price of democracy was estimated at some 800 corpses. The cost, to the PNP, was also exacted in another way: the hasty exodus of many of the gunmen who had nailed their colours unequivocally to the party's mast and who now feared a grisly revenge. Some fled to Cuba, many more went to the United States.

The migration was joined by JLP gang members too. Some seeking sanctuary from their enemies. Some eager to broaden their horizons in a country where ruthlessness with a gun could be a passport to achievement. Wherever there was an established Jamaican population – Miami, New York, Toronto, London – there was fertile soil in which the transplanted gunmen, hustlers, pimps and ganja dealers, could flourish. So, 'going foreign', as they called it, was no bar to continuing the same kind of activities which had underpinned their status in Kingston.

Bowyark brought his skills to North London (see Chapter 9), and during the 1980s, drug trafficking and armed robbery kept him at the top of the heap – until January 1987, when a British-born black decided to test him with a machete in a Jamaican shebeen. The supposedly impregnable Bowyark was left with eighteen wounds to his head and his wrist almost severed. For ten days, he lay in hospital, his life in the balance – while on the streets, his status plummeted. But Rankin Dread lived up to his reputation, discharging himself from his 'death bed' to reclaim his position. The legend became myth.

On the other side of the Atlantic, too, the 1980s were generous to the Jamaican refugees. Take Delroy 'Uzi' Edwards who is now serving a life sentence in a US federal penitentiary for six murders. As an enforcer for the JLP in Southside, Kingston, he was probably responsible for twice that number of deaths before his twentieth birthday. In the early 1980s, he materialised in the US on a tourist visa – and overstayed his welcome by several years. But during that time he made full use of his talents.

Like many of the Jamaican hustlers, Edwards started out selling nickel and dime bags of marijuana. His base was a grocery store in Rogers Avenue, Brooklyn, which belonged to his father, Lloyd. But, more than just street smart, Edwards had vision. Even as early as 1985, he could see that the big bucks were in crack. And, inch by inch, his organisation, the Renkers posse, stamped its control on the crack trade in Bedford – Stuyvesant, Flatbush and Crown Heights. At its peak, it had fifty workers, pulling in $100,000 each week for the corporate coffers.

And in keeping with the expansive spirit of the decade, the Renkers (the name comes from the smell of urine against a wall), continued to explore new markets, eventually supplying crack to Philadelphia, Baltimore, even the District of Columbia. Edwards sank some of his gains into old-world property – buying a $150,000 house in Amityville, Long Island, for which he paid in low denomination bills handed over to the astonished seller in a duffel bag.

Suzy, a Jamaican in her late forties, fits effortlessly into the nouveau riche world, which Edwards sought to inhabit. She is exactly the type of lady that a ghetto drug dealer would find alluring. But many have done so at their cost, for Suzy is an undercover agent, who has provided valuable information for both US and British police agencies. She looks the part. The mountainous sapphire and diamond rings winking and flashing from four of her fingers would make a formidable pair of knuckledusters. And gold bangles the width of handcuffs hulahoop around her wrists as she speaks. Suzy, originally from Tivoli Gardens, lives in New Jersey, and saw Delroy Edwards at close quarters.

'I think the people he mixed with led him astray. Their motto was: "Rich, wicked and powerful". Most of them were not smart enough to fulfil those dreams. But he was. By the time he had built up the Renkers, he owned racehorses and surrounded himself with beautiful women. He liked very pretty girls with long, straight hair. He don't like no wigs or weaves. That's why he liked me. In fact, a lot of people thought I was his special girl.

'Delroy had class – but he was a very, very dangerous man. He wore a Rolex watch and Cartier jewellery, but he always travelled with an Uzi automatic. And I seen him use it. One time in the Love People Club in Brooklyn, someone stepped on his toe. It was an accident. And the guy apologised. Didn't make no difference. Delroy started shooting – and the guy got taken out in an ambulance. If you mess with Delroy, he'll kill you with a wink.'

And the Renkers Posse imported the primitive 'justice' of West Kingston into New York with no concessions. A teenage crack seller suspected of stealing money and drugs from the gang was beaten with a baseball bat, scalded with boiling water from a furnace, and left hanging in chains from a basement ceiling. His corpse was dumped beside a garbage bin near a rival group's headquarters, where it was found two months later, frozen and partly decomposed.

In the end, it was the unrestrained use of violence which led to Edwards' downfall. In 1987, after his brother-in-law was killed by rivals, Edwards led his gang on a shooting spree which left one person dead and three badly injured. The law enforcers in New York sat up and took notice, and decided that if a drugs war was being fought on their doorstep, they would treat the Renkers Posse like the Mafia and attack it under the RICO statute. The acronym stands for Racketeering Influenced Corrupt Organisation. A RICO prosecution endows the authorities with greater powers and more flexibility to tackle criminal enterprises than any other piece of legislation.

Edwards was the first Jamaican gang leader to be hit with a RICO indictment and in the summer of 1989, he was found guilty on 42 charges, including 17 acts of racketeering, 6 murders, 15 shootings, a kidnapping, a stabbing, an armed robbery, an attempted robbery, falsifying a passport, money laundering, and a clutch of drugs and firearms violations. Delroy 'Uzi' Edwards was still only twenty-eight.

To celebrate the demise of Delroy Edwards, the team which put together the successful RICO prosecution held a victory lunch in an Italian restaurant in Brooklyn. Two thousand miles away, in Kingston, Jamaica, they were mourning the imprisonment of a favoured son who was seen in a very different light.

Renkers corner is a distinctive enclave within the ghetto of Southside. You can still see the message 'Free Delroy' scrawled on a wall amidst a rash of vivid murals. The corner is only a few streets from the sea, and the Renkers crew make what money they can from fishing. It is a job of sorts in an area where three out of four people have no work, but their daily catch is pitiably small. This was Delroy's community, and the two well-muscled youths, Tony and Kanga, who sit on upturned crates mending a fishing net, regard him as a departed hero.

'Delroy was a good man. He look after his people. He was a leader when he was here, and when he went foreign, he don't forget us. He sent back food and clothes for the kids and when he came back, he always handed out money and treats. We know what they said about him in the States. But we ain't gonna change our opinion of him. We loved Uzi.'

And despite what befell their leader, both Tony and Kanga are making plans to go to the States. 'Sure we want to go to New York. Why not? We got no jobs, no prospects here. It's gotta be better there.'

By the tail end of the 1980s, Delroy Edwards was merely one of many Jamaicans who had penetrated the mainstream of American crime. The Federal Bureau of Alcohol, Tobacco and Firearms, the so-called 'Untouchables', was so alarmed about the violence the Jamaicans had spawned, that it produced a confidential report on their activities. It calculated that about 30,000 posse members were active in the United States. And that is just those in organised crime groups. Some ATF agents say you could probably double that number if you counted

Jamaican criminals who function outside structured or semi-structured syndicates. The ATF estimated that, by 1992, the posses controlled about a third of the crack trafficking in the US.

And, alarmingly, many of those posse members identified by the ATF are just as much at home in Britain as they are in the United States. In 1990, for example, the police in West London raided a crack factory at Shepherds Bush. They arrested two men who both had British passports and presented themselves as businessmen. In reality, their names were Victor and Leroy Francis and they were both enforcers for the Renkers Posse in Brooklyn. Victor was wanted in New York for two murders, including the beating to death of the crack seller whose body was dumped in garbage sacks. They had slipped into Britain when federal warrants were issued for them in the States.

This pattern of movement between Britain and the States is a thread running through the Yardie story. Jim Harter, an experienced ATF agent in Miami, puts it like this: 'Our criminals are your criminals. The reason that I have such good relations with Scotland Yard is that we are targeting the same criminals. Not just people committing similar crimes, but the same people.

'At first, I found it hard to comprehend. After all, my world is Miami and Fort Lauderdale and I suppose you can include New Mexico where my mother lives. But the Jamaican world is Kingston, Miami, New York, Kansas, London – there are even posse members in Anchorage, Alaska, for God's sake. The gang members are equally at home in any of those places. It is a new crime phenomenon and many law enforcers just have not grasped it yet.'

But a new phenomenon which has appropriated many well-worn gangland clichés. At the funeral of a 'don' who was killed in a shoot-out with the police, the dead man's girlfriend placed a wreath in the shape of an M16 assault rifle on the coffin. The priest enraged mourners by tearing it in two, accusing them of 'glorifying macho gunmen'. Which might be considered ironic in a country where many still cherish the Colt .45 as a guarantor of liberty rather than a threat to it.

The 'Taste of the Islands' is a Jamaican restaurant in North Dade, in the suburban girdle surrounding Miami. Before the events of August 1992, it was just another Caribbean good-time joint where you could order a passable jerk chicken and party to some authentic reggae. But the 'Taste of the Islands' is now pointed out to tourists and sightseers as the spot where Jamaican gun law left its calling card.

It was around 3.30 a.m. on a Saturday morning. A reggae party in a private dining room upstairs was still in full swing. Maybe eighty or a hundred youngsters were cruising the dance floor when the gatecrashers burst in. Two or three men – in the confusion, no-one was quite sure – appeared in the doorway, their semi-automatics outlined against the light. For a moment or two, the entertainment continued unmolested. Then the thunder of the bass beat was overlaid by a fusillade of gunfire which raked the room like a searchbeam.

Hilda LaToy Reynolds had been celebrating her seventeenth birthday. She died in the arms of her elder sister. A few feet away, twenty-year-old Ricardo Mitchell lay mute – his lifeblood ebbing swiftly from a gaping hole in his jugular. Two others were killed. Eighteen wounded.

Jason Shippey was passing by as the survivors staggered outside: 'It was like a massacre. There was nothing but bodies everywhere.' He counted ten people lying on the pavement. Others were in the road and the restaurant parking-lot, bleeding, moaning. Even by the routine excesses of Miami crime, it was a nightmare.

'This shoot-out is a perfect, textbook example of how the Jamaican posse does business,' says Jim Harter. 'The Mafia does it differently. When the Mob wants to hit you, they just get you and they do it very cleanly. They're professionals. This group, the posse, makes big messes because they don't give a damn about anybody. They are going to take you out the first chance they get – whatever the circumstances.'

Metro homicide detectives confirmed one of the dead and one of the wounded to be posse members. It goes without saying that the mayhem was crack related. Those law enforcers with long enough memories see the casual violence of the posses as part of Florida's recent heritage of drug crime.

Ed Schumacher used to be head of the domestic interdiction squad at the Metro-Dade Police Department.

'The Jamaican gangs are behaving in the same way that the Colombians did twenty years ago. Their philosophy was: "If you had a problem, you killed your problem." Even the Mafia flinched at the violence of the Colombians when they moved into the drugs trade. Now, the South Americans look on the Jamaicans with exactly the same fear and suspicion. They don't like dealing with the posses because they are afraid of getting ripped off – or worse.'

And the Jamaicans have learned well from their predecessors. 'In the early seventies, it was chiefly the Cubans who controlled the cocaine traffic in south Florida. Then the Colombians arrived. At first, they used the Cubans as middle men because they had all the connections. But it was plain from the economics of the drugs business that that wasn't going to last. The Colombians were determined to maximise their profits.

'So, then we had the range wars. And given the firepower carried by the South Americans – and their ruthlessness – there was only going to be one outcome. The Cubans were forced out. Now, you can see the same trend happening with the Jamaicans.

'At first, they needed the know-how of the home-grown US blacks to set up their crack operations. Not any more. Using extreme violence and intimidation, they have ousted the indigenous dealers. And from what I hear, the same thing is beginning to happen in your country.'

Chapter Five

Jim Brown's Body

When Clint Eastwood first strapped on a holster and narrowed his gaze against the sun, he did more than create a movie legend. The stylised ferocity of the spaghetti westerns fed male fantasies around the world, but Jamaica, with its rootless urban young desperate for a sense of identity, was especially ripe for seduction.

Night after night, the tacky fleapit cinemas of Kingston echoed to the sound of celluloid gunfire. And with real guns seeping into the ghettoes, it was an ideal time for life to imitate art – no matter how grotesque the consequences. It became fashionable to adopt streetnames like Trinity or Outlaw, to call the gangs 'posses', and to settle everyday conflicts with the same callous amorality as the screen heroes and villains. The names of some of the posses reflected this surge of machismo. The Untouchables, the Hot Steppers, Red Ecstasy, the Land Raiders, the Twelve Tribes. Others reflected areas of Kingston – Rema, Jungle, Tel Aviv, Angola.

Some of these gangs have never ventured out of the ghettoes. Others, like the Renkers, the Spanglers, and the Gullymen, have sprouted offshoots in the United States, Canada and the UK. All of them are associated with either the PNP or JLP, though abroad, the demarcation lines have weakened to the point where drug dealing, not politics, is the glue which holds a group together.

Those who prefer their crime models neat and simple – typically, journalists, though some law enforcers too – have talked glibly of a black Mafia. This comparison is way off the mark. Whereas the *consigliere* is the undisputed chairman of the board of his criminal family, the Jamaican don owes his status to his own ingenuity and firepower. If he can't keep the drugs money flowing, he has no future and his posse will be left at the mercy of rivals. The man driving a top-of-the-range Mercedes on a Friday could be just another ragged arse pipehead by Monday morning if the weekend went badly.

When Jamaican criminals began arriving in significant numbers in the United States, they gravitated towards the trade in marijuana. After all, Jamaica has been a ganja producer since the 1960s, and it was a natural move for them. But it helped wrongfoot many law enforcers who took the view that only hoodlums involved in the serious drugs, cocaine and heroin, deserved real respect. By the time they woke up to the fact that whatever the source of profit, the Jamaican gangsters would pursue it with unrivalled single-mindedness, the battle was already half-lost. In 1984, in Florida, ATF Special Agent, J.J. Watterson, began investigating the origin of a batch of guns which had been smuggled from the US to Jamaica, and got a horrifying glimpse of the future.

'I started checking gun store records in Dade and Broward counties and discovered that the guns were part of a larger purchase of weapons, about seventy-five in all, which had been bought by Jamaicans in the States. Most of them had given false names but the ones I could trace all seemed to live in apartments or houses which were protected like fortresses.

'Within a year, these same guns began turning up in murder cases all over the States – Washington, New York, Detroit,

Miami, Los Angeles. And in each one, the connection was Jamaican drug dealing. When Sweet Pants – that's what I call Suzy, our informant – told me that the posses had arrived with a vengeance, I thought she was talking baloney. But she knew darned well what was going on.'

Watterson was the first American law enforcer to identify this new criminal threat and for the next five years, he became a dedicated crusader against the largest and most violent of all the gangs, the Shower Posse, which spearheaded the Jamaican assault on the US drugs market from his own backyard, Florida. The name, itself, carried the message. Quite simply, anyone who got in their way was showered with bullets. In cold print, it sounds melodramatic, but on 4 August 1985, the whole country was made aware of what it meant. It should have been a black Woodstock. Three thousand Jamaicans from all over the States congregated at a sports complex at Oakland, New Jersey, for a picnic cum reggae festival to celebrate Jamaican Independence Day. Lines of chartered buses could be seen for miles around ferrying in the partygoers. There were many women and children amongst them. But times had changed since 1969. Some of these celebrants were carrying 9mm pistols and sub-machine guns with their dope and booze. And the love and peace lasted for as long as it took the first argument to break out.

Suzy, the confidante of Delroy Edwards, was there with friends: 'We were really looking forward to it. But we could feel the tension when we arrived. There had been some trouble, a shooting, the night before and revenge was in the air. There were groups of Shower men eyeballing members of the Spangler posse, who are PNP gunmen. There were Renkers people there, too.

'The guy who started the shooting was called Samwell Brown – a Shower man. It was something to do with a robbery attempt

58

– after all, everybody was wearing their cargo. You could have drowned in gems.

'When the firing began, it sounded like a war. It was terrifying. I saw men blasting away with Uzis and M16s. Some folk trampled down a section of fence around a swimming club to escape and jumped into the pool – even ones who couldn't swim. We hid under a table. It was madness.'

Over 700 rounds were fired. Three people were killed and thirteen wounded. It was the first – but not the last – occasion on which the Jamaican clans proclaimed their murderousness beyond the confines of Kingston.

The brains behind the Shower Posse was Vivian Blake, an adventurer from Tivoli Gardens, who is equally at home in Miami, New York or London, where he once owned property. Of all the Jamaican crack gangsters, he probably comes closest to the traditional image of the Mafia don. A high-roller in hand-made suits and white silk scarf, he has built a reputation as a canny businessman – and a ladies' man. Suzy, 'Sweet Pants', has moved in his orbit, too.

'I remember the first time I was introduced to Vivian. It was at a "grass" house on 182nd Street in the Lower Bronx, around about 1982. He was living in Long Island then. He had some of his soldiers with him.

'He said to me: "You're a real beautiful lady. Stay with me." He wined and dined me. Champagne in a bucket. He loved champagne. Took me for a ride in his flashy two-door BMW. Made me feel real good. But you know, despite his reputation, I never seen him with a handgun, either then or since. Actually, he has a very nice personality. If he likes you, he likes you – nothing will change it. He is a Taurus, and that is typical of the sign. Mind you, they may forgive but they don't forget.

'I know a girl who was raped by Vivian Blake. She was all fired up afterwards, in a fury, and she wasn't thinking straight.

She made one helluva mistake. She went to the cops and filed a complaint. You don't do that to a guy like Blake. He took his revenge by having her brother killed.'

But in Jamaica, drugs wealth buys protection. Blake remained at liberty for longer than any of his rivals because he had friends in high places, to whom a Florida District Attorney's warrant on charges of multiple murder and drug trafficking was of very little moment. That is, until the beginning of 1994, when surprisingly, Vivian Blake was arrested in a pawn shop in Kingston. The Americans slapped in their extradition request within forty-eight hours of hearing the news.

Though Vivian Blake is thought to have been active on the international drugs scene for at least a decade, he remained until his arrest a shadowy figure, rarely photographed, often unrecognised. Indeed, it was widely rumoured that he had had plastic surgery to alter his appearance.

By contrast, the man with whom he built up the Shower Posse, Jim Brown – whose real name was Lester Lloyd Coke – was a towering presence, literally and metaphorically, whom no-one could ignore. And it was this high profile which probably led to his controversial death in a prison fire in Kingston as he awaited extradition to the United States. Some would say his end was entirely in keeping with a life of often incendiary violence. But the real story of Jim Brown is infinitely more complex than that, and it demonstrates that the criminal figures demonised by police officers in Britain and the United States are viewed very differently in their own back yard.

According to the Americans, Jim Brown was a vicious killer. And they cite the evidence to prove it. In Miami, in November 1984, he and Vivian Blake went over to the apartment of a Shower Posse soldier, Richard Morrison, a.k.a. Storyteller, to 'do some coke'. Storyteller was a Tivoli Gardens gunman who moved freely between Kingston and Florida.

After a couple of hours, they emerged onto the street and, as they walked to their car, they were robbed at gunpoint of their cash and valuables. The indictment sheet later issued against Brown explains that he believed that he had been set up by the occupants of the house which he had just left. The police say that, with Storyteller and two other gunmen, Jim Brown returned to the house and cold-bloodedly executed five of the six people inside by placing a .45 to their heads. The sixth, a twenty-three-year-old white junkie, survived the massacre, though she was shot seven times. The final bullet exited through her teeth. She lived with horrific facial injuries for eight years before committing suicide in 1992.

When agents of the ATF in Florida began delving into Brown's past, they discovered other telling examples of his ruthlessness. It was said that he once pulled a Kingston bus driver from his cab and shot him dead in front of his horrified passengers. The man's crime was to have been too heavy-handed on the steering. When a Jamaican politician wanted to acquire a site for development which was occupied by a Chinese restaurant, Jim Brown was entrusted with carrying out the 'negotiations'. Tragically, the couple who owned the restaurant were unaware of the nature of the man they were dealing with. They refused to leave. The story goes that two months later, Brown shot them both dead. The politician got his site.

In 1984, even the Jamaican police were forced to seek a warrant for Brown's arrest after the murders of seven defectors from the Jamaica Labour Party, which he had allegedly organised. There is no evidence, though, that the warrant was ever enforced. In Kingston, Jim Brown had a pat response when taxed – as he frequently was – with allegations of thuggery. 'I am a politician,' he would say. And since Jamaican politics embraces most extremes of human behaviour, it was a claim which could be justified – and was rarely contested. But the key to really understanding him lies in the area from which he came, Tivoli Gardens. When Edward Seaga dreamed of turning Tivoli into a community power base, Jim Brown was the means of achieving it.

Brown was a building contractor. The project took shape, using his workers. With 70 per cent unemployment the jobs which flowed from his relationship with Seaga gave Brown the role of community patron. In a system where government is able to do very little to mitigate the effects of poverty and deprivation, those who can provide for the community become enormously influential. As more and more contracts were channelled through his office, Jim Brown became the undisputed don of Tivoli, a protector against the harsh world outside, and an arbiter for behaviour inside it. Suzy, the undercover agent, understands the workings of Tivoli and knew Jim Brown.

'Jim was called "don dadda", a term of affection. Everybody loved him because he provided things for them. Little kids used to come up to him and say they were hungry and he would give them lunch money. I've seen old folks kiss him with their toothless gums because he had given them some cash or some help.'

This picture of the drugs trafficker as community benefactor is a common one in Tivoli. On May Bank Holiday 1993, a man called Christopher Bourne, better known as Tuffy, was shot dead in Brixton in South London. Tuffy was a gunman and crack dealer whose name had cropped up in half a dozen London shootings. He was killed by rivals from Kingston in a turf dispute. But in his own back yard of Tivoli, Tuffy was a hero. When he came home, he would spread his money around and, according to those who knew him, he would help keep the lid on disputes which might otherwise flare into violence. In short, he commanded respect.

In a place like Tivoli, though, you don't keep anyone's respect without being brutally tough. Suzy knows the score. 'I been in New York, London, Hawaii, all over. Stayed in the best hotels. But you can forget the rules of civilised living in Tivoli. There, it is strength that rules.

'I was there when a guy called Blood was killed. They said he was an informer. They shot him, tied him to a handcart down by the railway line, and "tagged" him – put a piece of cardboard on him, saying "this bwoy carried news to the police". That's justice in Tivoli.

'Another time, I saw an execution. We heard shooting – automatic weapon fire – and ran to see what was happening. A group of men, about six I think, had been lined up in a gully and executed. They were all tagged – this one was a rapist, that one, a "terrorist" – and dumped down by the railway line.

'These men had been held in underground cells inside Tivoli, before they were killed. Other people who had broken the code for a more minor offence were just shot in the foot as a warning. This is how the dons keep law and order.'

In Popcorn's liquor store on Spanishtown Road, you won't hear a bad word said against Jim Brown. Popcorn a.k.a. Carlton McBridge, is a slack-bellied man in his late forties, whose breakfast is a can or two of Red Stripe beer followed by a series of ganja spliffs. By lunchtime, the whites of Popcorn's eyes are slashed with crimson and he looks to be on the edge of losing control. But there is nothing which happens in the dusty streets around his store that escapes his attention.

Popcorn manages Tivoli's football team and was one of the area dons through whom Jim Brown exerted his authority. In the 1970s, he was a gun-runner.

'They say a good man don't live too long – and for me, Jim was like JFK. Died before his time. If any trouble broke out between people from Tivoli and another area, Jim would calm it down. If someone steals something and there is a complaint, Jim would sort it out, without the police being called.'

And if that meant summary justice, so be it. 'There are some things folks have to be punished for. You see this .25 pistol I keep in my pocket? If a man come and rape one of my daughters, I would go kill him. Simple as that. And nobody would blame me.'

When you put it to Popcorn that, according to the Americans, Jim Brown was a murderer and an international drugs trafficker, he looks away pained. 'I don't know nothing 'bout what he did in Miami. I'm telling you the sort of man he was here – amongst his own people. Things haven't been the same since he was killed, that's for sure.'

Suzy knows rather more about Jim Brown's life in Miami and recalls that whenever she saw him, he had a long-barrelled Magnum handgun with him.

'It was more for his own protection than to intimidate people. He had an awful lot of enemies. But despite what they say about him, he was never violent or arrogant around me. Seeing is believing – and I don't believe everything they say about him.

'Of course, he had baby mothers in the States, as well as his wife and kids back in Kingston but I have heard he was kind to his family and a good father. Jim Brown was not a wild Casanova or partygoer like Vivian Blake. He was more of a business type.'

From the 1970s onwards, Jim Brown's fortunes were tied to those of the Jamaica Labour Party under Edward Seaga. But both men prospered under the benign gaze of a force which made all the Uzis and M16s in the Kingston ghettoes look like so much slingshot.

Seaga entered the Jamaican parliament in the early 1960s

64

as the youngest ever MP, at the age of twenty-three. In the world of geo-politics, beyond Kingston, it was a momentous time as President Kennedy gambled with peace by eyeballing the Soviet Union's nuclear warheads out of Cuba.

The Caribbean continued to be a theatre of the Cold War into the 1970s and the alarm bells clanged furiously when the ruling People's National Party in Jamaica began to flirt with Fidel Castro. Cuban 'experts' arrived to advise on agricultural projects and work in schools and clinics, while moving in the other direction, some of the young activists and enforcers for the PNP were shipped to Havana for military training. Those who returned to Kingston – and some stayed away for many years – were rather more proficient in the art of killing than they had been and were given the name, Brigadistas.

For the policy analysts at the State Department there was little argument that the ideal bulwark against the leftish policies of the PNP was the resolutely pro-capitalist Edward Seaga. Some of Washington's support was open – some covert. How many members of the staff of the US embassy in Kingston worked for the CIA in this period is not clear – but there is strong anecdotal, if not written, evidence that the agency was engaged in running guns into Jamaica for use by the JLP, and that a crucial conduit was Jim Brown, whose contracting work at the port provided ideal cover for smuggling.

It is, of course, a delicious irony that a man whom the US authorities later spent considerable time and money trying to extradite was almost certainly given more than a helpful boost in his criminal career by the Central Intelligence Agency. Shades of Panama's General Noriega, who also repaid US patronage by dipping his snout into the drugs trough.

In the 1980s the criminal careers of Vivian Blake and Jim Brown really took off. Blake based himself in Miami, with Richard 'Storyteller' Morrison. Brown remained the don of

Tivoli, but travelled frequently to Florida. Initially, until about 1985, the profits of the Shower Posse were largely derived from smuggling ganja into the United States. Thereafter, the big earner increasingly became crack cocaine.

On the strength of this trade, the membership of the Shower Posse grew to well over 5,000 in a dozen US cities. New York City, Rochester in New York State, Washington DC, Detroit and Toronto – these were the principal heads of the cocaine hydra. Into its ravenous maw fell the crack junkies whose daily existence was defined exclusively in terms of when and how they could get their next fix. Blake and Brown made sure that the supply was constantly replenished. The addicts, their loved ones, and society at large paid the price.

And the size of the operation was startlingly impressive. 'From about 1985 onwards,' says J.J. Watterson of the ATF, 'the pipeline carrying ganja from Jamaica into Florida and cocaine from Florida on to the north-eastern states just never stopped flowing. There were suitcases of the stuff on every plane. For every one which was intercepted, another ten got through.

'The Shower Posse had maybe six to eight girl couriers on every New York-bound flight out of Miami, Fort Lauderdale, and Orlando. And there were six to eight flights each day. In the three years, 1985, 1986 and 1987, we estimate that 300,000 pounds of marijuana, and 20,000 pounds of cocaine passed through Florida heading north.

'Each consignment was fairly small – the couriers would probably never have more than three hundred dollars of the stuff on them. But it's like a water pipe running twenty-four hours a day. At any one point in the pipe, there isn't an enormous amount of water – but unless you turn off the stop-cock, it just keeps on running.'

And this was before the crack boom in New York had gone

into orbit. By the late eighties, the Jamaicans, the Dominicans and the Colombians had fine-tuned their trafficking operations to such a pitch that a Niagara of cocaine was cascading into the world's most voracious drugs market, with a sufficient overflow to begin to fill the demand overseas – principally, Europe. Here, too, the Shower Posse used the Jamaican connections in London, Bristol and elsewhere to grab a slice of the action in the UK.

And what was the law enforcement response? By 1988, J.J. Watterson had secured enough hard evidence to go before a federal grand jury. It reacted by indicting thirty-four members of the Shower Posse, including Blake, Brown and Morrison. The sixty-two counts included illegal arms purchases and racketeering as well as trafficking. Blake was charged with nine murders. In practice, though, the indictments meant little. At the time they were handed down, none of the three principals was within reach of federal justice. Blake was believed to be in London, the other two in Kingston. And the crack trafficking of the Shower Posse continued to thrive.

But for Jim Brown and Storyteller, time was a dwindling commodity. The process which led to their arrest in Jamaica is not clear but the decisive factor may well have been the election defeat in 1988 of the JLP. With the PNP in power, the gang boss and his crony were more vulnerable. It was also whispered that Brown's erstwhile partner, Vivian Blake, had betrayed him because he owed Brown a large amount of money. Whatever the truth, in 1989, Jim Harter, from the Alcohol, Tobacco and Firearms bureau, travelled to Kingston from Fort Lauderdale with two US marshals to make an extradition request regarding a clutch of murders and racketeering. The Americans did not expect prompt action nor did they get it.

'All over the world, extradition is a pretty slow and cumbersome process – but comparing the mechanism in the

US with Jamaica is like comparing the movement of a falling avalanche with a glacier,' says Harter.

'I don't mean this to sound patronising but the Jamaican cops are struggling with technology which the US and the UK discarded in the 1950s. Some of their rural police stations don't even have a telephone. And whenever some of our guys fly into Kingston, they take with them reams of Xerox paper as presents for government officials because they just cannot get hold of any.'

As 1989 became 1990 the extradition process was little further advanced. But there was at least one hopeful sign for the Americans. Jim Brown and Storyteller were arrested and incarcerated in the maximum security wing of the General Penitentiary in Kingston. They used every cog in Jamaica's legal machinery to fight the extradition warrants. When every domestic stage had been exhausted, they instructed their lawyers to prepare a final appeal to the Judicial Committee of the Privy Council in London, one of the few surviving relics of British hegemony over its former colony.

In June 1992, with the appeal still pending, Jamaica's Appeal Court Registry made an extraordinary error. It passed an order allowing Storyteller to be surrendered to US law enforcement agents. They could not believe their good fortune. Their prisoner was quickly transferred to Miami where he was arraigned on charges of murder, conspiracy to murder and possession with intent to distribute cocaine. The Jamaican government then made diplomatic and legal efforts to have Storyteller returned to their jurisdiction. But they failed and he stood trial and was convicted on the cocaine charge. In keeping with the draconian drug penalties available to American courts, the judge jailed him for twenty-four and a half years, without parole. He went down to the cells in the knowledge that another trial was being planned on the murder and conspiracy to murder counts. He was looking at thirty-five years to life.

Jim Brown, meanwhile, sat in his cell in Kingston awaiting the decision of the Privy Council in London. It came in January 1992. Five Law Lords, sitting in a high-ceilinged room at No. 1 Downing Street, ruled that under international law, the US courts had the right to try Brown. Less than a month later, he was dead.

Prison conditions in Jamaica are grim. A 1990 report by the human rights organisation, America's Watch, found that 'most of the cells measure six feet by nine . . . each cell has a concrete slab for sleeping on'. The General Penitentiary, where Brown was being held, is a red brick fortress in the Southside area, close to the sea. Its watchtowers are visible from far off.

Probably one in two of the males over eighteen in the surrounding ghetto have spent time in the Pen. They testify to the atrocious conditions and the brutality of the guards. But by all accounts, Jim Brown managed to secure rather more acceptable accommodation. To relieve the stifling heat, he installed a high-powered electric fan. He had a ghetto-blaster radio, pumping out ragga music, and three other appliances illicitly wired up to the mains. And it is said that free-basing cocaine helped while away the tedious hours.

Despite the creature comforts though, he had his worries. On the last occasion that his wife, Beverley, saw him alive, he was complaining that someone had been spying on him through his window. 'How is it that that can happen in a maximum security wing?' he asked her. 'I am going to take it up with the prison superintendent.'

Beverley – known in Tivoli as Miss Bev – went to see him twice a week. She had known him since she was fourteen and had borne him five children. Whether she knew about the other women in Miami, she isn't letting on. For her, Jim Brown was the perfect husband, strong, dependable, always cheerful, the rock of the family. Like the loyal Popcorn, she prefers to draw a veil over the other life which the Americans allege he led.

Suzy, the undercover agent, also visited him in jail:

'He was living like a king. Once a don, always a don. Even the PNP inmates gave him respect. He told me that despite his fight against extradition, he really wanted to stand trial in the US. He had a lot he wanted to get off his chest, about his relationship with politicians and so on. And for that reason, he always feared someone would try to kill him in there.

'I hear he was planning an escape. He was going to try to get away from the island by boat. But the beans got spilled to the Ministry of Justice and the plot was foiled.'

How the fire started has never been satisfactorily explained. But on 23 February 1992, the warders were alerted by screams and smoke emanating from two cells in F block. By the time they arrived – and there were allegations that help was deliberately delayed – Brown and one other inmate were charred almost beyond recognition. An autopsy report concluded that they had been asphyxiated. A Canadian coroner who examined Brown found scorch-marks on the lining of his windpipe, indicating that he had recently been smoking cocaine.

Inevitably, there were claims, principally from the Jamaica Labour Party, that Brown had been the victim of a political murder. The questions flowed endlessly. Why was it that a fire of such intensity had been confined to two cells? Why did it take at least fifteen minutes after the first alarm had been raised for the cell door to be opened? A possible answer to this was provided by a prisoner who told the inquest in tears that he had been pressured to cover up for warders who had deserted their posts as the cell burned. The inquest also heard that it took nearly two hours to remove Brown to a hospital which is only minutes away from the jail. Some also suggested that it was rather more than coincidence that he died the day before a last-ditch habeas corpus hearing was to have been held at Jamaica's Supreme Court. JLP lawyers launched an investigation into allegations that Brown had been tortured before he died.

Suzy is convinced he was killed to stop him talking in a US court: 'It was premeditated murder. The PNP wanted him out of the way because he knew too much about their links with some of the posses. They paid a prison guard to do it. Jim had friends amongst the guards, JLP supporters, but they were on duty during the week. The fire happened at a weekend when he had no protection.'

PNP sources say it was the JLP which organised Brown's death because he had threatened that if he was going down he would drag some of the politicians down with him. It is a theory supported by J.J. Watterson who says the escape plan was changed to one of murder when it was decided that Brown knew too much to be left alive.

Whatever the truth, when the Americans were told that Brown was dead, they were highly suspicious, fearing that it was a ruse to cheat them of their prey. Only a photograph of the dead body, received from a British source, accompanied by a fingerprint record, convinced them that it was indeed Brown and not some unnamed convict sacrificed to enable the gang boss to evade his pursuers.

Suzy was in the States when Jim Brown died: 'I didn't believe he was gone. He was a legend. I didn't believe it so I didn't cry. But later, I went to May Pen cemetery on Spanishtown Road – Tivoli's cemetery – and when I saw his grave, I cried.'

Tivoli Gardens came to a standstill as 35,000 people attended Jim Brown's funeral. At the head of the procession which wound its way to May Pen was Edward Seaga, the ex-Prime Minister and leader of the JLP. An interviewer from Jamaican television asked Seaga why he was mourning so publicly a man wanted in the United States on charges of drug trafficking and murder. Seaga replied: 'As long as you and other people keep looking at the man's background rather than where he stands in the community, you will always ask a question like that. Ask the lawyer if he looks at the background, ask the clergyman who takes a confession if he looks at the background. Look at the man in terms of how the community respects and treats him as a protector from their community.'

Fifteen months later, during an election press conference in Kingston, I put the same question to Seaga, and got almost exactly the same response. 'Community protector' may not be an epitaph which the law enforcers of the United States or Britain would choose, but the ghetto which nurtured Jim Brown is determined to have the last word, come hell or highwater.

Chapter Six

Operation Dalehouse

The Jamaican tourist brochures promise the winter traveller breadfruit and banyan trees. Multi-coloured hibiscus flowers as large as saucers. Croaker lizards and tree frogs. For warmth and colour, London offers the January sales.

It is late January 1992, four weeks before the untimely death of Jim Brown. On a street in Brixton, two shivering plain-clothes police officers are keeping a suspect under surveillance. He is a British crack dealer and they are trying to build a case against him. They film him deep in conversation with another black man, who is in his early twenties, expensively dressed and wearing a silver Rolex Oyster watch on one wrist and a chunky gold ID bracelet on the other. His name is etched in white gold on the bar.

As he moves his head, the spun gold of a Cuban-link chain glitters against the dark skin of his neck. Aside from the fact that he is flaunting several thousand pounds' worth of jewellery, the body language tells the watchers that he is the dominant partner in the relationship. The surveillance operation has been going on for several weeks and the police reckon that by now they can put a name to most of the contacts their target is meeting on the streets. But this is a face they have not seen before, and they are intrigued. That evening, one of the officers meets an informant at a cafe near the former 'front line' in Railton Road. He slides over a photograph of the unidentified contact and asks: 'Do you know him?' The response is unexpected. The informant looks agitated and nervous and whispers: 'Sure, I know him, man. That's Jah T. I tell you, if he here, you have trouble.'

As streetnames go, Jah T is on the portentous side but then his real name also carried an imperious swagger. Jah T was born Mark Anthony Coke and he was the son of Jim Brown, whose given name was Lester Lloyd Coke. With his father in jail, Jah T was the de facto don of Tivoli Gardens, inheriting his responsibilities and his enemies. What he was doing on a Brixton street in January 1992 is uncertain. He may have been setting up a crack deal. He may have been 'chillin' in London because the lead content in the Kingston air was just a little too high to guarantee his continued safety. Whatever, it is too late to ask him now because a fortnight after he was spotted in Brixton, an M16 rifle cut short his life in his home town.

Jah T's demise is a perfect illustration of the distorted code of values by which Jamaican gangsters live and die. It is a topsy-turvy world in which being 'bad' is good and in which status is maintained by behaviour which in any civilised society would earn opprobrium. The magic word is 'respect'. It is as much a talisman as the gun. Without respect from those around him, the emperor has no clothes. To disrespect (usually abbreviated to 'dis') the don is tantamount to subverting his authority beyond redemption. In Jah T's case, the process which was to lead inexorably to a violent death began at a beach party at Fort Clarence, ten miles down the coast from Kingston. In keeping with local tradition – a tradition which is now routinely imitated at Jamaican clubs and parties in Britain – the dee-jay proposed a gun salute to the local warlords. 'Respect to Jah T, respect to Phang,' he shouted, and then stood back as the M16s and Uzis chorused their approval.

Georgie Phang was a leader of the Jungle Posse. The Concrete Jungle is a colloquial name for Arnett Gardens, the power base of the People's National Party. Its gunmen were, of course, implacably hostile to the Shower Posse headed by Jim Brown and his son. To propose a salute to both sides was a diplomatic necessity but the dee-jay still committed a fatal error: uttering Jah T's name first was interpreted as a mark of profound disrespect to Georgie Phang. Phang's supporters sought immediate revenge by attacking the dee-jay. Jah T's cohorts retaliated with a random shooting of the enemy and that, in turn, was avenged with a prize scalp.

On 2 February 1992, Jah T went to visit his mother, Miss Bev, who lives in Barbican, a classy area well away from Tivoli Gardens, Jah T's power base. For security, he never travelled alone and he took some of his 'soldiers' with him. But they never got further than Maxfield Avenue which runs uptown from Spanishtown Road. As the group came round a bend on their motor bikes, they were ambushed by an assassin with an M16. Jah T was flung to the road in a cascade of oil and blood. Two of the bodyguards were also cut down. There were chaotic scenes at Kingston Public Hospital when the bodies were brought in. As news of the shootings spread, hundreds of gun-toting JLP supporters from Tivoli began arriving to vent their anger. The churning mass filled up the waiting rooms and spilled over into the wards, causing such confusion that, some allege, it obstructed the surgeons in their efforts to save Jah T's life. Within the hour, he had bled to death.

Twenty-one days later, the young pretender was laid to rest, in a prolonged display of public mourning. From 9 a.m. to midday, the body, dressed in a black satin suit and white gloves, lay 'in state' at the Tivoli community centre. The white casket with silver handles reputedly cost $4,000. At noon, Jah T was taken by hearse to the Halibethean church for the funeral service. His three baby mothers – including his common-law wife, Debbie 'Foxy' Golding – stood in the front pews, dabbing their eyes with lace handkerchiefs. Behind them, a phalanx of young men and women, dressed, according to the *Daily Gleaner* 'in the most stunning black designs, matched with gold accessories' sang hymns lustily.

Two hours later, the hearse moved slowly down Spanishtown Road towards May Pen cemetery, followed by a crowd of some 25,000. The procession was led by the JLP leader, Edward Seaga. The mourners, watched by lines of police and soldiers, shouted pro-JLP slogans and gave v-signs. Jah T was interred in a cemetery where a disproportionately high number of the graves bear the bodies of young men murdered in gunfights. And on the very same day, within hours of the funeral, his father, Jim Brown, met his own gruesome end in Kingston General Penitentiary. He was forty-seven. (Father and son now lie side by side in the cemetery.)

Miss Bev remembers being stunned with shock for days afterwards. 'When Tony (her name for Jah T) was killed, the only one I had to lean on was Jim. He was a tower of strength. After we had buried Tony, I went to the jail to see Jim and he give me great comfort. It was only an hour or so later, that someone tell me there's a fire at the prison and I rush up there. But it was too late. Jim was already dead.'

In Jamaica, death begets death: over the following week, more than a dozen people lost their lives and many more were injured as a vicious wave of bloodletting between the PNP and the JLP washed through the Kingston slums. Then Jah T's brother, Dudley, emerged to claim the donship of Tivoli and what passes for normality was restored.

* * *

The detectives who spotted Jah T in Brixton were not there by accident. They were working under the banner of Operation Dalehouse, the most successful police initiative launched against crack-related crime in the UK. By the time it was wound up in November 1992, the thirty-five detectives on the team had made 274 arrests for crimes in South London, embracing murder, kidnapping, armed robbery and drug dealing. More than a hundred of the drugs seizures were crack, with an estimated street value of £1,000,000. The Dalehouse database logged 3,500 names, a significant number of them Jamaican 'illegals'. And the information stored on computer was shared with detectives in other Met areas, who found themselves investigating fifteen crack-related murders in the months after Dalehouse came into being. But the extraordinary thing is that despite the American experience with the posses, and the shrill warnings from the ATF and other agencies, most police officers in Britain were still taken by surprise when the shootings and the stabbings began to claim more and more of their time.

Dalehouse came into being in August 1991 as the result of one particular crime committed four months earlier in April. Towards the end of a weekday afternoon, a group of five black men robbed a jeweller's shop in Brixton's Granville Arcade. As soon as they burst in, the owner, Charles Fisher, could see they were serious. He was not the type to pick an argument with a sawn-off 12-bore shotgun and he offered no resistance. When they told him to strip the display cabinets of all the trays carrying gold items, he moved with speed. But his compliance was academic. As the gang gathered up their haul, one of them leaned casually across the counter and blasted Mr Fisher at the range of two feet. His anguished scream could be heard the length of the arcade. By the time the police and ambulance arrived, the shop carpet was already sodden with blood and shards of flesh ripped from his groin. The wound was so serious

77

that the investigating officers fully expected the case to turn into a murder inquiry. But Charles Fisher was surprisingly robust and somehow, despite massive loss of blood, he survived.

The inquiry was put in the hands of Scotland Yard's Flying Squad but it was not long before a wholly new approach was set in motion. 'There was something odd about this incident,' says Detective Superintendent John Jones, who headed Operation Dalehouse. 'Fisher did nothing to obstruct the gang, yet they almost murdered him. It was as though the shooting itself was the primary object rather than the robbery. We decided that we needed to take a closer look at it.'

If the decision to wind up Dalehouse after sixteen months was an error, at least the right man had been chosen to lead it. There are some Met officers who would have interpreted the 'closer look' as an exercise in masonic secretiveness with the principal aim of scoring professional points and advancing a career or two. John Jones is emphatically not of that breed. He's an engaging man, who looks disconcertingly like the jazz musician, Kenny Ball, chain-smokes and drives a scruffy white Scimitar 1800 sports car. When the call came, he was acknowledged as a resourceful career detective with nearly thirty years' service. In October 1993, when PC Patrick Dunne was murdered in Clapham, colleagues were reassured to know that the officer in charge of the investigation was 'JJ'.

Planning how Dalehouse should proceed, Jones had – for the Met, anyway – fairly progressive ideas about sharing information and methods of working with other units, such as the passport specialists of the Yard's SO1 (3) branch, and the Home Office immigration teams. Some of his contemporaries told him flatly that he was being naive and that he would get his fingers burnt by keeping an 'open house' approach at Croydon police headquarters, the operational base for Dalehouse.

And, on reflection, he reckons that the efforts of his team were often undermined – the culprits, in his view, being Home Office civil servants who failed to prevent illegal immigrants from Jamaica with a history of violence from re-entering the country. But then, in the early stages, even the police had no real idea of the extent of the crime wave they were facing.

John Jones: 'After the shooting of Charles Fisher, we set up an AMIP squad at Croydon. (AMIP stands for Area Major Investigation Pool and is on permanent standby to handle serious crime inquiries, including murders.) Fairly quickly, we identified the people responsible for the robbery. They were members of a black group called The Syndicate. There were five or six of them, some Jamaican, some English-born, and the more we found out about them, the more astonished we became. We discovered that one of our key suspects had only recently been deported to Jamaica as an illegal entrant. But when we looked at the file a little closer, it emerged that he had been deported eight times in one year – and had returned to the UK each time using a different false passport.

'When we began interviewing people, they told us that The Syndicate had been responsible for a whole series of crimes, most of which we knew nothing about, and all of which were unsolved.'

It was said they had carried out a spate of armed robberies at dance halls, clubs and private parties. Some of their victims had been shot. Others pistol-whipped and beaten with baseball bats. Gas-guns had been fired, gas bombs thrown into crowded rooms. All those on the receiving end were black and none had gone to the police for fear of reprisals. In one incident, a heavily armed gang robbed 300 youngsters at a disco. Not one of the victims or witnesses reported it to the police. In June 1991, 400 people were attending a fund-raising event at a Brixton community centre when a group fired sawn-off shotguns and pistols around the room. Again, the affair went unrecorded. When the crime was so serious that the police had to be involved, desperate attempts were made to hide the evidence. A man was almost killed at the Academy dance hall in Brixton, but even as the ambulance crew was stretchering his body away, spent cartridge cases – and other forensic clues – mysteriously disappeared from the floor.

In the most notorious case of all, Mark Burnett was shot dead on the dance floor of the Podium nightclub in Vauxhall. The place was packed with 2,000 revellers. Yet, when the police started interviewing potential witnesses, either they had seen nothing or they were in the toilet at the time. 'Those toilets must have been jammed full if you believe these accounts,' says John Jones. Not only did those standing close to Mark Burnett deny all knowledge of who shot him at point-blank range, the first concern of many was to strip his dying body of the gold and jewellery he was wearing.

And when John Jones's officers arrested suspects, they were faced with more frustration.

'Most of them just sat there in the police interview room exercising their right to silence. Of the 274 arrests, I bet not more than twenty answered any police questions at all. And remember we are not talking here about professional villains who you would expect to exploit every legal loophole. These were just young thugs or hoodlums contemptuously sticking two fingers up and saying: "Sod you, mate." You can imagine how we felt.

'As well as the overt violence, the members of The Syndicate were also using their girlfriends, or baby mothers, to commit cheque and credit card frauds. We recovered stolen cheque books, credit cards, driving licences and passports. And the point of all this criminal activity was to raise funds to pay for a steady flow of couriers to bring in cocaine from Jamaica and the States.'

And they had been pretty successful. The police found cocaine valued at some £90,000 when they broke up The Syndicate – as well as a veritable arsenal of weapons, which explained why shootings in parts of South London were happening at the rate of three a fortnight. At the beginning of the inquiry, despite the unmistakable evidence of hospital admissions, some officers had been sceptical about this catalogue of violence. Was it really happening on their patch? But when they started pumping their informants, the doubts disappeared.

'We would get a report that a .32 or a .45 had been fired. Detectives would go to the scene and find no trace of an incident from talking to people. But when they started searching the area, they would discover spent cartridge cases. So it was clear that something had happened. It was just that no-one would dare tell us about it.

'Then we started going back over previous major inquiries in South London which bore similar characteristics and which remained unsolved. We used the HOLMES database to pick out distinguishing features. And by comparing this with witness and ballistic evidence from our own investigations, we came to the conclusion that there was a consistent pattern emerging. What's more, here was a growing class of serious, violent crime which the police were barely touching at all. It was quite an eye-opener for us, I can tell you.'

That pattern becomes starkly clear when you consider the evidence of a confidential and hitherto unpublished police report, submitted to Scotland Yard to underline the threat posed by crack-related gangsters. It details the following ten crimes committed in London over a period of twenty-seven months.

1. Shooting and attempted murder of Clifton Scott – 23.11.88.

81

2. Murder by stabbing of Marie Burke, a senior official of the US embassy visa staff – 24.5.89.

3. Kidnapping of drug courier, Julia Morris – 19.7.90.

4. Shooting and murder of Glen Abdul at Maxim's night club – 19.7.90.

5. Shooting and murder of Emmet Rattray and attempted murder of Clive Mackenzie – 1.9.90.

6. Shooting at and attempted murder of PCs Crawford and Macdonald at Myatts Field by Albert Hinds – 17.9.90.

7. Shooting of and attempted murder of Aubrey Rose, followed by the shooting at and attempted murder of two pursuing police officers at the Academy night club – 30.9.90.

8. Attempted murder of Fitzroy Francis by two men with a handgun in the street – 16.12.90.

9. Shooting of and murder of Nicholas Johnson and attempted murder of Joseph Waters.

10. Shooting of and attempted murder of Winston Delgado – 8.2.91.

The report then explains the links discovered between these crimes. It says: 'All these offences – except no. 2 – involved drug dealers seeking revenge.' Number Two, incidentally, shows the extraordinary audacity and brutality of the crack gangs. Marie Burke, a Jamaican, discovered that a colleague in the consular section of the US embassy was illegally providing visas to enable Jamaican crack dealers to enter the US. She was about to blow the whistle but never got the chance. She was strangled and stabbed at her home in Central London. Her killers were never caught – though their identity is known.

* * *

The report goes on:

> The same firearm used in nos. 9 and 10 (confirmed by the Met. forensic laboratory).
>
> Fitzroy Francis was one of the offenders in nos. 1 and 10. He was the victim in no. 8.
>
> The same firearm used in nos. 1 and 4 (Lab. confirmed). Dudley Johnson (an imported hired assassin from Jamaica) was the gunman in nos. 4 and 5.
>
> Abdul, the victim of no. 4, was an imported killer responsible with others for the murder of Marie Burke at no. 2.
>
> V.A., a major London crack trafficker, organised the shooting of Delgado at no. 10. (Delgado being a member of a rival gang which was flooding the market with cheap cocaine.) The gunman was a Jamaican Yardie brought from Birmingham specifically for this purpose. He also organised the Shenola shooting at no. 9 for which his brother and an associate were charged.
>
> The girl courier at no. 3 was bringing in cocaine from Canada for V.A. She dropped the drugs through fear of arrest but was then kidnapped by two men, associates of V.A, who were the promoters at the Shenola on the night of the shooting at no. 9.
>
> The gunman in no. 5 was another illegal immigrant assassin employed by V.A.'s organisation. The offender at no. 6 was also an employee of V.A. This man was arrested only after the police had been given a good deal of misinformation by another person who was the organiser of the false visa racket at the US Embassy and believed to have been a co-conspirator in the Marie Burke murder.

* * *

The report goes on to note that 'the following facts are of special interest':

a.   In two of the ten offences examined, police officers were fired on.

b.   In several of the offences, hired gunmen were brought in, sometimes from the other side of the world, to carry out the murders.

John Jones: 'Operation Dalehouse taught us what the US law enforcement agencies had discovered in the mid-eighties. That where crack is concerned, national boundaries mean absolutely nothing.

'In every one of the murders and attempted murders we investigated, there was clear evidence of the involvement of Jamaican gunmen. Some of them lived in the UK, some in the US, some in Jamaica. But nothing prevented them travelling between those countries to commit serious crimes. So, a number of our inquiries had to be conducted overseas as well as in South London. For most of the officers involved in the operation, it was a unique criminal investigation.'

John Jones is talking at Thornton Heath police station, an unlovely 1960s building a few miles from his headquarters at Croydon. The ground floor houses the Territorial Support Group and the dog handler section. We are on the first floor in a murder incident room. The operation has been given the name, Ferryden.

The names of the team members are chalked up on a blackboard. The numbers on the left-hand side of the board indicate how many 'actions', that is, lines of inquiry, have been instigated. The latest figure is 144. Behind a bank of phones, an officer called the 'receiver' is hunched over a computer terminal. It is his task to process all the information generated by the investigation so that some sense can be made of it. All this is part of the routine furniture of an incident room. But the data on the computer screen carries clues which tell the initiated that this is a *Jamaican* inquiry. The words 'Killer', 'Blue' and 'Indian', which crop up from time to time, are streetnames. And though they give the impression that this is some kind of elaborate video game, they may well be the most effective means of securing an arrest.

John Jones: 'If you show a photo of someone to an informant, the chances are that he will identify him by a streetname. And if you then say: "Well, who is he?" he will tell you that he comes from Manchester in Kingston. His parents live in Tivoli Gardens. He has got three children. But he won't be able to tell you what his proper name is. Even if he has known the man for thirty years.

'Now, what we do is put the streetnames together with other intelligence. For instance, an informant might tell us that someone called "Fingers" has entered the country illegally. And that may be the extent of his information. Meanwhile, we show a photo to another informant who says he doesn't know the name, but he does know that the guy drives a red BMW. From someone else, we may learn who his girlfriend is. So, gradually, we can piece together a picture. Eventually, and it may take a long time, we come up with the real name.'

Indeed, Operation Ferryden itself provides as good an example as any of the problems of identification posed by many crack murders. It also demonstrates how even when good police work produces arrests, reluctant witnesses can hamstring a prosecution. In this case, the challenge was to unravel the violent death of a man detectives came to know as Tom British.

Chapter Seven

The Murder of Tom British

It is a Saturday evening in Brixton. The date – 6 February 1993. Ragga is pulsing from the sound systems. At dance halls like the Vox, girls sheathed in Lycra and men in razor-slashed jeans and pumps are gearing themselves for a long, sweaty night. In the clubs and shebeens, domino contests are already cranking up the passions. The Caribbean cafes are struggling to satisfy a stream of impatient demands for curry goat, fried salt fish with onions, tripe and beans. Wherever you look and listen and smell, there is an excess of life. Except for one small corner of SW9, where a body lies bleeding to death.

Carrara Walk is on the Somerleyton estate, just the width of the railway line from Brixton's main artery, Railton Road. It is a series of box-like council-owned maisonettes clad in honey-coloured brick. At around 8.15, two black prostitutes called Janet and Sophie walk across the road to number 50. The registered tenant of number 50 is a man named Leon Grant. But he is away for some time. Officially, the flat is empty but since the turn of the year, two Jamaicans in their twenties have been using it, on an irregular basis, to smoke a few spliffs, drink and get laid. Both the whores are crack addicts and have become frequent visitors to their part-time neighbours across the street.

As the girls get closer, they realise something is wrong. Something is missing. Normally, at all hours of the day or night, despite the persistent complaints of the neighbours, waves of bass riffs surge from the flat like breakers. Tonight, there is nothing but silence. And then, they notice that the front door is ajar.

The body is lying on the floor of the sitting room. One bullet has been enough. A shot from a .32 automatic from close range has torn through the jugular and the breast bone, and exited through the back. There is still a faint pulse but the breath is coming in increasingly shallow spurts. Janet and Sophie run, trembling, to a phone box.

The dying man expired within half an hour of arriving at hospital. The first task of the police was to establish who he was. But the corpse offered not a single clue. His pockets contained a couple of hundred pounds and seven rocks of crack. There were heavy gold rings on both hands, wrist bracelets and a medallion looped around the bloodied neck. Nothing else which would help identification. He was a black man, aged around thirty, with a bullet hole in his neck. Not much to put on a report sheet.

About an hour later, the police received a 999 call from a man speaking from a public phone box. All he said was that there had been a shooting at number 50 Carrara Walk, Brixton. No names, no explanations. The operator tried to keep him talking but he hung up in under sixty seconds. The call was traced, though, and it came from Peckham.

The police found it interesting that the dead man had not been robbed of his jewellery, nor the £200 in his pocket. And then there was the question of the seven rocks of crack found on him. Detectives thought that the killers may have planted the drugs, following the pattern of a number of Jamaican murders in the United States. It is a ploy to divert attention

87

from the real motive – on the supposition that the inquiry team will not try too hard to solve the case if they think it is just another crack killing.

Janet and Sophie were not much help to the investigators. Neither had any reason to be friendly towards the police. They had never cooperated in the past. Sophie, who came from Harlesden in North-west London, was a former girlfriend of a man known as Yardie Ron, who was shot dead in a night club in 1989. She was the key witness then but declined to testify. No-one was ever convicted of that murder.

In this fresh murder inquiry, the women told the detectives that they had known the dead man by a kind of streetname, Tom British, and that he came from Jamaica. When pressed, they revealed that he had been using the flat with another Jamaican whom they knew only as Richie – sometimes referred to as Rich Kid. Apart from that, there was nothing else which they could, or would, contribute to the investigation. At first, the police thought that the victim was the registered tenant of the property, Leon Grant. That would have been neat and simple. But a routine check established that Grant was indeed away – he was in one of Her Majesty's prisons.

The first break came two days later. A black woman, who gave her name as Desrene Blake, walked into Brixton police station and said she had some information which might be of help in a murder inquiry. She was carrying a Jamaican passport, issued in the name of Starrel Powell. According to the entry stamp, Powell had arrived in the UK on 7 December 1992. The photograph was that of the dead man from Carrara Walk. Desrene said that he had been staying with her in Lewisham though she had no idea that he was also using a flat in Brixton or why he had been killed. The police were sceptical about that, especially when, under questioning, Desrene revealed a possible motive.

She admitted that before Starrel Powell had arrived on the scene, she had shared her flat with a character called 'Blue', who had a history of violence. Their relationship ended when 'Blue' was sent to jail. But he had recently been released and had turned up at the flat to reclaim, if not his woman, then at least his clothes, television set, and video recorder, which had been left behind for safe keeping. Unfortunately, Desrene was out when he called – and the door was opened by a Jamaican who declined to give his name and was less than pleased to meet his woman's former lover. Starrel Powell told 'Blue' to 'fuck off, if you know what's good for you, man'. Blue retaliated by pulling a gun and firing one shot into the ceiling and another through a window. He left with his clothes and TV set – but without his video recorder. Neighbours heard his muttered threats.

Not surprisingly, 'Blue' was a strong suspect. He certainly had a motive, though it seemed slightly improbable that he would pass up the opportunity to shoot Powell in the white heat of anger yet feel the need to kill him in cold blood several days later. Given 'Blue' 's antecedents, it also appeared unlikely that he would squander the chance to profit from the murder by leaving behind the dead man's money and jewellery. But the theorising became academic when the police learned that 'Blue' had a cast-iron alibi and that, in any event, a new element had entered the equation.

Steve Barker is a detective constable attached to the drug squad at Brixton police station. He has been brought into a number of Jamaican-related murder inquiries because some of his informants move in that shadowy world of crack, guns and illegal immigration, which is closed off to all but a few specialist officers. They call him 'John Wayne' on the street – a reference not only to his height but also to his tenacity when investigating a crime.

Three days after the murder, on 9 February, Steve Barker was talking to one of his regular informants and showed him a photograph of Starrel Powell. The response was very interesting. 'Sure, I know him, man. I was in approved school with him. He used to sell cheap jewellery. You would see him around Kingston on his bike. He was basically a con man. His streetname is Tom. That's the only name I have for him. I hear someone shoot him.'

The name, Starrel Powell, meant nothing to the informant, which reinforced the police view that the passport was a false one. It now became more important than ever to trace the mysterious Richie whose disappearance from the scene suggested that he knew more than a thing or two about the death of his friend – whoever he really was. Inquiries uncovered two Brixton characters known as Rich or Richie Kid, who might have fitted the bill. Somewhat confusingly, both had the same surname, Wallace, and it took some patient detective work to put one of them in the frame.

On the night of the murder, a black woman had gone to King's College hospital in East Dulwich asking for a patient called Tom British. The name meant nothing to the hospital staff but when she explained that he had been brought in with gunshot wounds from Brixton, they knew who she was talking about (though it has to be said that on some nights, the gunshot count amongst patients at King's College hospital is so high that far more specific information would be needed). By that time, the man from Carrara Walk was already dead, and on hearing this, the woman disappeared without leaving her name. Her description could have fitted two people in whom the inquiry had an interest. One was Desrene Blake. The other was a girl called Tina, who was known by the police to be the current girlfriend of one of the Richie Wallaces.

Desrene was quickly ruled out. It was clear that she knew

the dead man only as Starrel Powell. And from other information, it appeared fairly certain that she was not aware of the killing until the day that she went to the police with the passport. That left Tina and her elusive boyfriend, Rich Kid. It did not take the police too long to track them down. Officers drew a blank at Tina's flat but on 10 February, four days after the murder, they went to her parents' home in Peckham. Tina was in the living room and after a search, they found Richie hiding behind a secret panel in the bedroom. He had an axe and a machete with him but he came quietly.

When the police arrested Richie, they thought they had broken the back of the inquiry. He admitted that he was the person who had made the anonymous phone call shortly after the murder and he confirmed police suspicions that their prime suspect was a man known as Indian, who had serious form for violence. But in a crack-related murder, little is straightforward and if detectives had had an inkling of what frustrations lay ahead, they might well have been tempted to abandon the case there and then.

Richie's story went like this. He and his friend, Tom British, decided to make some quick money by going into crack dealing together. They planned to use the empty flat in Carrara Walk as their base. Tom had no cash to sink into the venture but Richie was prepared to put up £700. That was not enough to keep them going for long, so Richie approached Indian and asked whether he would like to stake them. Indian is the streetname of Asim Ahmed, a well-known Brixton hard man who moves in Jamaican drug-dealing circles and dresses like a Yardie, though, somewhat confusingly, he is of Pakistani origin. He agreed to put £1400 into the kitty.

At this point, Richie gave the police two versions of what followed. In the first, he said he was on his way to Stockwell with the £2100 to buy cocaine when he was mugged and robbed by two black men. Richie rang Indian to recount what had happened. Naturally, he was less than pleased to be told that he had handed over £1400 for nothing, and he gathered three associates – O., a Jamaican, P., a black Brit, and W., a tough, ex-boxer from North London who had just done time for armed robbery – to confront Richie face to face. The showdown took place at 50 Carrara Walk. Indian made it plain that he suspected Richie of inventing the story of the robbery to cover a blatant rip-off and he became increasingly agitated. (Some of this was later corroborated by a delivery boy from a nearby West Indian food shop who called at the flat as the temperature began to hot up.)

As the shouting turned to physical threats, Tom British – a man with a hair-trigger temper – intervened on Richie's behalf and tried to force the other four men out of the flat. But he succeeded only in drawing their wrath on himself. According to Richie, they made an attempt to wrench some of his jewellery from his fingers and began abusing him. One of the four, P., suddenly left the flat and went to their BMW parked outside. He returned with a .32 calibre automatic pistol and gave it to Indian. Without warning, Indian fired one fatal bullet into Tom British's neck.

That left Richie alone with the killers. They bundled him outside and Indian told the others what to do. P. was instructed to get rid of the gun while the other three jumped into the BMW, Richie squeezed between two of them on the back seat. He was told it would be a short journey – for him. They were going to kill him. Richie pleaded that that would be crazy. Indian would never get his money back if they did. Indian ordered him to keep his mouth shut. The car travelled less than two miles, to a park in Camberwell. Indian took a gun from the glove compartment, handed it to W. and told him that this would be a good spot to execute the hapless Richie.

The two men got out and watched the BMW speed away down the road.

Richie remembers standing by some railings preparing to die while W. checked the clip in the pistol. He saw the barrel being raised towards his head and was wondering if a sudden sprint might save him, when the bonnet of the BMW unexpectedly bore down on them. Its hub caps clipped the kerb and Indian casually leaned out and said: 'I've changed my mind. Get in.'

The car was now heading back towards Brixton while Indian explained that their first priority must be to destroy any evidence left at 50 Carrara Walk. They would set fire to it, with the body of Tom British inside. The car pulled into the first garage forecourt they came to and Indian and O. got out to buy a can of petrol. W., having earlier been deprived of his victim, had relaxed his vigilance and Richie needed no second invitation. He was through the door and running hard before the lumbering boxer had even emerged from the car. There was no catching him. Thirty minutes later, Richie slipped into a public phone box and alerted the police to the body lying on the floor of number 50 Carrara Walk. By the time that the flashing blue lights arrived at the flat, a hasty attempt had been made to set it alight. But it had been botched.

The detectives who took Richie's statement had no reason to believe anything he had told them. He had form for crack dealing and robbery and would have had few qualms about inventing a version of events to cast himself as victim rather than villain. But they felt he was unlikely to be a murderer. Moreover, local knowledge of Indian and his associates suggested that they were perfectly capable of committing the crime. The casual callousness of the shooting and the almost farcical aftermath also carried the ring of truth.

One of the murder squad said: 'That is exactly the sort of

thing which happens in these crack feuds. It was only £1400 after all. Not a killing matter, even for many criminals. But where crack is involved, the "rules" just don't apply. If someone has a gun, they are almost bound to use it.'

The day after he made his statement, Richie asked to change it. He told the police that the murder and subsequent events were exactly as he had described them. But he had been lying about the build-up to protect his girlfriend, Tina. She was the one who had been carrying the cash to buy the crack and had faked the robbery to rip off Indian. The plot had been hatched by Tina and O.'s girl, Florence. Richie had known nothing about it.

According to this version, the plan had been carefully worked out. Tina had gone into a solicitor's office in Kennington, apparently very distressed, saying that she had just been mugged on the pavement. She was too upset to speak on the phone but would the secretary be so kind as to ring a number for her and explain what had happened? The number was Indian's.

'Knowing Tina, I am pretty sure that this is what really happened. She is a conniving little bitch,' said one of the murder squad. 'Richie told us that the prime mover in this whole plot was Florence. But frankly, none of that mattered too much. Our job was to catch the killers.'

Within a month, three-quarters of the task had been completed. P., who had disposed of the gun, was arrested in Clapham on 23 February, O. and W. were picked up in the first few days of March. P. claimed that he had never been anywhere near the flat in Carrara Walk. The other two admitted they were there on the night of the murder but said that neither of them had fired the fatal shot. It looked as though the pieces of the jigsaw puzzle were gradually falling into place. There had even been progress on the vexed question of the dead man's identity.

Two weeks after the murder, a Jamaican woman had contacted Brixton police to say she thought she had some useful information. Her name was Carol Baker and the information was that the dead man was almost certainly her husband, Paul. Carol said they had been married in Jamaica but had split up a year earlier. She had seen him when he arrived at Heathrow in December, but not since. She knew nothing about his movements or associates. She gave detectives the name of her husband's mother in Jamaica and a call to her substantiated the story. Tom British a.k.a. Starrel Powell was, in reality, Paul Baker.

But in this murder inquiry, every step forward was followed by two back. Having captured three of the gang and finally settled the issue of the victim's identity, the police discovered that Indian had fled the country and was almost certainly in Pakistan, where he had family. Britain has no extradition arrangement with Pakistan.

Although the police investigate a crime, the job of taking the case to court has rested, since 1986, with the Crown Prosecution Service. In a murder charge, the first stage in the prosecution process is a remand, usually in custody, but occasionally on bail. The next step is the committal hearing, at which a magistrate is asked to send the case for full trial to a crown court.

The law states that no more than seventy days shall elapse between the arrest of a suspect and the committal for trial. In this case, the clock had started with the arrest of P. on 23 February and would be stopped on 3 May. In many prosecutions, that would present few problems. But this one was different. A CPS lawyer, who we shall call John Williams to preserve his anonymity, had the task of trying to square an awkward circle:

'Our information was that Indian had fired the gun but the others were equally guilty because they were acting in concert with him. It was what we call a "joint enterprise". But since Indian had escaped our clutches, we were running the charge without the principal party. It was like *Hamlet* without the prince.

'It seemed pretty unlikely that Indian would be found – never mind brought back – before 3 May so we had two options open to us. One was to go ahead with a weakened prosecution, and risk having the case thrown out at committal stage. The other was to withdraw the charges until such time as Indian was also in custody. But we were dealing with a murder here, and the second option seemed unthinkable. So we decided to press ahead.'

The committal hearing was set for 23 April at Camberwell magistrates court. If ever a case hinged on witness identification this was it. There was no expectation that either O. or W. would turn queen's evidence and implicate Indian. P. had exercised his right to silence throughout. There was little conclusive forensic evidence – the murder weapon had never been found. Other than those present in the flat, no-one had seen what happened. The evidence of Richie, therefore, was crucial.

In all too many crack murders, the key witness has either refused to give evidence at all or withdrawn testimony at the last minute through fear. More than one notorious crack gangster is walking around London at this moment because intimidated witnesses have backed away from pointing the finger in court. So it was clear that Richie had to be wrapped in cotton wool if he was going to be coaxed into court to nail the killers of Paul Baker. The police decided to put him in a South London hotel under close protection. Richie agreed on one condition – that Tina could stay with him.

'We had very little choice,' said a senior detective on the inquiry, 'because without Richie we had no case. But we knew damn well that Tina was a demanding little bitch and we were prepared to be milked by the pair of them in order to get Richie to court.'

And they were. A television in the room was not sufficient for Tina and Richie. They had to have a video recorder installed. They needed a mini bar as well – and it had to be plentifully stocked. They made phone calls all over the world at peak times. 'I tell you, they drank us dry and cost us a fortune. Correction – cost the taxpayer a fortune.' Despite such pampering, however, Richie began thinking twice about appearing in court to give evidence. On 8 April, a fortnight before the vital committal hearing, he disappeared from the hotel in the middle of the night, high-tailed it to Heathrow and caught a plane to New York. The murder inquiry team had a shrewd idea that if he left the country, he would head for New York, so while his plane was still in the air, a discreet call was placed to the immigration authorities at John F. Kennedy airport. Richie was held as an undesirable entrant and put on the first available flight back to Heathrow.

On 23 April, at 9.30 a.m., John Williams from the CPS arrived at Camberwell magistrates court hoping for a successful day. He had heard about Richie's brief escapade on the 8th but had been assured that he was back in the country and due to have met the police on the afternoon of the 22nd to check the arrangements for the committal hearing. Within ten minutes, however, the CPS knew the day was not going to be a good one. The worried face of the sergeant on the case told its own story. Richie had failed to show up for the previous afternoon's meeting. The hotel hadn't seen him. The police were searching all his known haunts.

By 10.15, the clerk to the court was getting restless. The

defendants were waiting to be brought up from the cells. Their counsel was ready. The stipendiary magistrate had a busy programme. He was prepared to take other matters first but, by noon, the Crown would have to decide what it wanted to do.

John Williams: 'I knew it was expecting a miracle for Richie to be brought in by then. So I had to apply for an adjournment. I asked for four days to give the police time to make inquiries. Defendants' counsel opposed the application – but it was granted.'

It proved a temporary reprieve only. Richie had gone thoroughly to ground and when the cast reassembled in the courtroom on the 27th, it was depressingly clear to the CPS that the case was crumbling to dust.

'I got up and said that without our principal witness, we were not in a position to proceed. Reluctantly, therefore, we would have to drop all the charges. It was a temporary stipendiary this time, and she looked astonished. I am not surprised. It is not every day that you have three alleged murderers in front of you and have to discharge them.'

O., P. and W. walked from the court smiling broadly, convinced that there was quite a lot to be said for British justice after all.

At this point, it looked very much as though, despite all the hard work, the murder of Paul Baker would have to remain on the file. It certainly wouldn't have been the first time in a drugs killing. Despite the public clamour for greater efficiency in the fight against crime, case-hardened officers know that, often, an arrest is only the beginning of their problems. The requirements of the justice system, such as disclosure of evidence, and witness intimidation can nullify even the most assiduous detective work. The inquiry team were prepared to put this down as yet another one which had got away. But then, out of the blue, some good news for a change. A telex arrived from Pakistan informing the murder squad that Indian had been arrested and was willing to return to the UK. A detective inspector and a sergeant were on the first available flight to Karachi to interview him.

'Put it down to the international brotherhood of police officers,' said one detective. 'With no extradition treaty in force, we had no leverage. But at whatever level, some kind of pressure was obviously exerted over there.

'From what I am told, Indian was being held in pretty appalling conditions – even kept in chains some of the time. And he was only too glad to get out of jail – even if it meant facing a murder trial. He signed a consent form pretty damn quick and we had him on a flight back to Heathrow. Mind you, he wasn't so fazed that he forgot about his right to silence. He said nothing at all when he was interviewed and formally charged.'

The return under escort of Indian solved one problem but highlighted another with which the harassed CPS lawyer, John Williams, now had to wrestle: 'First it was *Hamlet* without the prince. Now, we had the prince but not the supporting cast.

'An old-style committal hearing was arranged for 18 June, but without our star witness, Richie, we were pessimistic about our chances of getting Indian to a trial. It was beginning to look as if our luck was permanently out on this case.'

But not completely. With three days to spare, on 15 June, the police finally tracked down Richie and 'sat on him' until the hearing at Camberwell. On the 18th, Richie duly came to court, said his piece and, to much relief all round, Indian was committed for trial to the Old Bailey.

John Williams: 'I must say that, even with Richie's evidence, the case only just about came up to proof. But the important thing was that we had our committal.

'Having got Richie back in the fold, we decided to look at the possibility of re-arresting the other three. I took counsel's opinion and, after a series of meetings, we decided to go for it.'

To their utter amazement, O., P. and W. were all scooped up by the police and once again, charged with the murder of Paul Baker. They were remanded in custody until 26 July, the date set for committal. John Williams found himself back at Camberwell magistrates court and suffering a bad bout of déjà vu.

'At ten past ten, when Richie hadn't shown up, I knew that we were in for a replay of 27 April. And although there was no sign beforehand that he was not going to appear, I already had the feeling that he was far less interested in seeing O., P. and W. put on trial than in nailing Indian. It was Indian who had shot his friend, and I think he had far less of a grievance against the others. Perhaps, in his mind, they weren't really guilty of anything serious.'

The police immediately contacted Tina, who said that Richie had 'gone walkabout' the day before. She didn't know where he was. John Williams was becoming increasingly frustrated: 'I had my summer holiday booked for the 29th and I could see it disappearing in this mess. I was getting pretty frantic.

'So I applied for an adjournment until the morning of the 28th. The police were confident that they would find him by then. I wasn't. But they were right. They got him on the 27th and he promised to turn up. We had to rely on the promise – we couldn't keep him under lock and key, after all. We were well and truly in his hands.'

The police court duty officer who went to Richie's flat on the morning of the 28th to collect him rang the door bell for several minutes before accepting that nobody was at home. Then a neighbour poked her head out and said that, shortly before, an ambulance had turned up and taken a young couple to hospital. From the descriptions, it was clear that the young couple were Richie and Tina.

By 10.30, John Williams was in a position he knew only too well – sitting at court trying to placate a fractious clerk who was close to the end of his tether. 'When I got the news from the police, who had gone to the hospital, I thought it was a wind-up. Richie had slipped getting out of the bath and twisted his back. Can you believe it?'

The only good news was that Richie had been discharged from casualty by mid-morning, and the clerk was persuaded to re-schedule the hearing for 2 p.m. At five minutes to two, Richie hobbled into the court on crutches, accompanied by two police officers. The defendants were brought up, and for the first time since the night of Paul Baker's murder, the four men confronted each other.

What happened next defied all expectation – even for a case which had, long ago, moved into the realm of the bizarre. John Williams asked Richie a routine opening question merely to establish his connection with the events under consideration.

'Where were you on the night of 6 February, this year?' There was a long, long pause. Then the reply: 'I don't recall.' 'Were you in Brixton?' Another lengthy silence, then: 'I don't recall.' 'Did you know a man called Paul Baker also known as Tom British?' Silence. Then: 'I don't recall.'

'And so it went on,' said John Williams. 'For twenty minutes, I bombarded him with questions and he answered every one with "I don't recall". At that point, I applied to have him made a hostile witness. That means that you can put someone's statement to them to jog their memory. But the magistrate refused. He said Richie was being unco-operative but not hostile.'

The distinction seemed increasingly arcane as the hapless lawyer ploughed on. 'After another fifteen or twenty minutes,

I had run out of questions and was just asking anything which came into my head. "What does a gun do?" was one I remember. And towards the end, I even asked him what day it was. The answer was exactly the same as to all the others: "I don't recall." '

At times, before uttering yet another 'I don't recall', Richie would pause dramatically and look around, as though he was about to say something more substantial. 'I got the feeling he was probably enjoying it. There was a packed public gallery who were enthralled by the spectacle, and the defendants were absorbed by his performance. The atmosphere was quite electric. I have never experienced anything like it in court.'

If Richie had been too frightened to give evidence, the Crown could have made an application under the 1988 Criminal Justice Act to have his witness statement put before the court. 'That would have cast a different light on his behaviour because, earlier in the inquiry, he had given chapter and verse on what had happened at Carrara Walk.' But it was quite clear that fear was not the explanation for what was going on. 'I think Richie saw it like this. Indian was going to stand trial. He was the killer – and Richie had no interest at all in seeing the others in the dock.' After forty-five minutes, the lawyer sat down, drained, and watched passively as the magistrate ordered the three astonished defendants to be freed – for the second time in the case.

The trial of Asim Ahmed, a.k.a. Indian, on a charge of murder, was set for 4 October, 1993, at the Old Bailey. But the defence applied successfully for a deferment on the grounds that there was a body of undisclosed material, of potential relevance to its case, some of which it had not had time to examine. To underline his point, the defence counsel attempted to lift a mountain of documents which stood a foot high on the table in front of him. Duly persuaded, the judge set a new date – 4 January, 1994.

Given the labyrinthine history of this case, there was no great surprise when 4 January also turned out to be a phantom starting date for the trial. And the reason? Richie Wallace, on whom the Crown's hopes rested, failed to appear at court. Indeed, the police had not seen him since 15 December when he had disappeared from the 'safe house' in which he had been staying as an involuntary guest of the Brixton constabulary.

Judge Michael Coombe was not amused and issued a bench warrant for Richie's arrest. Two weeks later, on 18 January, the police finally tracked him down. Judge Coombe was in no mood to entertain his explanation that he had been given a different starting date for the trial. Nor his claim that the police had tried to force him to testify by threatening to disclose his address to Indian. Richie was found guilty of contempt and dispatched to Belmarsh prison in South London for eight weeks. A third starting date was set – 16 March.

The defence counsel, David Farrington, must have entered Court 8 at the Old Bailey on Wednesday, 16 March, with high hopes. A Crown case which depends on one witness, whose credibility is already in tatters, and no forensic evidence, would attract little side money even from the most improvident gambler. Certainly, the man who led the inquiry, Detective Inspector Reg Field, was fairly pessimistic as he took his seat in the courtroom. And when he glanced at the slight, unthreatening figure of the defendant in his spectacles and neatly pressed white shirt, he wondered gloomily what the jury would make of it.

It was several hours before he even had a chance to find out because the defence moved straight away to have the case thrown out for abuse of process. 'It is vexatious and oppressive', declaimed Mr Farrington, 'for the Crown to put forward as a witness a man whom they have already branded a liar. Mr Wallace has crossed the Rubicon of credibility. There has to be a benchmark beyond which the Crown cannot go in presenting someone as a witness of truth and reliability.'

Judge Coombe readily conceded Richie's unwillingness to come to court and his history of lying and prevarication. Nevertheless, he felt it right that the facts should be heard by the jury, who should determine the strength of the prosecution case. So, after lunch on the 16th, Richie was brought up from the cells to face Indian for the first time since the committal hearing ten months earlier.

In the same way that a play is often tested out in the provinces before transferring to the West End, what happened that afternoon suggested that Richie felt his masterly stonewalling at Camberwell at the committal hearing of O., P. and W. deserved a wider audience. As Crown counsel, Michael Worsley QC, asked question after question, the refrain, 'I don't recall' reverberated around the oak-panelled courtroom. By the time the day's proceedings were over, Richie had given no ground at all and the following morning, resolutely carried on where he had left off.

It is hard to be certain why Richie, having testified at the committal hearing against Indian, should have put up the shutters again. The best guess is fear. Indian's brother was a baleful presence in the public gallery and stared meaningfully at the witness every time he was asked a question. Richie also confessed concern that, after using him to help convict Indian, the police would bring a separate charge of crack dealing against him and even put him in the cell next to Indian's.

At lunchtime on the 17th, an exhausted and dispirited Worsley confessed to DI Field that he was close to 'throwing in the towel'. 'He told me that he couldn't see how he could take the case any further unless Richie was made to talk. I could understand how he felt although it was clear to me that the jury wasn't taken in by Richie's performance. In fact, two or three of the blokes looked as though they could have cheerfully strangled him if they had been given the chance.'

The judge's intervention in the cross-examination (if that is what it could be called) led to an exchange which might have come unedited from a Marx Brothers film.

Judge Coombe: 'I must warn you, Mr Wallace, that there could be serious consequences for you if you carry on like this. Do you understand?'

Wallace: 'Yes.'

Judge Coombe: 'Tell me, is there anything medically wrong with your memory?'

Wallace: 'Yes, I have a bad memory.'

Judge Coombe: 'Have you seen a doctor about it?'

Wallace: 'I don't recall.'

At the end of the afternoon on 17 March, the judge made an order that a prison doctor at Belmarsh should examine Richie Wallace before he returned to court on the 18th. If the doctor could find nothing wrong, and the witness continued refusing to answer questions, he would be committed to jail for contempt. And this time, the judge went on, Wallace was looking at the maximum term, which was two years.

The threat carried extra weight because that same day the newspapers carried a story about a judge on the North–Eastern circuit who had imprisoned an uncooperative witness in a case of attempted murder, for twenty-one months. Judge Coombe also agreed to a prosecution application to have Wallace declared a hostile witness, which meant that his earlier statements in which he had implicated Indian, could be put before the jury.

No-one knows what it was that worked the miracle but on Friday, 18 March – to the astonishment and relief of the Crown

– Richie's faulty memory unblocked itself.

DI Field: 'It may have been because we were able to play to the court tape recordings of an earlier interview. He could hardly deny that that was his voice and from then on, bit by bit, he began to respond to the Crown's questions.'

Although Richie never actually said in as many words that he had seen Indian pull the trigger, his evidence placed the defendant in the room with Tom British, with the gun in his hand. And, despite a claim by the defence that the .32 had belonged to Tom British and had been removed from him by the hired muscle, W., who fired the fatal shot with it, the Crown team felt that at least they had been able to present something worthwhile to the jury rather than a confection of wishful thinking.

Richie's evidence was supplemented by that of his girlfriend, Tina Baxter, who was also brought to court against her will and declared a hostile witness. And the delivery boy from the West Indian fast food shop, David Martin, testified to hearing the name, Indian, used by the group of menacing individuals gathered at the flat in Carrara Walk on 6 February, the night of the murder. With a longer than usual break for Easter, the prosecution case ended on 12 April, in somewhat better shape than it had begun.

Once again, the defence made a submission of 'no case to answer' on the grounds that Wallace had been discredited and that without him, the Crown was holed below the waterline. It was the twelfth such submission during the trial and, though the judge took three days to make his ruling, he dismissed it as he had dismissed the previous eleven. On 20 April, Judge Coombe summed up the case.

DI Field: 'When the judge finished his summing up, I don't mind admitting that I was gutted. It was absolutely fair but at the same time it was devastating. Richie was presented for what he was – a crack dealer and a congenital liar. And though the judge pointed out that that didn't necessarily mean that he wasn't telling the truth about the murder, it more or less convinced me that we were going to lose.'

At 10.47 a.m. on 21 April, the jury of nine men and three women retired. At the beginning of the afternoon they sent the judge a note seeking clarification of the term 'reasonable doubt' and asking whether they could convict on circumstantial evidence only. Later in the afternoon, when it was plain that they were deadlocked, the judge called them back to say that he would accept a majority verdict. By 4.15 p.m., with no verdict in sight, he summoned them once more and sent them to a hotel overnight.

DI Field was at the Old Bailey at 9.15 p.m. on 22 April, prepared for the worst. After exactly one hour – almost twenty-four hours from the time the jury had been sent out – the clerk told him that the court was reassembling. 'I couldn't bear to look at Ahmed when the foreman delivered the verdict because I expected it to be "not guilty" and I knew he would be gloating. You could have heard a pin drop in the courtroom.'

But, against the odds, the verdict was 'guilty', by a majority of eleven to one. There is only one sentence for a murder conviction, life imprisonment. The judge said that in view of the seriousness of the crime, he would be recommending a minimum term of twenty years. Until that point, Asim Ahmed had remained cool and detached. But then the mask slipped.

DI Field: 'As I was in the box giving his "previous", I glanced at Indian. He was broken, his head just slumped into his shoulders. But when he was being led out, he gave two lengthy glares at the jury and suddenly you could see the evil in the man. The figure who had sat passively throughout the trial, trying to make a good impression, looked really frightening, just as he had done on the streets.'

Asim Ahmed, a.k.a. Indian, began his life sentence in Wormwood Scrubs and, perhaps not surprisingly, instructed his solicitor to prepare an appeal. At the time of writing, it was still several months away. Given the history of this extraordinary case, only the foolhardy would attempt to predict the outcome.

Chapter Eight

A Crack in the Market

'The first hit is always the best. Eyes just opening. Head goes back. It just freezes you. I've never had anything like it. If I leave it for a couple of days, I get that hit back. With crack, once you've got that hit of the day, no matter how much you take, you don't get it back.' – Crack addict in Nottingham.

Yes, but what exactly is this thing called crack, the very name of which sounds like a bell tolling for the end of sanity and civilisation? At various times, it has been called a cocaine derivative; a synthetic form of cocaine; a cocaine-based drug; a new drug. It has been written about as some kind of mutant which slithered from a nameless laboratory to enslave the world. An invention of the devil. It is none of these things. Crack is a very clever way of making an expensive stimulant, cocaine, appeal to people living on welfare cheques, and social security. If you think of it in terms of food, it is a beefburger compared to a sirloin steak. They both contain meat, but in different forms. And in exactly the same way that fast food had to be aggressively marketed to earn its niche in the high street, so crack was sold as a pre-packaged take-away which would nourish the brain like nothing else around.

Powdered cocaine, or hydrochloride, comes from the coca

leaf. The bitter-tasting white crystals are the result of a production process which first releases the drug from the leaf and then turns it, with the aid of chemicals, into a refined powder. When it is absorbed into the bloodstream, it stimulates euphoria, excitement and increased activity. It is taken in two ways – either intra-nasally (i.e. snorted), or dissolved in water and injected.

Cocaine hydrochloride is unsuitable for smoking because it is non-volatile and much of the active drug is destroyed at high temperatures. However, at an earlier, intermediate stage, the cocaine – after being soaked with kerosene and sulphuric acid, and softened with limestone – is in the form of a paste. In this condition, it is still full of harmful impurities but it can be smoked. In South America, they generally call it *basuco* and during the 1970s Peru, Bolivia, Ecuador, Colombia and Venezuela all had a growing number of addicts. (In the eighties, at least one consignment of coca paste was seized in the UK.)

Smoking coca paste never caught on in the largest market of all, the United States – despite attempts by some of the more enterprising cocaine wholesalers to promote it. The Colombians, for example, would include paste in kilo-size batches of cocaine powder as a loss leader and instruct the dealers in New York to give it away free to see how the customers liked it. But perhaps because it was too harsh for their taste, the response was unwelcoming.

However, by the late seventies, the ingenuity of the American consumer had already found another and more attractive way of taking cocaine – freebasing it. This involved working backwards from the finished hydrochloride to create a powder which was smokable. First, the acid had to be neutralised by an alkali and then the residue mixed with a solvent such as ether to capture the base cocaine. It is a process which can produce a substance with a purity level of 95 per cent or higher.

Always searching for nirvana, users on the West Coast began to embrace freebasing in growing numbers. Some found that heating the compound with an acetylene or butane torch speeded up the evaporation of the ether and guaranteed a higher level of purity of the base cocaine left behind.

It was also extremely dangerous because ether is one of the most flammable solvents. The risks were dramatically highlighted on the night of 9 June 1980 when the celebrated black comic and actor, Richard Pryor, almost killed himself while freebasing at his home in California's San Fernando Valley. Exploding ether inflicted third-degree burns over the entire upper part of his body and parts of his face. The incident not only destroyed Pryor's career but provided an impetus for the discovery of a safer way of producing smokeable base cocaine.

It is striking how, all along, the Caribbean has played such an active role in the crack story. Jamaican dealers have fanned out from Kingston to set up crack networks in the United States, Canada and Britain. Jamaican enforcers have ridden shotgun to protect their investment and to cow the opposition. And there is good evidence to suggest that the Caribbean islands themselves were the testbed for the emergence of crack as the street drug of the eighties and nineties. Some researchers believe that the dubious honour of being the first country to produce a crack prototype may belong to the Dutch Antilles. In the version found there around 1980, coca paste was converted into a smokeable residue using baking soda, water and rum. The result had a variety of names, including 'roxanne', 'base-rock' and 'baking-soda base'. Freebasing was also well established in Jamaica by about 1980, though at that time, it was only the elite of society – musicians, politicians and the ghetto dons – who indulged. And it wasn't long before reports of a substance called 'rock' were emanating regularly from the Caribbean.

A Florida medical examiner, on a visit to the tiny British dependency, the Turks and Caicos Islands, heard tales of a drug 'that looked like a pebble, and people would smoke it and go crazy'. But the first traces of a fully developed pattern of crack usage and distribution seem to have been found in the Bahamas. The hundreds of islands and cays had been a convenient stopover on the cocaine transshipment route between Colombia and Florida for some years and, inevitably, by the early eighties, an increasing amount of the powder was seeping into local consumption. Freebasing gradually became more commonplace until a network of 'base' or crack houses was established.

The users found that a Coke can was a convenient receptacle for the rocks and they would lie around sucking in the smoke through the ring pull until, in some cases, their brains became addled. Indeed, it was a sharp and sustained rise in the number of psychiatric admissions to hospital which alerted the authorities to the epidemic on their hands.

This frenzied growth in freebasing did not come about by accident. The deluge of cocaine arriving in the Bahamas inexorably forced down the street price of the drug – to the point where a gramme could be bought for a fifth of its previous cost. The dealers, facing substantial losses, reacted by pushing crack for all it was worth. The hook was that crack was sold in amounts as low as a fifth or a quarter of a gramme, making it appear far more affordable than cocaine powder, which would never be retailed in quantities of less than a gramme. Of course, there was a catch. Although the freebase provided an incomparable rush of exhilaration when it hit the brain, you needed to take far more of it to sustain a high. So the real cost of crack addiction was much greater. By the time the suckers had worked this out for themselves, it was too late. They were well and truly impaled on the hook. And to guarantee that the strategy worked, the dealers made sure that powdered cocaine virtually became unobtainable. The strategy worked.

By 1985, crack was already well established on many of the other islands. Sammy Lewis, who later made a successful living as a trafficker in North-west London before his dramatic arrest in 1991, was living in Barbados at this time and could see what was happening around him.

'We called it "washed rock" and the dealers were pushing it hard. When I went to Trinidad, I found the same there. And I heard tell that Jamaica was the same. When it comes to drugs, the islands don't need lessons from no-one. They're way out in front, man. It took the UK a few years to catch up.' Sammy Lewis played his part in the process.

In essence, the marketing savvy which established crack in the Caribbean was the template for the assault on the biggest prize of all – the United States. Take New York. The city's cocaine trade was dominated by Colombian importers based in Queens, and Dominican retailers who had carved out a niche in Washington Heights. A shared language, Spanish, oiled the wheels of the alliance.

From the early eighties onwards, a Dominican immigrant called Santiago Luis Polanco-Rodriguez began to demonstrate sharper and more deadly entrepreneurial skills than his rivals. In 1982, he was selling cocaine powder through a chain of outlets, cheekily using the slogan 'Coke Is It'. But by the middle of the decade, he and his half-brother 'Chiqui', had decided that the route to real wealth lay with crack.

Another snappy marketing label helped kick-start the switch to the new product. The brand-name was Based Balls, and the crack sold under that imprimatur came in distinctive red-capped phials with a high level of purity. It was a roaring success.

Between the summer of 1985 and 1987, the Based Balls empire just kept on growing. At its peak, as many as 10,000 of the phials were being sold every day. Employees even handed out business cards, reading 'Based Balls – Cop and Go', which listed retail sales outlets.

Elsewhere, other would-be crack moguls were also employing business techniques of which Dale Carnegie would probably have approved. A big-shot called 'Vamp' Hargress emerged from the Los Angeles gang nexus and decided to spread his wings. He set up crack houses first in Seattle, then Oklahoma City. Nothing was left to chance. An area would be rigorously test-marketed to see if it was receptive to the product. One of the Hargress team told a detective that, in a previous job, he had sold vacuum cleaners door-to-door, and the principle was pretty much the same.

Meanwhile, in Kansas City, a fast-growing dealing network used the sales pitch, 'Stock up on Mother's Day', meaning the first of the month, when the welfare cheques are mailed. The exhortation struck home. Before too long, a burgeoning number of daily shopping lists had crack way out ahead of bread and milk as a priority buy. The Kansas City crack operation was run by the Waterhouse Posse – Jamaicans from the Waterhouse area of Kingston. And the man who led them into the promised land of middle America was Errol Wilson, who had been a gunman for the People's National Party before turning his sights towards foreign drug dealing. Wilson was another product of the generation which had gorged itself on a diet of spaghetti westerns. He assumed the streetname, 'Dogbite', a fair reflection of his ferocity. But he was no fool. He recognised that the conservative heartland, if at first sight unpromising for a dreadlocked invasion, offered immense potential.

Unlike New York or Los Angeles, where the competition was armed and street-smart, Kansas had plenty of unfulfilled demand and few rivals equipped to stay the course with the posses. Those that tried found themselves outgunned. By 1986, the Kansas City police were investigating fifteen murders connected to the Waterhouse Posse. The first thing that Wilson did was to bring in his own enforcers, utterly loyal to him. Then he recruited teenagers in the Jamaican communities of New York and Miami, gave them plane tickets to Kansas, and assigned them to work in the crack houses or on the streets on the promise of earning at least 500 bucks a week. In many cases, wages on that scale were a mere pipedream but few dared to argue. You broke your 'contract' with Dogbite Wilson at your peril. With low overheads and an expanding customer base, the posse showed a cute head for business and some of the crack dens were taking in up to $15,000 a day.

A stream of female Jamaican couriers brought cocaine powder up from Miami in one or two kilo amounts, some of them making the journey several times a week. The crack sold in Kansas City was always top grade and the Jamaicans sold bigger rocks for the price than anyone else. In a legitimate business, it would have been applauded as a classic example of risk-taking reaping its just reward. Indeed, even the law enforcers had grudging respect for the resourcefulness of an organisation which created a drug demand in a city where narcotics had not previously been a serious problem. The police were only being half-ironic when they referred to 'Dogbite' Wilson's safe house – 3100 Pirie Avenue – as the 'corporate offices' of the Waterhouse Posse.

Major David Barton, of the Kansas City police narcotics squad, watched in awe as the posse put down roots in his town: 'They do everything that a good business would do. They do market research. They advertise. They provide twice the substance for the same amount of money. They give away free

115

samples. They do all they can to establish a market for the product.'

And that included looking overseas to boost the turnover. Britain was the first stop on the trade route, and the price of drawing the UK into the warm embrace of the company was an air ticket to Heathrow or Gatwick.

Customs officers are trained to identify a number of warning signs which might indicate that an air passenger is carrying drugs. People who pick up bags from the luggage carousel, put them down, and then pick them up again. People who walk rapidly through the channels, averting their gaze from staff. People whose luggage seems out of keeping with their general appearance.

On 23 March 1989, a Virgin Airways flight from Miami landed at Gatwick Airport. Miami flights always attract a high degree of attention and sniffer dogs are routinely sent on board to nose out drugs. On this occasion, the interest of customs officers was drawn to a young, unaccompanied woman walking towards the green channel. She seemed excessively nervous and ill at ease. Despite her protests, the officers insisted on a luggage and body search. They found two kilos of cocaine hidden inside a stocking and under a swimsuit. The passenger's name was Twyla Wilson and she came from Kansas City.

After such a find, it is customs policy to seek to maximise success by persuading the passenger to carry on into the arrival hall in the hope that he or she may be meeting someone else involved in the smuggling operation. Twyla Wilson was not being met at Gatwick. But she revealed that she was supposed to hand over the cocaine to a man later in the day at the Strand Palace Hotel in London. She agreed to keep the rendezvous. The plan called for her to take a room in the hotel and wait to be contacted by telephone. Under the watchful gaze of customs investigators, she played out her role, if a trifle hesitantly, and took two calls from men identifying themselves as 'Johnny' and 'King Kong'.

After a short wait, her contact arrived. But she hardly had time to open the door when he sensed a trap and fled down the corridor. The customs men gave chase and caught him before he could escape into the busy West End street. He said he had been visiting a friend and had knocked on the wrong door. It certainly was the wrong door for him. He was arrested and charged with importing cocaine with a street value of a quarter of a million pounds. By the time the case came to court, customs investigators knew that the man they had caught was called Melvyn Rowe and that he was a trusted lieutenant of Dogbite Wilson in the Waterhouse Posse. Melvyn Rowe was sentenced to fifteen years in jail.

The capture of Rowe was an irritant to the Waterhouse Posse but the attempt to gain a bridgehead in London went on. They were under heavy pressure in Kansas – by 1989, more than 200 members had been picked up by the police – and the higher crack prices of a fledgling market made the UK an irresistible magnet. If a courier picked up a kilo of coke in Miami for £10,000, it would treble in value just by virtue of having crossed the Atlantic. Allowing for losses during conversion into crack, that same kilo could generate as much as £800,000 when parcelled into quarter gramme rocks to be sold on the streets. For that kind of profit margin, the Waterhouse Posse was prepared to take risks in trying to develop a crack pipeline into the UK. Even if it meant organising courier shipments under the noses of the law enforcement agencies. Jamaicans like Samuel Gumms planned for expansion overseas despite the certain knowledge that they were under surveillance by the Kansas City narcotics squad.

Seeking to distract his watchers, Gumms flew to Los Angeles

to oversee a cocaine service to London. He didn't realise, though, that even there, his telephone was being tapped. A later examination of his bill showed a daily stream of calls to his base in Kansas City and to numbers in London. The plan was for the cocaine to be carried by courier to Britain. Jacqueline Cody, an English prostitute from Bristol, flew from London to LA to meet Gumms. He supplied her with a kilo and a half of high-quality cocaine. To minimise the risk of detection, Cody was instructed not to return directly to Heathrow but instead to take an internal flight to New York. She arrived at La Guardia airport and caught a cab to JFK international airport – unaware that she was being tailed by federal narcotics agents (who at one desperate point lost her). They waited until the last possible minute in case she was meeting anyone else and pounced as she was about to board Flight 182 to Manchester.

The Americans estimated the value of the cocaine she was carrying – on the basis that it was intended to be divided up and sold as crack – at three-quarters of a million pounds. But since it was intended for the UK market, a truer reflection of its worth is £1,500,000. Like Twyla Wilson, Jacqueline Cody, frightened and a long way from home, proved cooperative under questioning. She disclosed that she had been supposed to make her way to a flat in Stoke Newington in North London to hand the cocaine to a dealer. She willingly supplied his address and streetname.

When the police raided the flat, they found an imitation gun and half a kilo of cocaine. They arrested the dealer, Philip 'Flip-Flop' Baker, and learned that, from his safe house, he had been running several couriers. They had already brought in cocaine worth more than £1,000,000, some of which was sold on to other dealers, who converted it into crack and also made a healthy profit. Baker, who was wanted for murder in New York, was jailed in Britain for fifteen years.

The Waterhouse don in Kansas City, Errol Wilson, was indicted by the US authorities on charges of engaging in a continuing criminal enterprise and distributing cocaine. But that was a minor inconvenience which hardly interfered with his expansion plans. He simply went underground, surfacing from time to time in a number of places, including London, in the summer of 1989. And even if he wasn't around in person, his authority was represented by lieutenants such as Melvyn Rowe and Lennox Benain. Benain, a Jamaican whose streetname was 'Mempo', was a man of considerable violence, who emerged from the Concrete Jungle in Kingston, where only the most ruthless survived.

'Men like that,' says Suzy, the undercover agent who has worked extensively for the British as well as the American authorities, 'are what we call "terrorists" – they are rapists, robbers and murderers. They rip off other drug dealers, they even rip off their friends. The only loyalty they have is to money – and themselves.'

Benain is now in Jamaica but in the late 1980s his attributes were much in demand in London, which he visited regularly, using false passports. He was involved in crack dealing in a number of areas, including Harlesden, Brixton and Stoke Newington. It was no accident, of course, that these were the areas to which the Waterhouse and other posse members were drawn. They all had significant Jamaican populations and some of the groups which supplied marijuana were easily persuaded that crack cocaine offered far more handsome returns.

It was also singularly good timing for the dealers because there was a law enforcement void in the territory they were seeking to colonise. The savage events of 1985 in Brixton and at Broadwater Farm still cast their shadow over the predominantly black estates. A Metropolitan Commissioner, Sir Kenneth Newman, described these areas – in a widely quoted phrase – as 'symbolic locations'. Symbols of the inability of the police to exert their authority. It was a period when Scotland Yard was pinned back on the ropes – and began to behave like a punch-drunk boxer. At one and the same time, treading on eggshells for fear of provoking another racial conflagration, yet lurching into ludicrously excessive counter-attacks, such as Operation Condor, a drugs raid on the Afro-Caribbean Club and twenty-eight other premises in Brixton (including a nursery!), which was launched from a train on the track above the street.

The Jamaican drug dealers were not slow to pick up on this air of police uncertainty and exploit it to their advantage. Officers on local divisions began to report an increase in the amount of violence and intimidation as a number of powerful individuals, who had 'respect', flexed their muscles. In their name, robberies, rapes, assaults and rip-offs were carried out, and few had the nerve to stand up and testify against them. Before long, the media, too, caught the mood. Crime writers nostalgic for the good old days when the Richardsons and the Krays ruled swathes of London by fear, began writing articles in the tabloids and middle-of-the-market Sundays asking whether a new breed of organised criminal was at work. A black breed. The time was ripe then for a new Scotland Yard initiative. It was called Operation Lucy.

Chapter Nine

Operation Lucy

Roy Ramm has detective written all over him. Stocky, auburn-haired, matey. A man at home meeting his snout and securing the kind of copper-bottomed intelligence which produces arrests, convictions, and commendations from the boss class. By 1987, he had worked his way up from detective sergeant at Stoke Newington, through chief inspector in the Criminal Intelligence branch at the Yard to superintendent staff officer, answerable directly to the Deputy Assistant Commissioner, Special Operations, Crime (DACSO).

His reward was three months at the prestigious FBI academy in Washington, studying organised crime. Who better then to look at whether a black Mafia was putting down roots in London?

Ramm: 'The idea of a Black Mafia was a headline writer's dream. And there had been at least one newspaper article – in a Sunday supplement, I think – which made people at the Yard sit up and take notice.

'So I put together a team, with officers drawn from places like Stoke Newington and South-east London, who had good informants or other special qualifications. We also had four or five black officers who brought an interesting dimension to the operation.

'And very quickly, we began to identify a number of individuals, who had "respect". The kind of guys who could walk into a club dripping with gold and leave unscathed, in the kind of areas where anyone else would be mugged for a neck chain worth a few pounds. We started to look at the pattern of car hire activity, where a vehicle would be rented on a Friday night and do a thousand miles over a weekend. Or cars which were on permanent hire to young black men who were ostensibly unemployed. That was a scam picked up from drug dealers in the States who used rented cars to conceal what they were doing from the law enforcement agencies.'

Close contact with some of those agencies – like the Bureau of Alcohol, Tobacco and Firearms – produced invaluable information on the kind of firearms which the Yardies favoured and the illegal use of passports to gain easy entry to the UK. It also established the point that it was not a black or Afro-Caribbean crime problem, but a specifically Jamaican one.

'As far as we could see, there were no Antiguans or Bajans (Barbados citizens) involved. Or anyone from the other islands. The people we were after were from Jamaica and they usually had links to the political parties there, either the PNP or the JLP.

'All these characters seemed to have unlimited cash, lots of gold, drove around in BMWs and ran female couriers – mainly white hookers – who brought in the cocaine from Miami or Kingston.'

With this intelligence, the Lucy team – by now, nicknamed the Yardie squad – planned their first operations. The ethnic dimension of the problem meant they had to tread very carefully. Aggressive policing, which was perceived as targeting black suspects, had bedevilled race relations in some of the 'symbolic locations' for years. The infamous Operation Swamp, an attempt to tackle street crime in Brixton by flooding the area

122

with police, was cited as one of the triggers for the 1981 riot. The Lucy team were aware of the risks they were running in planning raids on black estates.

'We tried to convince the local boys, from the divisions, that we were there to support their efforts to clean up high crime areas – not to do another Swamp and leave them with a legacy to clear up. So we made it a matter of policy to use local officers in the arrests, based on intelligence which we had gathered.'

Peckham, just south of the river Thames, can lay claim to the privilege of being the first borough in which a crack 'factory' was discovered. With a large black population, many of them West Indian, it provided the dealers with the ideal background to blend into. In August 1988, Sergeant Charles Griggs, a community police officer, was involved in a surveillance operation on a flat on an estate in north Peckham.

'There was so much activity in and out of this flat, it was amazing. Maybe forty or fifty callers an hour. When we raided it, there were three Jamaicans inside. Two had just arrived from Kingston. The other was from the Bronx in New York. Our view was that this estate, and others with a large black community, had been specifically targeted by foreign dealers as places where they could sell crack.'

When the first crack dealer to be convicted in Britain appeared in court, the jury heard how security conscious the new breed of traffickers were. Thirty-year-old Edward Reynolds had been operating from a flat on the nineteenth floor of the Milton Court estate in Deptford, South-east London. The flat was protected by a cast-steel outer door, fitted with a series of Chubb locks, and a steel-cased inner door, with six rigid steel bolts. There was also a sophisticated alarm system. Dealing was done through a slit in the outer door so that clients never saw their supplier. A coded sign beneath the slit indicated when the premises were open for business. When the police raided it, they had to cut off the outer door with oxyacetylene burners and smash the inner one with hydraulic rams. Inside, Reynolds was in possession of forty-three rocks of crack, a quantity of cocaine powder, and a substantial amount of cash. It was an investment well worth protecting.

A number of the dealers raided by the Lucy team were known to have been taking payments for the drug in stolen goods, encouraging addicts to commit robberies and thefts to feed their habit. In a council flat in West London, where crack was being produced and sold, detectives recovered a collection of stolen electrical equipment, jewellery and designer clothes. It was a potent sign that crack was already making its mark on the black economy.

Conscious that the Yardie squad was supposedly looking for evidence of a Black Mafia, the press lapped up the activities of Operation Lucy with slavering enthusiasm. And on 14 April 1988, the connection with organised crime seemed to have been established with one of the largest raids of all. The target was the man who had cut a violent swathe from Tivoli and Rema to Hackney in North London – Rankin Dread, a.k.a. Bowyark.

Rankin Dread's 'Yardie' pedigree was impeccable. He had learned his trade under Claudie Massop, a don who controlled Rema on behalf of the JLP in the 1970s. When Massop was dispatched to an early grave by the Jamaican police, Dread – real name, as far as can be ascertained, Robert Blackwood – assumed his mantle as the 'top rankin'. His curriculum vitae includes the murder of a number of PNP gunmen in Kingston and attacks on police officers. One of those on the receiving end was a policeman, Keith 'Trinity' Gardner, who features later in this narrative. Rankin Dread blew half his teeth away, which Trinity made light of by chasing his assailant for nearly half a mile before he escaped.

The role of 'don' – even if it offered only a tenuous hold on power – carried obligations too. And like other gunmen who have gone 'foreign' and become successful, Dread met his responsibilities by giving out money to the poor and needy of his ghetto. However, he clearly preferred playing Rasputin to Robin Hood. And stories abound of his monstrous appetite for excess. How he organised the poisoning of thirty political opponents in a revenge attack. How he raped five women in one night. Much of it may have been myth but it was highly potent.

A British immigration officer describes him like this: 'He's slim, presentable, looks like a well-preserved boxer, maybe welterweight. Often seen in a black Crombie and Fedora. I call him the Daniel Boone of the Yardies because he was one of the pioneers. He's got a touch of class about him. Still (in 1993) only thirty-seven. And he's one of the very few who've put a chill up me.'

The reputation of the man was embellished by a foray into the world of music. In the early eighties, he released a reggae record called 'Fatty Boom Boom' which crept into the charts. And even in 1988, at the time of his arrest in Clapton Way, Hackney, a confidential Scotland Yard report described him, amongst other things, as a 'reggae musician'.

The raid on a dilapidated squat at number 19a Clapton Way was probably the first time that a Yardie operation generated banner headlines in the UK. Reporters and photographers went in with the assault party at 5 a.m. and responded in suitably Ramboesque vein. 'Police Raid Yardie Stronghold' (*The Times*); 'Police Hunt for Yardie Godfather' (*Daily Mail*); 'The Godfather of the Black Mafia known as the Yardies was seized . . .' (*The Sun*) and so on. All of the newspapers – tabloids and heavies alike – carried pictures of the police shock troops, the newly-formed PT18 squad, in their visors and body armour, handcuffing a disparate group of black men and women. In amongst the weapons and the debris of beer and lager cans, sniffer dogs nosed out seventeen wraps of cocaine and a larger amount of cannabis.

The police had rehearsed the raid by storming a replica house at their riot training centre in Hounslow. Roy Ramm was quoted as saying: 'We expected a lot of people there to be armed and violent, and indeed we found a fearsome collection of weapons, including a two-foot-long machete and the largest lock knife I have ever seen.'

The purpose of using the PT18 squad was to 'dominate the scene physically and psychologically – to intimidate' as one of its officers put it. And that was achieved. By the time any of the seventy party-goers inside the house were even aware of the raid, they were spread-eagled on the floor having their wrists bound with plastic cuffs. But when the dust had settled, what did the operation achieve? Only five of the twenty people arrested were charged. Two of those deported as illegal entrants, Donovan Williams and Donald Michael Brown (known as Run-Eye because a bullet had creased an optical nerve causing spasmodic weeping) wasted no time in returning to the UK. And neither of the two most dangerous characters in the house ended up in jail.

Rankin Dread, the 'Godfather' of the police briefings, escaped justice in a manner which has become all too familiar – a breakdown of communications between the police, the Crown Prosecution Service and the Home Office. The police wanted him to face charges of possession of drugs but the CPS offered no evidence on the grounds that he was going to be deported. Police and immigration officers were furious. They were hoping to see him in jail for several years, and then deported.

And then there was the egregious Devon Plunkett, a.k.a.

'Foodhead', a Shower Posse man who was wanted for a number of murders in Miami, including that of a six-year-old girl, killed by a stray bullet as she emerged from an ice-cream parlour. The ATF believed that Foodhead controlled weapons shipments for the Shower Posse right across the States. He had already been removed from the UK once in the name of Adrian Price, but at the time of the raid on Clapton Way, he was using the alias Frederick Gordon, and simply slipped through the net. Waving his six-month British visitor's passport, the man whom the Americans would dearly have wanted to extradite, walked free from the police station. In his case, though, freedom was short-lived. In October 1988, a sharp-eyed uniformed constable stopped him and two others in a car in Clapham and discovered half a kilo of cocaine under the driver's seat. Foodhead fled and was chased for half a mile before being caught. He was jailed for six years. While inside, Foodhead did two things. He began writing a panoramic narrative which is a thinly disguised version of his life story as a Tivoli street enforcer who became a drug gangster in the United States. And he got married to a woman called Yvonne Marshall, with whom he had been living in Clapham before his arrest.

Immigration officers suspected that Marshall was harbouring Jamaican 'illegals' at her flat, and carried out a raid. During their search, they found letters written by Foodhead from Wormwood Scrubs in which he discussed organising the murders of a detective with the Operation Lucy squad and ATF special agent, J.J. Watterson – both of whom he deemed responsible for his incarceration. Watterson took the threat so seriously that he retired.

The highly publicised arrests at Clapton Way demonstrated some of the problems which afflicted Operation Lucy. Its remit, to explore black organised crime, led to expectations – certainly, in the media – that every raid was striking a blow at a limb of the Black Mafia. On the strength of that view, there were some memorable excursions to the wilder shores of reporting. Some copy put out by the Press Association quoted speculation that London Yardies 'may be trying to infiltrate black political and trade union organisations and that police have already discovered links with the IRA'. A newspaper described the Yardies as a '*cult* which owes much of its power to the violence of its followers'. In short, it was open season on Yardies. A new name had entered the lexicon of contemporary crime.

This was both irritating and distracting for the Operation Lucy team. After eighteen months, their conclusion was that, though a growing number of Jamaican criminals were active in the UK, exploiting the profits to be made from cannabis and crack, they could hardly be compared to the organised syndicates, such as the Mafia or more recently, the Triads. In a memorable phrase, which is no less apt for being repeated so often, it was a case of 'disorganised organised crime'. Or, as a senior officer has since described it: 'The Yardies are like an amoeba which forms for the purpose of crime and then splits into smaller segments, re-forms and splits again.' Nevertheless, it was crime which left victims dead or injured, families bereaved, and fear and intimidation in many black communities.

In response, Operation Lucy had begun to build up a profile of a new type of target who brought in drugs via baby mothers and prostitutes; who slipped into the country on false passports and out again when the heat was on; who had easy access to guns. And who were black. And this, the ethnic dimension, proved to be the toughest problem of all for the police to handle. Chief Superintendent Roy Ramm could understand the concerns:

'Here we had a squad which was investigating black crime. The fact that the people committing this type of crime were almost exclusively Jamaican was seen as irrelevant. The question being posed in the higher echelons of the Yard was: was this kind of operation racially divisive?' The answer which came down from on high was: yes, it was.

The decision to disband the Lucy team, in the second half of 1989, left a number of its members feeling disenchanted. They had made or inspired some 400 arrests and obtained a number of convictions for serious offences. They had built up a database of more than 3,200 records on Jamaican drug-related crime. Fifty illegal immigrants wanted for serious offences in both Jamaica and the United States had been deported. Valuable information had been garnered about the amount of crime centred on Caribbean clubs and dance halls. The Yardie squad had established a burgeoning link between drugs and firearms, which has developed into a social scourge. And they had identified an intelligence void between the regional crime squads and the divisional level which has since been exploited by some dangerous 'disorganised' criminals.

But the bosses at the Yard felt they had to take a wider strategic view. Complaints from black groups and civil libertarians played on sensitivities about policing which could be portrayed as 'racist'. And in this respect, the Yard's own use of the media can be seen to have been counter-productive because photographs and video footage of mainly white police officers handcuffing and arresting black suspects reinforced every negative stereotype imaginable.

There is no disguising the fact that police PR was in a quandary. The kind of criminal which Operation Lucy was targeting lived and operated in those areas – Stoke Newington, Harlesden, Brixton – where there was a high Afro-Caribbean population. As we have seen, these are the communities where the Jamaican crack hustlers have been able to establish themselves. By attacking the problem in a high profile manner with raids like Clapton Way, Scotland Yard was laying itself open to charges of racism. But by standing back and doing nothing, it could be argued with equal plausibility that the police would be taking the racist option. If the same level of robberies, assaults and drug crime were being perpetrated in white areas, with white victims in hospital wards, then wouldn't the police response be swift and vigorous?

Scotland Yard's public affairs department tried to square the circle by taking local 'representatives' on raids as impartial observers and distributing leaflets, pointing out that, by removing those who preyed off the weakness and vulnerability of their neighbours, the entire community would benefit. And it is certainly true that many black citizens were heartily grateful that action was being taken to harass the drug dealers on their doorsteps and outside their children's schools. But for all that, the central argument about whether it was a form of crime which warranted the existence of a special police squad which bore down most heavily in black areas, continued to fester, and ironically, did so even after Operation Lucy came to an end.

Beyond the politics of race, Operation Lucy also had to contend with the internecine politics of the Metropolitan force – a factor of considerable weight, which three years later was to push Scotland Yard off course again in the fight against crack. Local officers, in the five Met areas, have no great liking for the 'glory boys' of the Yard's specialist units. Roy Ramm tried to address this by involving divisional police in arrests, based on intelligence gathered by his own team. But there were still members of drug squads who felt aggrieved that they had been robbed of some plum jobs. That disaffection was communicated to Assistant Commissioner level and also played its part in the decision to pull the plug on the Yardie squad.

'It's the same old story,' says one ex-member of the Lucy team. 'You do a good job. You identify a problem. You start to tackle it. And then they go and change the rules. In the Met, it's always the internal politics which counts in the end.'

Allowing for the cynicism of the foot-soldier, it is undeniably true that the country's largest police force lost its way after Operation Lucy was wound up. Though Scotland Yard need not shoulder all the blame because, from April 1989, the course was being navigated by the Home Office, from directions supplied by a dynamic American.

Chapter Ten

There Ain't Enough Noses

In his own words, Robert Marvin Stutman is a 'pudgy, moon-faced Jew' from the New England mill town of Providence, Rhode Island. At the beginning of 1989, few British law enforcers had ever heard of him. By the summer of that year, his name was on everybody's lips and the Home Secretary, Douglas Hurd, was visiting him in his New York office. It is one of the more astonishing stories of UK drugs policy.

The Association of Chief Police Officers is the body which represents the views of chief constables, their assistants and deputies, and officers of commander rank in the Metropolitan force. It usually holds three separate conferences a year to formulate policy. Traditionally, the spring gathering is a forum on drugs. In April 1989, the ninth ACPO drugs conference was held at Colwyn Bay, the headquarters of North Wales police. Stutman was then head of the New York office of the Drug Enforcement Administration and was invited by ACPO to give a presentation about the new drug, crack.

Roy Ramm had met Stutman before and knew the stamp of the man. At forty-five, he was remarkably young to be heading the largest drugs office in the world, with a thousand agents and civilian staff under his command. His crusading and lobbying on drugs policy had made him a familiar figure on

Capitol Hill. He was a man who had spent years in the field, knew his own mind and spoke it fearlessly. But none of this was known to his audience in Colwyn Bay, as they awaited the three o'clock speaker on the last day of the conference. Indeed, one of those present recalls a sense of foreboding when he saw Stutman striding to the platform without any notes. 'I honestly thought it was going to be a bleeding disaster. Here's this unknown Yank, lecturing an audience of fairly conservative British police officers – and he hasn't even got a prepared speech.' And after lunch, too, when the eyelids are heavy. Not for long on this occasion, though. 'It was electrifying,' says the aforementioned member of the audience. 'All around me, there were people in suits who'd been slumped back in their seats, suddenly straightening up, ears straining, eyes wide open – looking at each other. I've never seen anything quite like it.' Another senior officer, not given to hyperbole, says simply: 'It was like a Billy Graham rally. A fire and brimstone presentation. Amazing oratory. He just painted an awesome picture.'

What Stutman did was to confront his audience with the devastation which crack had brought to the United States. Addiction on an unprecedented scale – 'three hits and you're hooked'. A massive rise in child abuse and domestic violence as families split apart in its grip. Stabbings and shootings on the streets. The murder of law enforcement agents. And all this from a drug which was virtually unheard of before 1985.

'Let me start off by pointing out what I think is probably the most amazing thing about crack that I can tell you. The first newspaper article done about crack in New York City was published in the *New York Times* on 25 November 1985.

'In the past three and a half years, crack has . . . become THE drug of abuse in the largest city in the United States. There is no other drug trend in history that has come close to spreading that quickly across a society.'

Stutman pointed out that in 1985 and 1986, even while crack was changing the face of New York, many Americans decried the possibility that it could spread to other cities. 'They looked around and said: "It's you crazy people who live in New York, you all got crazy accents, you're all nuts, it can't happen anywhere else and it will certainly never leave the ghetto." '

Now, he said, it was available in forty-nine of the fifty states 'even in the heart of conservative middle America – Houston, St Louis, Kansas City, Dallas'. And like all good communicators, he put the sting in the tail:

'The only thing I would ask you is the following: learn from our mistakes. We have screwed up enough times to write ten thousand books but I would hope all of you don't have to go through the same thing that we went through. Don't be like the people of Kansas and Texas and California, who said: "It can't happen here".

'I will make a prediction and, as you all know, predictions in this business, you've got to be crazy. But I will personally guarantee you that two years from now, you will have a serious crack problem, because as the gentleman before me said – we are so saturated with cocaine in the United States, there ain't enough noses left to use the cocaine that's coming in.'

On the last day of the ACPO conference, the Home Secretary usually attends a private, black tie dinner. It is a civilised way of keeping in touch with the latest police concerns. The then Home Secretary, Douglas Hurd, arrived in Colwyn Bay about five o'clock. He quickly discovered that the only topic of conversation was Stutman's presentation. Hurd called for a transcript and found the stark message as compelling as the chief constables had. As he told readers of the *Daily Mail* several weeks later: 'It made a deep impression on me'. So much so that this former diplomat with a reputation for taking stock before action, immediately set about trying to influence policy on cocaine – not just in the UK but throughout Western Europe.

The following month, May, Hurd convened an extraordinary meeting of ministers who sit on the Pompidou Group of the Council of Europe. The urgency of the Home Secretary's opening address must have surprised a gathering of interior and justice ministers preoccupied chiefly with terrorism, cross-border crime and immigration. Especially when he called crack, a drug about which most knew next-to-nothing, 'the spectre hanging over Europe'. To reinforce his case, Hurd – or his advisers – lifted verbatim chunks of the Stutman presentation. In fact, it was a reprise of the American's ACPO address, spoken with an Eton and Cambridge accent.

And with a zeal quite out of character with his usual approach to politics, Douglas Hurd kept up the impetus over the summer. On 24 July, he delivered another warning on crack to the Action on Addiction Conference. Within ten days, he was at it again in his role as chairman of the Ministerial Group on the Misuse of Drugs – this time, confirming an earlier promise to host a major international conference in London on ways of reducing demand for drugs, especially cocaine. His campaign was reinforced by the Commons All-Party Home Affairs Committee, which weighed in with an interim report on crack published on 19 July. Again, many of Stutman's statistics – especially concerning the impact of crack on child abuse – were reprinted, as part of a searing indictment of US failures to contain the epidemic which had transfigured its society.

If Stutman's message had had a profound impact on the political front, it was matched by a similar sense of urgency amongst police strategists. Indeed, given the fervour with which the Home Office had responded to the warning, it would have been surprising if Scotland Yard had dragged its heels.

Two senior officers, Commander Roy Penrose, and DAC Wally Boreham were dispatched to the States in June to see the situation at first hand and come back with recommendations. They spent a fortnight in New York, Washington and Boston, asking law enforcers what they would do if they were in Britain's position. Roy Penrose says the response was unequivocal: 'They told us that their first mistake was not to take crack seriously at the very beginning. And that led to the second. A failure to put in place any kind of intelligence machinery which could drive effective arrest and seizure operations. We came back convinced that these were lessons we should learn from.'

By the autumn of 1989 then, both the politicians and the police had agreed on the overwhelming case for a powerful new strategy to combat crack. It was being reported that approval had been given for a joint police-customs unit which would have its nerve centre in London but with some officers based in Manchester, Birmingham and Bristol. This, in itself, was revolutionary given the mutual rivalry and suspicion between the two organisations. And at Scotland Yard, the Penrose/Boreham recommendations were coalescing into a new intelligence unit which would replace Operation Lucy with a much broader remit. Taken together, it was argued, these two moves would address the key issues in Bob Stutman's ground-breaking address. But, though few realised it at the time, the foundations of this new edifice were flawed. Britain might not have been repeating the mistakes of the US but it was certainly making some costly new ones of its own.

The seeds of the problem can be identified as early as Douglas Hurd's first public response to Stutman – the address to the Pompidou Group in May. After borrowing Stutman's examples showing the destructiveness of crack, Hurd moves straight on to deal with cocaine trafficking and the saturation of the US market. His primary answer to the predicted crack epidemic is to put in place a range of measures to stem the flow of South American cocaine destined for Europe. And spelling out what he means, he lists confiscation of assets, cash contributions to a United Nations Trust Fund, and aid to help law enforcement in the cocaine producer countries.

Now, the significant thing about these initiatives is that they were all part of British government policy *before* the Stutman speech. Stutman was by no means the first American to warn that Europe was next on the list for the Colombian cartels. From the mid-eighties onwards, every British politician, police or customs chief who went to Washington came back with just that message. Europe will be next. That much in Stutman's presentation was already accepted wisdom. But there was also within his remarks, an inner core of analysis which was much more uncomfortable for a British audience to absorb. This is the critical passage.

Crack is controlled by a fairly large number of organisations, basically of two ethnic backgrounds. Number one, Dominicans; number two, Jamaicans.

After defining which group controls retailing and which wholesaling, he hits the solar plexus with this critical observation: 'I don't have to tell any of you gentlemen this – you have a large number of Jamaicans in this country, many of whom have relatives and friends in New York and none of whom are very stupid if they are dope peddlers to start with.

'These guys don't have to be geniuses to realise they don't need to import crack from the US. They can go out and buy a baby bottle at a department store and you certainly have water here and you certainly have bunsen burners here. They can make their crack right here in Great Britain and increase their profits by something like three hundred per cent.'

In other words, Stutman was issuing a warning that Britain's particular problem lay not just with the South American cartels targeting Europe – which they were bound to do through the laws of supply and demand – but because there were ethnic factors in British society which would accelerate the spread of crack. It was the most explosive argument in an explosive address – and British policy-makers reacted by doing what they do best when confronted by the unpalatable. They buried their heads in the sand.

As a guileless foreigner, Stutman himself was unaware that he had said anything contentious: 'I had made thousands of speeches on drugs in the US and the issue of race had never been raised. To say that Jamaicans controlled the wholesale traffic in the States was not considered a bigoted comment. It was fact.

'But when I got back to New York after the ACPO address, I began hearing whispers that my remarks about Jamaicans had angered some people. Somehow I had breached a code or convention.

'It didn't really mean a lot to me at the time but later in the year, the Lord Mayor of London visited New York and invited me to come over again to deliver a speech at the Guildhall. And when I began discussing with people what I might say, I was told, in no uncertain terms, that I should not refer to crack as a Jamaican problem. In fact, I was told I shouldn't introduce the ethnic line at all.'

The abiding irony is that the comments which people wanted to ignore turned out to be remarkably prophetic, while some of the much-quoted claims which influenced a nation's strategy could not be substantiated at all.

The recommendations with which Roy Penrose and Wally

Boreham returned from the United States in the summer of 1989 went up to Commissioner level, and in October, the fruits became apparent when the Crack Intelligence Co-ordinating Unit came into being. The man chosen to head it, Detective Superintendent Chris Flint, was faced with a daunting task. 'I had heard a tape recording of Stutman's speech – in fact, every relief in the Met was instructed to listen to it – so I knew all the horror stories. But we were still pretty unsure of what was expected.

'No-one really had a clue what crack was. I had never seen it. We didn't know how it was sold – whether it was in phials or in clingfilm; we didn't know how much a rock weighed; we didn't even know how we would describe it on a statement for court purposes. It was a steep learning curve, I can tell you.'

The Crack Unit moved into Tintagel House on the Albert Embankment, occupying the same office space as the now defunct Operation Lucy team. It inherited five members of that team – almost a quarter of its complement. But there, officially, any connection ended. The Yardie squad had targeted the people involved in crack-related crime, and got its fingers burnt in the process. The remit of the Crack Unit was to look at the product itself and to try to limit its reach. It would do this by gathering intelligence on the extent of crack dealing in London, analysing it and passing that information down to the divisions as an aid to local enforcement. But bearing in mind Stutman's strictures about the devastating addictiveness of crack, the unit was also instructed to develop links with other agencies, such as the psychiatric wings of hospitals, in an effort to monitor the way in which the drug was making its mark.

'There was considerable unease,' says Chris Flint, 'amongst treatment agencies and others when we tried to make contact. Not unnaturally, they suspected us of being interested only in arresting people rather than the wider picture. In time, things got a little more friendly though I don't think there was ever universal acceptance of what we were doing.'

In theory, the new crack initiative should have been on safer ground on the law enforcement side. But here, too, the doubts began to creep in. Given the fanfare of attention which had followed the Stutman address, there was a strong expectation that the arrest and seizure figures would begin to reflect the seriousness of the problem. But when the 1989 figures came out, they showed that only about 250 grammes of crack had been seized. Compared to sixty tonnes of cannabis and 500 kilos of cocaine powder, it was such a puny total that people began wondering what had happened to the much-vaunted crack explosion. They also started to cast doubt on some of the shock figures which Stutman had thrown at his ACPO audience.

To underline his point about the addictiveness of crack, Stutman said: 'A study that will be released in the next two to three weeks, will probably say the following – that of all those people who have tried crack three times or more, seventy-five per cent will become physically addicted at the end of the third time.' But when journalists and drug researchers began asking questions about the study, there was a mysterious absence of information which would identify its authors or where they worked. Another statistic widely quoted from his address was this: 'Of all the kids who died by battering in New York City, seventy-three per cent were the children of cocaine/crack using parents.' This time, it did prove possible to trace the source of the material – and the figure turned out to be wrong. It was, in reality, 46 rather than 73 per cent. Of more relevance though is the fact that, in absolute terms, the number of children was just two. Despite this, Stutman remains unapologetic: 'Even if the statistics I quoted in my ACPO speech were wrong by fifty per cent, what difference? It was still a horrible situation I was describing.'

But by the time he returned to deliver his speech at the Guildhall, he faced a rather more sceptical audience. Indeed, at one point, he lost his temper with someone who accused him of exaggerating the problem.

'I told this guy he was displaying a degree of arrogance which I found breathtaking. Here was someone saying I had got things out of perspective, when the evidence in the States was all around us. I had seen the movie, read the script. Now, people in Britain said: "It can't happen here, our slums aren't as bad as yours, we don't have as many guns in circulation as you." But hell, it's not the presence of guns which causes drug dealing, it's the other way around.'

Meanwhile, the faultlines caused by the racial argument were making their presence felt. It was said that while the politicians and policy-makers wanted to keep the ethnic link out of view, the impact of Stutman's presentation had made that impossible. And Stutman himself was pilloried for having an undue influence on those police officers who were at the sharp-end, doing surveillance and making arrests. It is absurd, though, to level this particular charge at him. A report on Yardies in 1986 by the National Drugs Intelligence Unit shows that British officers were aware of the Jamaican link nearly three years before Stutman addressed the ACPO. And, of course, the Crack Intelligence Co-ordinating Unit could hardly ignore the groundwork done on this by Operation Lucy. Nevertheless, by the middle of 1990, it appeared to many that the police were concentrating their efforts on those inner city estates with a large black population, yet making what looked like a derisory number of seizures, compared to other hard drugs. The critics had more than enough ammunition. Once again, it was said, Britain had fallen for a large dose of American hype which carried the additional risk of poisoning race relations.

The first casualty of the mood change about crack was the

decision in August 1990 to disband the joint police-customs unit set up the previous December. The official line was that it had never been intended as a permanent fixture. The unit, with its twenty-four officers, had been given the remit of establishing how much crack was being imported into the country, and who was supplying it. It seized one shipment of four kilos of cocaine powder, intended for conversion to crack, and a few smaller amounts. But no rocks of crack. This should not have come as a surprise since Stutman had pointed out that people did not need to import it in rock form. The conversion could easily be done, with a few household ingredients, in the kitchen of any flat.

So, the unit was never likely to be a powerful front-line weapon in the fight against crack. Its real purpose seems to have been an attempt to weld two agencies with different, often conflicting, traditions into one outfit. Judged on this basis, it was a signal failure. The personalities clashed and the two approaches – the customs officers relying more on analysis, and the police on streetwork, making use of informants – never gelled.

With hindsight, it's also evident that the Crack Intelligence Co-ordinating Unit had significant design flaws and this is where Robert Stutman's influence can fairly be criticised. Stutman's ACPO address had concentrated on the unique properties of crack as a drug and as a trigger for crime and violence. This was the message received loud and clear by Britain's policy-makers and they responded by setting up the crack unit under Chris Flint, with a specific remit to focus on the places where the drug was dealt and the means by which it reached the streets in rock form.

The object, to put it crudely, was to allow the Home Secretary to tell the Commons in a year's time, that, as a result of resolute action, a new and dangerous drug had been prevented from wreaking the same kind of damage in Britain as it had palpably done in the United States. But this ignored – or at the very least, downplayed – the other aspects of the phenomenon which, even in 1989, were allowing a new breed of criminal to gain a foothold in many cities. Such as immigration flaws which enabled Jamaican gunmen to slip into the country on false passports; the astonishing ease with which guns were circulating; the police service's lack of skill or experience in handling black informants; the absence of witness protection programmes; the need to look at robberies, burglaries, and other crimes, which may have been crack-related. In short, concentrating on crack alone placed blinkers on the police, allowing a problem which may have been manageable at the end of the 1980s to slip beyond control in the nineties.

A former member of the Operation Lucy team, who declined to join the crack intelligence unit when he saw the remit which it had been given, puts it like this:

'It seemed to me that the unit was encouraging the collation of information rather than real detective work on the streets. The decision to let the area drug squads do most of the arrests was political – but it wasn't helpful. Once you are at arms-length from what's happening, you are storing up trouble.

'My other complaint is to do with Stutman. Sure, he made everyone sit up and take notice. But he focused attention on the US experience. And you will always find people in positions of influence in this country who will take comfort in the fact that we are not like the States and never will be.

'The point was that we already had all the evidence of a growing Jamaican crack problem by the time that Operation Lucy was up and running. And yet by stigmatising that as "disorganised, organised crime", most of the answers were shoved away in a drawer at Scotland Yard and forgotten. And I am afraid we are still paying the price.'

By 1991, when Yozzer Hughes was shot at Church End, there was more confusion than clarity about crack. Were the dealers and addicts mainly black? Was it a local cottage industry, or could it be tackled on the same basis as other hard drugs which generated vast profits? Had the much-heralded epidemic simply failed to materialise? Or could that be attributed to the policies put in place during the autumn offensive of 1989?

The truth is that it was far too soon to provide definitive answers to these questions. Even at the time of writing, in autumn 1994, the picture is still unfolding. But one thing is clear. Stutman's ACPO address led to a concentration of attention on crack as a drug rather than as a means of providing a lucrative lifestyle and a source of extreme violence. To pose one last question – did we take our eye off the ball?

Chapter Eleven

The Addicts

The Six O'Clock News on BBC Radio Four on Monday, 25 January 1993, carried the following item. 'Detectives in California are investigating a bizarre drugs case in which a newborn baby boy was sold for ten dollars. The child was offered to eighteen-year-old Robert Garcia as he walked through a car park in Tustin. He paid over the money in order to protect the child. He said afterwards that the addict was "pretty messed up" and had even said the baby was a girl. The infant is now being cared for in a children's home.'

The same story was carried in one or two of the newspapers the following morning. Amongst the additional facts they included was that the baby-seller was the child's mother – and she was a crack addict. It was, I thought, the perfect example of crack as a symbol of amorality. Here was a drug whose spell could not be defied even by the most powerful of natural bonds, that between mother and child. I was contemplating this horrible proposition as I drove to work, when the eight o'clock news came on. This was the last item: 'Police in America say an eighteen-year-old who claimed he'd bought a baby in a car park for ten dollars, has now admitted he made up the story. He told police that his girlfriend had given birth to the baby herself. They then concocted the story because they were afraid to tell their parents the truth.'

I dare say most people would wonder at the psychopathology of someone who could invent such a tale. But I am far more interested in the willingness of others – me, of course, included – to believe it. And why was it believed? Because the drug concerned was crack.

Amongst the many statistics with which Bob Stutman, of the DEA, shocked his police audience in North Wales in April 1989 was this set.

'In a survey of seventeen thousand crack users, forty-seven per cent had been involved in a physical fight under the influence of crack. Thirty-five per cent had been involved in assaults with weapons. Twelve per cent had committed child abuse. And one per cent had actually been involved in murders. This is a drug which, unlike any other drug we have ever seen, produces those kind of numbers.'

In the months after his speech, when sceptics began to ask if some of the shells in Stutman's devastating bombardment had actually been duds, the veracity of some of these figures was called into question. Was crack, people demanded to know, capable of exerting such a malign influence over the human personality? Could it operate the levers marked 'bestial' and 'psychopath' even when every other instinct of decency and self-restraint was pulling in the opposite direction? The experts were divided. A consultant physician wrote in a journal: 'Among all the hard drugs, crack will remain at the top as a killer because of its addictive potential.' His article was described by a criminologist as 'one of the most ill-informed and irresponsible pieces of writing on the subject'.

The example of real events is no more conclusive. One of the most horrific crimes committed during 1992 was the sexual assault and attempted murder of a twenty-seven-year-old fashion buyer in Brixton. She was abducted on her way to work one morning and dragged into an empty squat by a man high on crack, Anthony Ferrira. Ferrira subjected her to a series of degrading sex attacks, throttled her with a scarf and slashed her throat with a broken bottle and knife. Then he set fire to the room and escaped. Miraculously, his victim survived – a neighbour broke down the door after smelling smoke – and she was in court to see Ferrira jailed at the Old Bailey for twenty years. A senior detective on the case told me later:

'In my view, the ferocity of the crime was due to the crack. He was still high hours after the attack and, in that state, he went to a nightclub in Streatham. He caused such trouble there that a bouncer hurled him through a window and he got several shards of glass up his rectum. One was a fraction from a major artery and he had to be carted off to hospital.

'While he was in casualty, a nurse told him he needed an anaesthetic injection so that they could remove the glass – and he went berserk. He grabbed a pair of scissors and he would have stabbed her, perhaps even killed her, if the medical staff hadn't leapt on him. That kind of irrational, totally unpredictable behaviour is characteristic of crack.

'After he had been arrested, and was on remand awaiting trial, he tried to commit suicide. I think it was remorse at what he had done while he was being driven by the crack.'

It sounds plausible until you examine Ferrira's previous criminal history: convictions dating back to his teens, including robbery, burglary, indecent assault, carrying dangerous weapons, wounding and, in 1985, manslaughter, when he stabbed a fellow prison inmate to death with a pair of scissors. With a record like that, is it really possible to say which came first, the drugs or the violence?

A drug which sensible people believe is capable of forcing a mother to sell her child, or a man to behave like a jungle predator, clearly has to be understood – even if, at the end of the process, some of its supposed properties are consigned to the realms of mythology. And where better to go than to the crack addicts themselves?

Cal is a white guy, thirtyish, plenty of bottle without looking like a bruiser. He was born in Canning Town, in London's dockland. Mean streets, mean estates, where you have to be able to take care of yourself to survive. Cal still lives there and he has 'respect'. He has been a crack addict for six years and does a little dealing now and then.

'You wanna know what someone is capable of doing on crack? I'll tell you. I was round this guy's house once, mate of mine called Fred, and we were both doing a pipe. He had a sixteenth, I had a sixteenth.

'He had a friend there who I didn't know, and this guy kept asking me for a draw. I told him to fuck off. But he kept on asking. I said: "You carry on and I am gonna do you, mate." Well, he didn't stop, did he?

'I stabbed him with a screwdriver. Put a lot of force behind it. Went straight through his collar bone and out his back. He needed seventeen stitches. He was much bigger than me but, I tell you, I never give it a second thought. When you're on crack, you don't give a fuck about anything, anyone.'

If anyone was born to be a drug addict, it was Cal. 'My old man was a coke dealer. That and other drugs. I saw the stuff at home all the time. I used to come back from school and he and his mates would be in the front room shooting up. Sometimes it was so crowded, it was like a fucking train station.

'One time, I wandered into the kitchen and one of his mates was fiddling around with some coke and some bicarb, ammonia and a test-tube. I asked him what he was doing. He said: "Washing up a bit of charlie".

'I suppose I was about fifteen then and I didn't know nothing about crack. It was just "washed charlie". We never did call it crack. Everyone on this manor talks about "goodness". They'll say: "Had a bit of goodness the other day." Anyway, this mate of me dad offers me a lick. "Save you getting it on the streets," he says. It was pukka. Quickest buzz I ever had. When you're young, it really does the business.'

Cal's dad was in the big-time. An East End wide boy who'd moved into drugs ahead of the game. In time-honoured style, he owned a scrapyard. 'That's where the drugs were stored. He could get hold of anything. Coke, cannabis, whizz. He would go away about five times a year – usually, New York, later on, Jamaica. Do a bit of business, make connections. He was taking home ten big ones a week at that time.

'He's a smart guy, me dad. Never did his dealing from home. He used to break into squats. Change the locks and make up his rocks there. But he never stayed too long. The secret was always moving on before it got too hot.

'The filth used to pull him in every now and then. But he only ever got done for possession of cannabis. One time, they kept him in for thirty-six hours at West End Central. They said they were letting him go. The bastards re-arrested him straight away and kept him another thirty-six. But they had nothing on him.'

Naturally, automatically, Cal drifted into crime, too. Left school at fifteen. Got slung out for smoking cannabis and speed in the toilets. Time to take life by the scruff. 'I did a bit of everything. TDA, selling motors I'd nicked. Burglaries houses, shops. It was opportunist mainly. I worked alone and I took the rough with the smooth.' The rough was six months in a detention centre, Aldington in Kent, for malicious wounding.

'I gave this geezer some cash to buy some powder for me and he never came back. So I went round to his drum and bashed him up. Stuck a Stanley knife in him a coupla times.'

Cal's first contact with the penal system was during Willie Whitelaw's 'short, sharp shock' experiment. It may have brought on a few orgasms at the Tory conference but it merely embellished Cal's criminal pretensions.

'When I came out, I was into drugs three or four times a week. Me dad's mate would supply me. Didn't matter what time of day you wanted it. Three or four in the morning – it was all the same to him.

'Here's me typical day. Get up about nine. Meet me mates. Sit round for a bit, have a couple of pipes. Then go and earn some money to pay for all the gear we were getting through. By earning, I mean robbing. Smoking beforehand took away all the fear, you know. Made me feel powerful. Gave me confidence.

'If we felt really wicked, we'd go down to the bank and see what we could snatch. We watched one guy paying in cash at the Midland in Commercial Road every day for two weeks before making our move. Two of us pulled him to the floor, grabbed the dough and were away on a motor bike. Four thousand quid. No witnesses, no comebacks.

'Mind you, that money didn't last more than a week. Spent it all on cocaine. Plus a bit of smack to make coming down a little bit easier. Sounds a lot of money, four grand. But if you consider me habit, and the fact that I had to clothe and feed myself and pay the rent cos me dad wouldn't give me a penny – well, it didn't stretch far.'

Cal moved in with his girlfriend when he was eighteen. Had his first child, a boy, when he was twenty. Another baby, a girl, came along five years later. But what would be milestones in a normal life were just another drain on resources. Another distraction from the main purpose – feeding the habit.

'I was into rocks and powder in a big way. And if I had it in front of me, I couldn't leave it. I had to use it all straight away. The kids didn't count. Crack took the place of me family. It was me life. The girlfriend didn't use it. She didn't even smoke fags. And she tried like hell to get me off it. I used to tell her to shut up.'

Cal turned the kitchen of his tiny council house in Canning Town into a mirror image of the drug den in which he'd grown up with his dad. 'I used to shut the door on the family and make up me rocks in there. Me girlfriend would stay in the front room watching tele. Often she would take the kids round to her mum.

'It suited me better to be on me own. Everyone knew that if the light was on in the house, they could get a smoke. It didn't matter what time of night. They used to knock on the front door at two, three in the morning. If it wasn't crack, it was cannabis. I had the contacts and people knew I could always get the gear.'

The price of addiction was at least £100 a day, seven days a week. A rock cost £20 and Cal and his mates would buy it in one-sixteenths. Five rocks. That would last four of them no more than an hour and a half. When that was gone, they would beg, borrow and steal – invariably, steal – to buy some more.

'We decided hanging around outside banks was a bit risky so we took to mugging people on tubes. Especially Friday when they'd just got their pay packet. I did the Central Line mainly – it was handy for the East End. I had a knife with me and some acid in a bottle. I'd show 'em the bottle and say: "This will strip the skin off you."

'It usually worked a treat. I once got away with £300 from a guy. I couldn't believe he had so much dough on him. It takes nerve to mug someone in a crowded carriage or on a platform.

But the crack was better than a shot of whisky. You could handle anything.

'You wanna know how I feel when I'm smoking? It's like taking a dull sensation and suddenly turning it into a lively one. You're more aware of everything. Your surroundings seem to change. The focus is sharp as a pin. It's a much more intense buzz than you get from the powder.

'It makes you feel wicked. You're bursting with confidence. You can communicate more clearly with other people. That high is six to eight minutes of magic.'

But what sounds like nirvana is actually nihilism. If crack is a passport to another world, it is one where all the normal standards have been warped beyond recognition. And Cal knows it.

'It starts with the paranoia. When you've got crack in the house, you feel as though you're being watched or threatened. You start using it up even more quickly to prevent someone nicking it. I used to open the toilet window and peer out to see if the cops were coming. Then, I'd open the bathroom window and do the same thing. I'd do it with the bedroom window too. You feel as though you're going bonkers.'

And then, there is the aggression.

'If you're smoking crack with someone else, you pick an argument for nothing. I would stab people for trivial things. Like speaking out of turn. And I've been stabbed so many times myself over crack. It just makes you reckless.

'Once, I gave this guy £200 to buy me some crack from Rock City, that's an estate in Bermondsey where everyone goes. I don't even know its real name. You get lost there and you ask for Rock City – anyone will direct you!

'Well, this guy comes back with Polos in twists of silver foil which he's bought from some black geezer. It's a common scam and they reckon you'll be too scared to face them out. Not me.

I went back with my guy to the house where he bought the stuff.

'Black guy opens the door and gives me some shit about: "When it left here, it was gear." I said: "If you don't let me in, I'm gonna do you." He called out to his mates and three or four black guys appeared from an inner room. The first one pulls out a bayonet and stabs me in the shoulder.

'But I'm so fired up, I start fighting instead of getting the hell out. I jump on the geezer who stabbed me and we start rolling on the ground. I'm trying to gouge his eyes and I've got my fingers down his throat to choke him. I must have been crazy. They kicked the shit out of me. I lost a lot of blood, ended up in hospital overnight. It was a stitches job.

'They wanted to keep me in for observation, but I discharged myself the following morning. Me mate came and picked me up and we made some petrol bombs. We went straight over to Bermondsey – it was about eleven thirty in the morning – and threw them through the front and back windows of the house. The guy who done me came running out in his underpants and I stabbed him in the back with me Stanley knife.

'The fire burned down the entire front passage of the house. He lost everything – all his gear. Taught him a lesson. As it happens, two weeks later, I was over at Rock City, but keeping well clear of him, on the other side of the estate. I'd just got me stuff and was leaving when, fuck me, there he is, with a pit bull on a leash. As he walks up to me, he's giving me the old bunny, daring me to do something. You'd have thought he'd had enough. I squirted him straight in the face with some ammonia I was carrying for protection, and he and the bleeding dog scarpered.'

Successfully dispensing a bit of vigilante justice was an aphrodisiac in itself. Freaked out on crack and self-righteousness, Cal began to see himself as an enforcer. 'I was in a pub in Bethnal Green when me mate, Paul, came in. He said his house had just been done over. Video and gold taken. And they'd stabbed his dog, a Yorkshire terrier, to death. Paul said he knew who'd done it and he asked me to give him a hand sorting the bloke out. Why did I get involved? Listen, after a few pipes I was fuckin' superman.

'So we pick up two other hard lads and go over to this place in Wickford Street and knock on the door. Guy opens up and Paul chins him straight away. We went into the front room and there's four geezers watching TV. One of them rushes us and Paul sticks him in the leg with his blade and twists it several times.

'Another one jumps me and I stab him fourteen times with me Stanley knife. It's got two blades strapped together, so you can't stitch up the wound. Evil, it is. There was claret everywhere. All up the walls.

'We're not satisfied, though. One of our lads, Frank, eyes a heater in the hall and pours about half a gallon of paraffin over the guy who organised the burglary – then flicks a match on him. He had forty per cent burns. Needed a skin graft. The guy who'd done the robbery had seventy-eight stitches in his head. And forty-eight in his back.'

There are limits even to East End retaliation – and this was one piece of mayhem which Cal couldn't just shrug off. Three of his group, including Paul, were picked up within days. One of them buckled under questioning and gave a description of Cal. But because he wasn't local, the police failed to track him down. He thought he'd got away with it.

'I was told via the grapevine to stay clear of Bethnal Green – and I did. It must have been six months before I was over that way again but I got into a spot of bother and the cops picked me up. It didn't take plod too long to sus I was the missing link on the other job and they charged me with attempted murder.'

Because there were four defendants, the CPS knew they would have difficulty proving who had done the stabbing. In the end, Frank and Paul were charged with attempted murder and got seven and three years respectively. Cal had his charge reduced to malicious wounding with intent. Considering that the Old Bailey court was shown pictures of the room after the attack, looking like an abattoir, he reckoned he'd done well to escape with twenty-one months inside.

The pock-marked kid who'd got his initiation in one of Willie Whitelaw's detention centres was now a fully-matured stakeholder in Brixton and the Scrubs, where a reputation for being swift with a Stanley knife counts for nothing. Half the people around him were druggies and, for the first time in his life, he began to see his own degeneracy through the eyes of his peers.

'I'd lost my girl and my kids, and my family had disowned me. I had nothing left. So, I made a kind of pledge to myself in there that this time, I'd try to keep to the straight and narrow when I got out.'

Back on the outside, his resolution held up for as long as it took him to find his first rock. With the charge surging through his bloodstream, he grabbed a knuckleduster and would have used it on someone's skull if he hadn't been stopped by the police and arrested. This time, the choice was stark.

'The judge said that, with my record, it was a custodial offence. But he was going to give me a chance, because he believed that the root of my problem was the crack. If I agreed to go to a drugs agency and sign up for a course of treatment, I would stay out of nick.

'It was the turning-point for me. Not because I couldn't face more time inside. I could have got through the bird. It was the fact that I was forced to admit what I'd known deep down for years. I had a crack problem. Sounds simple to say it.

Tackling it is something else. It's a question of what's stronger – me willpower or the crack. Come and see me in five years – I'll let you know.'

'What's the difference between butane gas and crack?' asks Donny, a black beanpole whose gelled hair shoots up in spiked tufts. 'I'll tell you. The fuel will kill you instantly. The crack is a slow, lingering death. It is the death of your soul. And you betta give that crack respect, man. Cos it's like climbing into a ring with Mike Tyson. Sure as hell it will batter the life out of you.'

At the age of twenty-seven, Donny had seen the best of times and the worst of times – and crack has been his partner for many of them. Six years ago, in the same awful week, his best friend was stabbed through the heart in the East End of London, and his Jamaican-born mother committed suicide in the Bronx. Donny couldn't spare too much time for grieving. He had a five-year-old son and a king-size cannabis habit to support. His only vocational experience had been a YTS scheme and three months in a hamburger joint at Paddington Station. He considered his trade to be nicking car radios and cassettes.

'I was one of the best, you ask anyone. I could remove a radio in thirty seconds or less – even if the car was alarmed. I'd flog them down the pub. A decent machine would fetch a oner (£100). It was going along very nicely until this guy started undercutting me – selling them for £50.

'That was about the time I turned to the crack. They call it a "recession lifter". And that's what it does. Takes you out of yourself when times are bad. It's not like charlie up your nose. It's not like Es (Ecstasy). Crack is like the best sex you've ever had. What can I say? It's just a more-ish drug.'

It is also a scary drug. 'It may take you a mile high. But when you come down, the guilt trip and the depression take

156

you two miles deep. That first time, my body was tingling all over after the initial rush and it scared me bad. I didn't go near it for two or three months afterwards. But somehow, at the back of my mind, I knew I was fighting a losing battle to stay away from it.'

In 1989, Donny got a break and landed a job on a building site. Suddenly, he had money of his own to burn. 'I was making £500 a week and I was in clover. I spent it on a motor bike, skiing, flash clothes. Then someone introduced me to the rave scene.

'I was dropping Es left, right and centre, doing a bit of speed, poppers. But I couldn't forget the memory of the crack. There's this place called Marie's, a wine bar in Forest Gate. I bought the stuff there and very soon, it was a regular weekly order. I would fork out £200–£300 every Friday on rocks.

'I was living in a hostel at the time and I would smoke it in the toilets. At the start, it would last me all night long. But gradually, I was getting through it quicker and by 2 a.m., I would be walking the streets looking for some more. I would be totally wasted by Saturday morning.'

Amazingly, he managed to confine his crack binges to Friday nights and continued working during the week. But £500 quickly became inadequate to feed such a voracious habit and he turned to crime.

'There's no way I would have had the nerve to rob a bank or anything which took real balls. But even so, I was desperate for cash so I found a hammer, pinched a pair of my girlfriend's stockings for a mask and went down to my corner shop. I beat on the counter with the hammer and screamed my head off and the little Indian shopkeeper was so terrified, he opened the cash till straight away. It had thirty-five pounds in it and two cheques. I grabbed it all and legged it. It bought me one and a half rocks. It's pathetic when you think about it.'

Later, he stole £60 from his father and bits of jewellery from his sister. But the timidity which was deep in his psyche put a brake on anything more serious. 'I knew that a friend of mine had a couple of hundred quid in his flat so I went round there when I thought it was empty. I kicked the door in and was just starting up the stairs when his girl appeared on the landing screaming blue murder. Some crack addicts I know would have battered her and grabbed the dough. But I couldn't do it. I was out of there like lightning.'

If the examples of Cal and Donny are at all typical, then crack has a spectacular effect in heightening instincts which are already part of the personality. With Cal, it brought out the latent aggression which had been with him since childhood. In Donny's case, abandoned by his parents at the age of thirteen, insecurity was turned into crippling paranoia by the crack.

'Smoking crack is all about chasing that first hit, recapturing the incomparable feeling you had the first time. It's an impossible dream. It's like regaining your virginity. It can't be done. But the addict is too dumb to realise it, at first.

'And when it gradually dawns on him, it takes people in different ways. Some get eaten up with anger which comes out in violence. Others turn it all inwards. I got to a point where I just wanted to shut the world out of my head. I had no money, no friends, no family – nothing.

'And I remember one night, in the hostel, when I felt so low, I think I would have killed myself if I had had the guts. It was the middle of winter and I was lying on the bed wrapped up in carpet underlay to keep warm.

'All my senses seemed super-charged. My hearing was so acute, I could pick up tiny sounds which buzzed around in my ears. It was driving me to distraction. My eyesight was so sharp, I could see through the curtains and I thought the shadows outside were people trying to get inside to attack me.

'I was on the verge of a cocaine psychosis and frankly, I was on that very thin line which divides sanity and craziness. It was the worst night of my life. Someone once said to me that when you're on crack, you're just a puppet, with the drug pulling the strings. I knew what he meant that night.'

Cal and Donny's stories are illuminating not just because they show the effects of living with a crack habit, but also because they begin to explain the link between crack and crime. It is a link which a number of senior police officers, abetted by the Home Office, have been loath to acknowledge, even though the evidence is staring them in the face.

I have spoken to junior police officers in a number of cities who despair at the attitude of some of their superiors. Standing in the blackened shell of a confectionery shop which had been burgled and set alight, a constable said to me: 'I know that eighty-five per cent of the burglaries in this area are committed by teenagers feeding their crack habit. I can't prove it – but I know it. And my colleagues on the beat will tell you the same thing.

'But my divisional superintendent tells the media that we don't have a serious crack problem in this city. Now, either he believes that – which makes him a bloody fool. Or he's lying, because if he admits there's a problem he's got to do something about it by committing manpower and resources to it – and, as we all know, police budgets are under severe strain. If you ask me straight, the second explanation gets to the truth of it.'

The point is underlined by a chief inspector in the Metropolitan force. 'It's all very well launching a blitz on burglars called Operation Bumblebee and carrying out dawn raids, but it's tackling the effect rather than the cause. A vast number of those burglaries are committed to feed a drugs habit and I think the public is being seriously misled about the scale of the problem.'

Criticism of the police can be applied equally to the Home Office, which has consistently played down the impact of crack addiction in England and Wales in its attempt to prove that government policy since the Stutman warning has been successful. Indeed, a press release issued with the 1992 Bulletin of Statistics of Drug Addicts adopts a remarkably self-congratulatory tone when it detects 'no sharp rise in cocaine notifications, suggesting that the UK is not experiencing an explosion of cocaine misuse problems on the US scale'.

The problem, though, is that the notifications come mainly from family doctors who fill out a standard survey form every year. And the sad fact is that the vast majority of crack addicts are not the kind of people to share their secret with their GP – always assuming they are registered with one. After all, what incentive do they have? Heroin users, if they live in the right area, can get a prescribed substitute – methadone. But there is no recognised substitute for crack other than willpower, and there are only a tiny handful of clinics which are prepared to prescribe cocaine powder to their patients.

The truth about crack then is not contained in the statistics but the experience of the streets – and the treatment agencies which see the addicts. The Newham Drug Advice Project in East London has been treating crack users since the late eighties and its director, Viv Reid, is full of scorn for government policy.

'The stuff put out by the Home Office is just window-dressing, to convince people that something is being done. If you want to get to crack addicts, you have to aggressively target them. You can't just sit back and wait for them to come to you – because they won't.

'We are seeing more and more crack users and we have not reached the lowest point in this cycle yet – not by a few years.

It is no good government officials pointing out that crack is an expensive drug and that there are cheaper alternatives like amphetamines. People take crack because of the unique buzz it gives them. They may use other drugs as well – but nothing else compares with crack. And they will do anything to get it.'

Nineteen-year-old Duane Daniels, a would-be Yardie, is a case in point. When he appeared at the Old Bailey just before Christmas 1993, he admitted to 600 burglaries, 130 muggings and 220 car break-ins to fund a crack habit on which he was spending well over £300 a day. It was the largest total of offences ever dealt with at the Old Bailey.

Before his arrest, Daniels's average daily intake of narcotics included 20 rocks of crack, half an ounce of cannabis, 10 cans of extra-strength lager, two doses of LSD and 14mg of a tranquilliser. Daniels told the court that he dearly wished to give up the crack – but the judge, for one, did not think that very likely. He handed down a jail sentence of ten years.

While there are children of eight and nine who can accurately draw a crack pipe and who are exposed to the persuasive techniques of the pushers outside their school gates, and even inside their playgrounds, it is not being alarmist to suggest that anyone who feels safer merely because Duane Daniels is behind bars is living in a fool's paradise.

Chapter Twelve

If You Can't Catch Jack

The elderly caller said there had been strange noises at the back of the block of flats in London's East End, where she lived. She suspected a burglary. It was 4.30 on a Friday afternoon, 23 November 1990. Despite the dramatic resignation the day before of the Prime Minister, Margaret Thatcher, the fine detail of everyday life went on. As usual, there was heavy traffic flowing eastwards and the patrol car sent from City Road nick arrived at the Holly Street estate in Dalston at a shade after five o'clock. When the two uniformed officers got to the rear of Welbury Court, the blackness yielded nothing but a distant whimpering – like an animal in distress.

Their torchbeams picked out a shape on the flattened grass which could easily have been a bundle of rags, had it not been for the contorted movements which raised it a few inches in the air at intervals. It was a woman and she was far more dead than alive.

'It's my nephew, it's my nephew,' were the first comprehensible sounds she uttered. Then, more faintly: 'Number 31, that's where I was.' It did not take long to establish that number 31 was on the fourth floor and that the woman had either fallen or been pushed the fifty feet to the ground.

When the officers entered number 31, they found it virtually empty of furniture but there were signs of recent habitation. In the kitchen of the two-level flat, there was an upturned handbag. Upstairs, on a stained mattress, was a gun (which turned out to be a replica). Downstairs, there was a cushion with traces of blood on it and more blood around the dimpled neck of a Ribena bottle. A wire coat hanger was protruding from the arm of a scruffy settee. Rust-coloured pinpricks on it appeared to indicate more blood. Lengths of wire flex were lying on the floor.

An hour later, the two officers reported back to their DI, Gary Southgate and there was much discussion about what had been going on in the flat. The favoured theory was that it had been occupied by a 'tom' (a prostitute), who perhaps was into heavy-duty bondage sessions. Maybe an over-excited client had pushed her out of the window. If that was the case, it could turn out to be the sort of inquiry where the victim, despite appalling injuries, does not wish to press charges.

The following day, DI Southgate mentioned his problem to a detective sergeant coming on for his weekend shift at City Road. It was the lucky break that most successful inquiries need rather more than brilliant deductive skills. The DS was John Brennan and there wasn't a police officer throughout the Met who was better equipped to provide answers to the puzzle of the bloodstained flat in Welbury Court.

John Brennan was a late entrant into the police. He wanted to be a professional footballer and between the ages of fourteen and seventeen, he was on Aston Villa's books. Despite playing once for England schoolboys, he found himself surplus to requirements in the mid-seventies when Tommy Docherty became manager of the Villa. Brennan decided to take his A-levels, got to university and then became a teacher, specialising in PE and biology. But there was something in his character which teaching couldn't fulfil and at the age of twenty-five, he switched careers and joined the police.

Brennan was a member of the Operation Lucy team. Indeed, he was the officer whom Devon 'Foodhead' Plunkett so hated that he wanted killed. And as Brennan became an increasingly familiar figure in the shebeens and clubs, he even acquired a streetname – Blondie. His interest in the Yardies is such that he wrote a thesis on the phenomenon, for which he was awarded an MA in Criminal Justice Studies at Exeter University.

When you immerse yourself in a world of skewed standards – where sadism and ferocious retribution are qualities to be admired not despised – there is no behaviour too perplexing to make some kind of sense. As he listened to DI Southgate's account of the scene at 31 Welbury Court, a faint outline of understanding was already taking shape. For a starter, the discovery of a body which had plunged from a flat window held distinct echoes of a case he had investigated in 1986. Within spitting distance of City Road, a Nigerian called Innocent Egbulefu had been hurled ninety feet from his eighth floor flat in Islington. When he hit the ground, he was still clutching the remote control unit from his television. He had paid the price for selling some bad ganja to a group of Jamaicans.

When Southgate mentioned the wire coat hanger with blood on it, that, too, was familiar. There had been several cases where a hanger had been crudely fashioned into a weapon of torture to terrorise those who had transgressed in some way. Another refinement which Jamaican crack dealers had brought to the business of crime.

Brennan asked what accent the woman victim had spoken in before she had slipped into a semi-coma. 'Sounds American to me,' said Southgate. Brennan said: 'I suggest you go and ask her if she's from Jamaica, guv. Meanwhile, why don't I take a look at the scene of crime?'

Brennan needed only a few minutes at the flat to be certain

that this was going to be a Jamaican investigation. When he opened a wardrobe, eight pairs of Travel Fox shoes spilled out onto the floor. On an upper shelf, there was a hat bearing another familiar Kingston label, Kangol. A pile of cotton Kangol sweaters sat on a lower one. In the bathroom cabinet, he found a can of pink hair spray – a common cosmetic accessory amongst Jamaican women – and the SOCO team recovered pink hairs from the sink. From the flat he went straight to Homerton hospital where the victim, who had been identified as Nellie Allen, had had her injuries diagnosed as three broken vertebrae, a cracked pelvis, a badly broken ankle and numerous lacerations. Nellie's streetname, by which everyone knew her, was Gem.

'Who did it, Gem?' asked Brennan. 'Pam.' 'Do you mean, Fat Pam?' 'Yeah.' Then, as confirmation, 'Fat Pam, that's Yardie P's girl?' 'You got it in one, boss.'

Fat Pam, a.k.a. Pam Pinnock, but born Evelyn Victoria Mason. Baby mother to a dope dealer called Yardie P, a.k.a. William Alexander Young – she was no submissive moll, Pam. She was a drugs peddler in her own right, cunning and manipulative and a vicious enforcer when crossed. When Brennan knew that Fat Pam was involved in the case, he told his boss, DI Southgate, that they should move swiftly and bring her in. He didn't like to think of her on the loose, like an aggrieved tigress, for any longer than was necessary. Southgate said he wanted a full statement from Gem before he sent in the heavy mob to lift Pam. As a result, John Brennan spent the next twenty-six hours at Gem's bedside in Homerton hospital listening to a harrowing story of naivety, deceit and dreadful revenge.

Gem has an apartment in the Bronx in New York but, as with so many Jamaicans, the concept of 'home' is a nebulous one. It is wherever she happens to be. She travels frequently to

Kingston, where she was born, and to England where she has many contacts. Gem is what the Jamaicans call a 'higgler' and what the Americanised West Indians tend to call a 'pegler' – a kind of licensed, freelance trader, who is allowed concessions on import duties by the Jamaican government on the goods which they bring into the country.

Gem specialises in Marina costume jewellery, gold bracelets, chains and the like, but she will turn a penny on any item which is in demand. String-vests, for some reason, always find a ready buyer amongst Jamaicans and, having disposed of her jewellery amongst the exiles in London, she would always return to New York with a pile of Marks & Spencer underwear to flog. The status of 'higgler', with its necessary access to different countries is, of course, a perfect cover for less savoury activities – especially drug smuggling. And Gem knows far more about the traffic in cocaine than anyone with a purely innocent interest in the matter has a right to. On this visit to England, however, Gem was not carrying powder, but her nephew, Tony, the author of her tribulations, was.

On Sunday, 18 November 1990, Gem and Tony arrived at Gatwick on American Airlines Flight 557 from New York via Miami. Gem was carrying jewellery in her hand luggage which she declared, at the cost of excess duty. Even so, customs officers did a thorough search of her. She was clean. Tony, on the other hand, was carrying two kilos of white powder in a body belt, which he did not declare. But he was not searched. Whether Gem knew that her nephew was smuggling cocaine is a matter of conjecture. She says not. Most of the law enforcers who have dealt with her say she probably did. What she did not know was that Tony was about to perpetrate a rip-off which would all but cost her her life.

Tony's full name is Frederick Anthony Dawson. He was then twenty-four, a good-looking hustler with a honeyed tongue, who had turned the gullibility of others into a round-the-clock cash machine. Tony was the prince of rip-offs and he had high hopes about this trip. As long as he could make the right connection, he was confident he would be leaving Gatwick with a suitcase full of notes.

On their arrival, aunt and nephew headed for Bletchley Court, N.1, the home of a Jamaican called Danny Green. Like Gem, Green came from Denham Town in Kingston, close to Tivoli, though they had forged a relationship only since about 1984, on one of Gem's earliest visits to London. Gem and Tony had arranged to stay with Danny and he would ferry them around in his car. Late that night, the three of them got dressed up and went to a popular Jamaican club in Kingsland Rd, Hackney, called Maxims. The way Gem tells it, she was surprised when Fat Pam walked in. But it appears to have been no accident. Pam was the connection which Tony was looking for.

After the introductions – Gem and Pam had been at school together, though at thirty-nine, Gem was a few years older – there was some inconsequential chat before Tony and Pam wandered off to a corner by the bar and sat talking animatedly in low voices for some time. It had gone 2.30 in the morning before the group left the club. They agreed to meet later in the day, the Monday.

Tony was still half-asleep when Danny roused him with the Vodafone mid-morning. 'It's Pam, for you.' They fixed their rendezvous for a Jamaican restaurant called Fitz's in Shepherd's Bush. Danny dutifully chauffeured his guests there for a late lunch. When Pam hadn't shown up after an hour, the others decided to eat. They had all but finished their meal when the door opened and Pam's familiar fleshy figure swaggered towards their table. She was rattling her car keys and eyeing Tony in a provocative way. No words were exchanged. He simply got up and followed her out. Gem stayed at Fitz's for most of the afternoon selling her jewellery and chatting, and Tony and Pam reappeared towards six o'clock. Tony was carrying a shoe box and wearing an expensive leather coat. By way of explanation, he said they were gifts from Pam. She had also given him £500 spending money.

That night, the group reassembled at Maxims and sat around drinking and bantering until 2 a.m. When they left, Pam whispered something to Tony and they broke away from the others, walking in the direction of Pam's distinctive cream Mercedes, parked thirty yards away. Gem noticed that Tony was carrying the shoe box. The young man and the older woman sat in the car for several minutes. Every now and then, Tony's head could be seen swivelling from side to side, scanning the street for any action. Eventually, the passenger door opened and Tony re-emerged. He no longer had the shoe box but he was clutching a blue Panache bag close to his chest. As he drew near, Gem noticed the traces of a smirk on his face.

On the Tuesday, after another session at Fitz's, Danny, Tony and Gem went to a flat in Shepherd's Bush, belonging to a Jamaican friend called Rupert. Danny had his Vodafone with him, and they had been there only five minutes when it rang. 'It's for you,' he said, passing it to Tony. Tony cupped the mouthpiece and conducted a long secretive conversation in which he gradually switched from calmness to a state of some agitation. Within seconds of pressing the off pad, it rang again. More agitated words, a voice shrilling down the line. A conclusion, and then the ringing tone once more.

After forty minutes of this, Gem said: 'Wha happ'n, Tony?' 'The bitch won't leave me alone,' was the only reply she got. It didn't make a great deal of sense. Danny left shortly afterwards, taking the Voda with him. But by six, he was back, highly distressed. 'It's Pam. She callin' all the time, non-stop. She threatenin' me, saying I'm dead. She say Tony has robbed her of £10,000 and where the hell is he? She real vex, man.'

Gem turned to Tony. 'Is it true? Did you take her money?' 'I didn' take no money. The bitch is lyin'.' Danny was trembling, knowing Pam's reputation only too well. Gem says she suggested they call the police – though that seems barely believable. But when Pam rang again, a few minutes later, she grabbed the phone from Danny.

'Listen, Pam. I'm coming to see you. We'll sort this out. Just cool it, man.'

They decided to take two minicabs. Danny and Gem in one, with Danny's dog. Tony and Rupert in the other. Tony persuaded them to go via Danny's where they packed their luggage and put it in Tony's minicab. The two cars moved off in the direction of Shepherd's Bush, where Pam lived – Tony's vehicle leading the way.

As they were negotiating the one-way system around Shepherd's Bush Green, Tony's cab suddenly swerved into the side of the road and Rupert was violently ejected. As Gem struggled out of her car, Tony half-emerged, shouted: 'Fuck off' and ordered his driver to pull away as fast as he could. The maroon cab jerked into the Chiswick-bound traffic flow, carrying not only Tony, but all of Gem's clothes, as well as her passport.

Tony was laughing to himself. Pam had contracted to buy half a kilo of coke from him for £10,000. With the street price of cocaine at thirty grand per kilo, she thought she had got herself a good deal. But she didn't know Tony well enough. The package in the shoe box was one-tenth genuine coke, and nine-tenths talcum powder, plaster of Paris and sugar.

Gem did not know what her nephew had done – but she knew she was in deep trouble. Tony had clearly ripped off Pam and presumably was heading for the airport, leaving his aunt to face the consequences. She should have expected it. On a previous occasion, Tony had slept with a girl in a hotel bedroom, and decamped in the middle of the night with her jewellery before she woke up. He was a past master at the double cross.

Gem's immediate concern was to stay out of Fat Pam's clutches. Danny Green was too shell-shocked to be of any further use. In any case, Pam knew where he lived. Gem could think of only one other person, with whom she could 'chill out' – Andrea Bailey, known because of the hue of her skin as Red Audrey. Audrey didn't seem overjoyed to see Gem but agreed to accommodate her at her flat in Harrington Hill, Upper Clapton. On the following day, the Wednesday, the two women went shopping to the West End. Gem felt safer among crowds.

It was early evening, and the two had their shoes off on the settee, when there was a ring at the bell. Audrey's Rasta boyfriend opened the door. Two black men stood there. The smaller of the two was carrying a large handgun. Gem recognised him immediately as Pam's younger brother, Patrick. He ignored the Rasta and Audrey, made straight for Gem and placed the gun against the side of her head. 'Pam want you.' 'What Pam want me for?' Patrick returned a glassy stare. 'Come on, man. Pam want you, let's go.' Then, half turning to the Rasta, he added almost as an afterthought: 'Stay cool, man. Just a bit of business, that's all.'

Under the pressure of the gun barrel, Gem was armlocked, kicking and screaming, to the door. As she was yanked into the hallway, she turned her head to make one last appeal for help, but the Rasta just stood motionless in the centre of the room and Audrey had melted into the kitchen – not so much to take refuge, says Gem, but to cover her shame at having betrayed her friend. (After all, no-one else knew where she was staying.) Gem was dragged down the stairs and flung into the back of a saloon car. Patrick gave the gun to the other man, while he drove. Gem asked over and over where they were taking her. Patrick said nothing. The only answer from the tall man was a clubbing on the head with the gun butt.

Neither Gem nor the police are sure exactly where that journey ended. She was taken to another apartment belonging to a mixed-race couple – a white woman living with a Jamaican. There were further assaults from Patrick and his companion and then Pam arrived, spitting fury. She kicked Gem in the head and the body, and beat her with the gun butt. At this point, the white woman, who owned the flat, intervened: 'I don't want this in my house,' she pleaded. 'Please go someplace else.'

Another short car ride. More violence, more threats. And then the ordeal transferred to yet another apartment. 'As they forced me out of the car, people were looking, and Pam was making out like I was under the influence. "I told ya not to drink to drunk," she kept saying. "How many times have I told ya?" I could hardly stand on my own by then.'

This apartment – again, neither Gem nor the police know where it was – belonged to a Jamaican girl. All Gem recalls about her is that she wore her hair in braids (that was insufficient for the police to make an identification). She had no objections to her home being used as a torture chamber. Gem was tied hand and foot with flex – 'they trussed me like a hog' – and bound to a chair. Pam shouted over and over: 'Where's Tony? He rip me off. Where's Tony?' punctuating her questions with kicks and blows. 'She was like a mad woman,' says Gem. The tall man was no slouch either, doing his fair share of kicking and, at one point, skewering Gem in the thigh with a kitchen knife.

By the early hours of Thursday morning, even the captors were exhausted and they finally left Gem for a few hours, still trussed, on the floor. A rim of crusted blood clung to her lips, her forehead swelled into a purple obelisk, and every rib and bone in her body throbbed from the kickings. She had had nothing to eat for seven hours and the only liquid offered her was some tap water sluiced into a plastic bottle retrieved from the garbage can.

'I thought I was gonna die. I really did. I knew they won't let me go unless they catch Tony. An' he was too smart for that. So, they gonna kill me instead of him.' Not for the first time during that night, she thought of the Jamaican saying: 'If you can't catch Jack, catch his shirt.'

But there was worse to come. The following day, realising that their treatment had produced no results, they took Gem into a bedroom. Patrick unbuckled his trouser belt and forced her at gunpoint to have oral sex – 'Come on babe, I want ya to clean me up' – while the others, Pam included, stood around taunting her.

'I beg them to kill me, I beg them,' says Gem. 'Patrick, he say nothin' but he took a bullet from the gun and he told me to swallow it. And I stretch my hand out to take it – but he say: "No, you die too fast, too easy, like that."

'The tall guy, he say he gonna rape me, and he start pulling down his pants. But I was having my period at that time. It was the only thing that save me.'

Patrick took a cushion and placed it on her lap and said he was going to shoot her kneecaps through it. The cushion would muffle the sound. In desperation, Gem decided to pretend that she knew, after all, where Tony could be found. Whether they believed her or whether even sadists need fresh air from time to time, they accepted her offer to lead them to her nephew. Still tied hand and foot, she was taken down to the cream Mercedes again.

'The only place I could think of to go was my friend's place in Shepherd's Bush. But I don' know the way, so we drivin' aroun' for ages, up and down these streets while I try to find the way. Suddenly, I see a police car coming towards us and I try to attract their attention by lurching against the window, bangin' my head on it and hollerin'.'

It didn't work. The police car drove on by and Gem was thrust onto the floor with Pam's heavy shoe resting on her neck. 'This time, bitch, we gonna kill you,' she said.

The flat at 31 Welbury Court was ideal for their purposes. At one time, Pam had lived in it before moving to West London. It was now empty and in the bedroom on the upper level, no-one was likely to hear Gem's cries. Another prolonged beating took place during which Pam – nearly fourteen stone of her – stomped on her back several times. A Ribena bottle, lying on the drainer, came in handy as an auxiliary club. Another night slumped on the floor, slipping in and out of consciousness. Wondering if she would survive to see the Bronx again – or Kingston.

In the morning, Pam found a new way of tormenting her. She re-shaped a coat hanger to act as a makeshift meathook, one end through the settee, the other impaled in the flesh of Gem's upper arm. She blacked out.

By early afternoon on the Friday, Gem summoned up her remaining strength for one last throw. She told them that she was now prepared to co-operate and she gave them the name of a hotel where Tony was, supposedly, staying. Why they didn't ring first before checking it out is not clear. Nor why they all left together rather than posting someone behind on sentry duty. It is possible that, after some sixty hours, they felt that their victim was so thoroughly terrorised that her will was entirely subjugated to theirs.

When the four of them left the flat and she heard their footsteps descending the stairs, Gem hardly dared believe that they had left her unguarded. She lay still for fully thirty minutes before easing her upper body gingerly away from the settee to free herself of the wire hanger. The next task was to unravel the flex which bound her wrists. Slowly rubbing her palms together, she generated sufficient movement to relax the tension from the bonds. As she felt the circulation beginning to return to one wrist, she realised that she had succeeded in slipping the knot.

Pam and her henchmen were not entirely wrong if they believed that their relentless brutality had robbed Gem of the ability to think straight. Even when she pressed her ear against the door and heard nothing, she refused to accept that one of them wasn't waiting outside to batter her unmercifully if she emerged. She stood there irresolutely for several minutes before deciding that only one course lay open to her. She made for the window.

Gem knew she was on the fourth floor of the block. She did not know how high up the flat was until she opened the window in the sitting room. But she could also see that the window of the flat immediately beneath was within striking range of her feet if she had the nerve to crawl out and hang from the ledge. And she could hear sounds of movement and human voices which indicated that, at least, someone was in down below. It was a perilous decision to take. But of all the fears crowding in on her, the most potent, by far, was the possibility that delay would leave her at the mercy of Fat Pam and her brother.

'I knew the way Pam was acting that if she came back and found me in the flat, she would kill me for sure. And in an empty flat, maybe nobody would have found my body for weeks. I tell you, when you're thinking like that, you will do anything – however crazy.'

Gem crawled out onto the ledge and slowly released her

legs until her full weight was being borne by her arms. The voices in the flat below were more distinct now. She could tell that they were not speaking English. It sounded like French and, to her concern, there was no response when she rapped her toes against the downstairs window. She swung back her heel and hit the window with more force. But there was no alteration in the timbre of the voices to give any sign that she had been heard. The more intently she listened, the more apparent it became that the inhabitants of the flat were in a back room. Gem began to panic.

The tendons in her wrists, already inflamed from the flex, began to throb unbearably. The soft tissue around her shoulders was stretching like elastic and as the seconds stretched into minutes, a numbing weariness began to envelop her. For the first time, she looked up rather than down and realised, to her horror, that had she but realised it, there was a flat roof within climbing distance of the ledge from which she had emerged. It was academic now. There was no way back.

'I can't say how long I hung there. I know it was many minutes. I was shoutin' and I was kickin' but I was gettin' weaker all the time. I jus' knew I couldn't hold out. I almost wished that Pam would come back and haul me inside again. And then, suddenly, I had no choice but to let go.'

Sometimes, the human brain has a capacity to blot out the very worst memories. Gem can't recall those few agonising seconds as her body went spinning downwards, nor the crunching impact as she hit the grass. She does remember trying to struggle up to run away and finding instead that she was rooted to the spot. The muscles which operate the back felt as though they had been severed with an axe. She began screaming.

'Above the sound of my own voice, I heard someone say: "Bring a sheet" and then "Don't move, an ambulance is on the way." And then just before I passed out, the last thing I recall seeing was a pair of shiny black shoes. It must have been the policeman.'

Chapter Thirteen

Patience Rewarded

Detective Sergeant John Brennan finished taking Gem's statement at 3 a.m. on Monday morning. Despite the length and the detail, there were many unresolved questions. What was the exact nature of the rip-off which Tony had perpetrated on Fat Pam? Where was Tony now? Where was Pam's brother, Patrick? And who were the tall man and the girl with the braided hair?

The first priority, though, was to arrest Pam. Her address was known – St John's Way, Holloway – and within two hours, a Metropolitan police raiding party was on its way, with support from the firearms branch, SO19. When they arrived, they noted with satisfaction that Pam's cream-coloured Mercedes was parked in the road. Inside, they found Pam with a woman called Greta Austin (not her real name). There was an imitation gun in a downstairs room and, scattered throughout the flat, an extraordinary array of high-class ladies clothing, valued at some £200,000. (Pam was already known to the police as a shoplifter.) From the many photographs showing Pam and her husband, Yardie P, holding guns, it seemed that she liked to flaunt her reputation for violence.

The photos also provided a strong link to the abduction of Nellie Allen because under the settee of the flat in Welbury

Court, the police had found a strip of negatives, which, when developed, showed Pam in various poses and locations. They came in useful when Pam later denied having been to Jamaica in the recent past. When the photos were enlarged, Kingston street names were clearly visible.

Detectives made a rather more significant find in the bedroom of the flat in St John's Way. In a fingertip search, they prised the wardrobe away from the wall and, behind it, found a purpose-built recess which served as a safe. They pulled out a silver box, containing a sheaf of documents – marriage certificates, birth certificates, housing benefit books, in short, all the paperwork needed to establish one or more false identities. Much of the material was in the name of Valerie Brown, a white woman from Newcastle-on-Tyne. Pam admitted to stealing her identity.

As Operation Ferryden showed, investigations into crime involving people who use streetnames and false identities are strewn with problems. Very few police officers can find their way through this maze of aliases but there is a guide they can turn to and his name is Brian Fotheringham.

Fotheringham is a Home Office immigration officer and even his best friends would acknowledge that he is a stubborn individualist. He ascribes his failure to get promoted to punching a superior but even the Home Office can probably recognise that people like him are far more effective close to the action than in a management capacity. Fotheringham has a photographic memory when it comes to matching faces with names. He is also prepared to bide his time. He tells the story of a Jamaican called Delroy Hines, a.k.a. Alfonso Recordo Stewart, who was refused entry at Heathrow as an illegal immigrant in 1983.

In 1986, he tried again and was put into detention at

Harmondsworth to await deportation. But he escaped from custody and went to ground. Fotheringham hadn't forgotten about him though and when he was arrested for a criminal offence in Dalston in East London in 1988, the hunter was back on the trail. Once again, though, Featherman – as the immigration officer is known to his adversaries – was frustrated. Hines did a runner. He spent a profitable two years manufacturing and dealing in crack – hence his streetname, 'The Chemist' – before falling foul of the law again in Peckham. Incredibly, despite his antecedents, the fugitive was granted bail and disappeared.

But in 1992, the indefatigable Fotheringham spotted his man in a bookmaker's in Stoke Newington. He was arrested and charged with possession of crack and dealing. His previous breaches of bail and his status as an illegal immigrant contributed to the three-year sentence which he received. He will be deported when he completes his term – though Fotheringham confidently expects to see him back in London before too long.

When Brian Fotheringham was told that Pam Pinnock had been using the name Brown, it struck a chord. He knew of an Eldon Patrick Brown, who had been deported to Jamaica as an overstayer and who had been involved in crack dealing in Stoke Newington. Brennan put it to Pam that this was her brother and she did not deny it.

A search of Brown's usual haunts, especially around Shepherd's Bush, produced nothing except the strong suggestion that he had fled the country and was probably already back in Kingston. Pam refused to answer any questions about the tall man or the girl with braided hair, and Brennan was none the wiser about their identity. Surprisingly, though, she did admit knowing the victim, Gem. He decided to concentrate on that angle and especially her nephew, Tony.

Tony had made a series of phone calls during the brief time he was in London – some of them on Danny Green's Vodafone. A print-out showed that one of these calls was to a number in New York. It was the only slender clue to Tony's mysterious disappearance. Once again, Brennan decided to make use of the brotherhood of Jamaican crime specialists. He rang Jimmy Killen in the District Attorney's office in New York.

Killen has the wonderful title, Senior Rackets Investigator in the Homicide Investigation Unit. He's a bluff, sandy-haired second-generation Irishman, who spent twenty-four years in the New York Police Department, the last eight or nine in Harlem, becoming increasingly frustrated as the body count from the activities of the posses began to rise. Now, he handles long-term investigations for the DA and, like Brian Fotheringham, he's regarded as a professional's professional.

On John Brennan's behalf, Killen checked out the location of the New York number which Tony had rung from London. It turned out to be the address of a house in Ozone Park, which is in the borough of Queens – and it was an address which had also figured in one of Killen's own investigations into Jamaican crime. A woman who lived in the house, Yvonne Dodd Hill, had put in a complaint that her boyfriend had stolen her BMW. Yvonne's boyfriend was Gem's nephew, Tony.

In March 1991, John Brennan and his boss, DI Gary Southgate, got permission to fly over to New York to pursue their investigation. They went to the house under a warrant obtained by US immigration officials, who believed that more than one of the occupants were Jamaican 'illegals'. They were right, and one woman turned out to be a close relative of Red Audrey, who had betrayed Gem in London. There were other connections too. The woman had an ex-boyfriend, living in Brooklyn, who was one of the characters holding a gun in some of Fat Pam's photographs. Brennan thought for a time that this might have been the unidentified tall man who had abducted Gem, but he was not.

Of more significance to the English detectives was a letter found during a search of the house. It had been written to Yvonne Dodd Hill by Tony. When they looked at the back of the envelope, they realised that their search for him was over. The stamp said: Metropolitan Correctional Center, Manhattan. Tony was already behind bars.

Jimmy Killen takes up the story: 'It turns out that what Tony had done in London, he had just repeated in New York. He and a fellow named Steve Moore sold two kilos of coke to a coupla guys. It was what we call a "beat" package. In other words, it was mainly made up of plaster of Paris and sugar. Could have netted Tony and his friend a lotta dough.

'Unfortunately for them, the buyers were agents for the DEA – Drug Enforcement Administration. Tony was arrested and banged up. I arranged for Brennan and Southgate to go see him but he didn't wanna know. Wasn't interested in co-operating in any way.

'We had another line of inquiry though. We knew that Pam Pinnock had a sister in New York, name of Peaches – Peaches Peterkin. We had a phone number for her and established that it was in the Bronx. I would say that out of the entire Pinnock family, she is the only one who's legitimate. And she was helpful to us.

She knew Gem and she knew what had happened to her in London. And it was our belief that Peaches's son, Steve, who lived in London, was the unidentified tall guy who abducted Gem with Patrick. I took a photo of Steve to Gem and, sure enough, she picked him out as the guy.'

Before he left New York, Brennan was keen to explore one more angle, but one which carried a high level of risk. Yvonne Dodd Hill, Tony's girlfriend, had powerful friends – indeed, just about the most influential friends that a Jamaican in New York could have. She was a former baby-mother of the Shower Posse don, Vivian Blake, and it was widely rumoured that she still controlled much of his vast wealth. If anyone knew where the bodies were buried – literally – she did.

When Yvonne sent word that she was prepared to meet the English police sergeant at a convenient, discreet location, Brennan accepted with alacrity. As in all the best Mafia films, she proposed a little Italian diner in Queens. Which merely confirmed Jimmy Killen's worst suspicions that Brennan was being set up for a hit.

'Jimmy only agreed on condition that he came with me and was wired for sound. And that we had a small army of cops with guns staking out the place in the car park. Of course, in the best traditions of the British police, I was unarmed.'

In view of the elaborate preparations, the confrontation was something of an anti-climax. Far from bringing any shooters, Yvonne was accompanied by her mother. It was clear that her purpose was not so much to impart information as to discover what the two detectives knew. After establishing that Yvonne worked as a ticketing agent for American Airlines and that she had booked the flights to London for Gem and Tony, there was little more that they were able to carry away from the meeting. Except the certainty that her job provided a very useful cover for someone wanting to organise regular cocaine shipments out of New York.

For much of the time that John Brennan and DI Gary Southgate were investigating her kidnapping and torture, Gem was recovering in hospital. After more than three months of treatment in London, she was passed fit enough to return to her home in the Bronx. She was still in bad shape but, given the nature of her injuries, she was just grateful to be alive.

'When they took me into hospital, they called my daughter

182

here in New York and told her to come over if she wanted to
see me again. They thought I wasn't gonna make it. In fact,
they moved me to a ward where they put folks who gonna die.

'The doctor said if I tried to walk too soon, I gonna be
paralysed from the waist down. So I just lay flat on my back for
weeks. I prayed real hard during that time. But I didn't know
if I would ever walk again.

'It's still very painful to walk. I gotta steel plate in my ankle.
My back and my pelvis ache terrible most of the time and it
usually takes me more than an hour to get movin' around in
the morning. But I'm still here. So, I reckon it just proves God
weren't ready to take me yet.'

The psychological scars ran just as deep. When the police
told her they wanted her to return to give evidence at Fat Pam's
trial, she said she couldn't face it. Pam's husband, Yardie P,
lived in New York and other members of Pam's family had
threatened her with retribution if she went into the witness
box. In her fragile state, she just felt like withdrawing into her
shell.

'But then I heard from a friend that while Pam was in jail
on remand, she had been bragging about what she had done.
Laughing about it. And that made me real mad. I was
determined to get even. So I said I would come over for the
trial.'

She also learned that Pam had been on cocaine for some
time before the kidnapping and she strongly suspects that that
partly accounts for the venom of her behaviour. It is probably
the only explanation for the fact that Pam never slept during
the three days that she held Gem hostage.

In May 1991, Jimmy Killen accompanied Gem to London
for the trial of Fat Pam. Gem wasn't sorry that she had agreed
to testify. Pam behaved with the same degree of brazen
arrogance in court as she had on remand. 'Her attitude seemed

to be: "If I had to do it again, this time I would kill you". She was found guilty of abduction, robbery and causing grievous bodily harm, and was jailed for ten years. Brennan had hoped that the 'tall man' would be standing trial too, as a co-defendant. But there, he was disappointed. Peaches's son, Steve, was arrested in London and took part in an identification parade. Despite what Gem had said in New York when shown his photo, she failed to pick him out in the flesh. It appears that she identified him earlier, only because she knew he was related to Pam and, in her all-encompassing anger, that was good enough at the time. She had cooled a little by the time she returned to London. Steve was released.

Six months after the kidnapping and torture of Gem, the identity of both the 'tall man' and the girl with the braided hair remained as much a mystery as they had at the beginning. The only viable line of inquiry which remained open concerned the whereabouts of Eldon Patrick Brown. Once more, John Brennan turned to his contacts.

They say that the Jamaican police are the 'biggest and baddest' posse on the island. Since they shoot maybe 150 people a year, few would dispute that description. A number of police officers are heavily into cocaine and ganja smuggling, others take rake-offs and bribes, a few have built up reputations at least as colourful as some of the ghetto dons – and, among this company, Keith Gardner, a.k.a. 'Trinity' stands out.

In the late 1970s, Gardner was an enforcer for the JLP. News footage filmed during the bloody election of 1980 shows him out on the street with his machine-gun, blazing away at PNP rivals. As a police officer, he has been just as profligate with the gun. Three years ago, he even killed his wife with it during an argument. The prosecuting authorities accepted his defence that she was a 'bad woman' and the charges were quietly dropped.

Trinity and Brennan already had a 'friend' in common – Rankin Dread, who had shot the Jamaican cop in the mouth back in 1980, and escaped justice when arrested by the Operation Lucy team in London in 1988. Since then, the two police officers had formed an occasional alliance when the need arose. So, when Brennan received reliable information that Patrick Brown was in Jamaica, he rang 'Trinity' who promised to provide any help that he could. On the strength of that, Brennan and Southgate got authorisation to fly to Kingston. They were not expecting instant results. Despite the cop-to-cop arrangement, the inquiry had to go through formal channels and the Jamaican Constabulary has not been notably co-operative towards foreign police force investigations which might disturb its own equilibrium. Indeed, a number of murder and drugs inquiries initiated at Scotland Yard or with US agencies like the FBI have run into a bureaucratic brick wall in Kingston. Sometimes, the intention to obstruct has almost certainly been deliberate. More often, though, it is the consequence of a lack of resources and technology which makes efficiency and competence virtually beyond reach.

An American investigator seeking information in Kingston on a drugs dealer who had been arrested in Miami wanted to find out if the man had ever been imprisoned in Jamaica. After the ritual closing of many doors in his face, he eventually gained access to the court records for the General Penitentiary. And a door was, literally, opened.

'It was the door to a dingy basement room in an old colonial building. It felt like entering a torture chamber from a horror movie. And inside, the scene was incredible. There were piles of documents everywhere – on the floor, spilling over tables, stacked to the ceiling in places. Each document bound with a piece of string or tape and each one relating to a criminal case. The cases went back to 1848.

'It took me four hours to find what I was looking for – and, to this day, I'll never know how I came across it in that clutter. This is their idea of record keeping.'

And, too often, their idea of criminal investigation is to break down a few ghetto doors, drag away the 'usual suspects' and beat them up or shoot them. Since evidence and reliable witnesses are all but impossible to obtain, it is seen as an acceptable instrument of deterrence.

Despite the occasional critical newspaper editorial, Jamaican society seems prepared to tolerate this system of justice, except when the law enforcers overstep the mark. In 1993, when police officers chased two suspects into Kingston General Hospital and shot them while they were handcuffed, in front of horrified doctors and nurses, the outcry was rather stronger than usual. But only because the killing had taken place uptown rather than in the ghetto, where it was generally seen as justifiable.

Against this background, the two London detectives were not at all surprised to wait in their Kingston hotel for four days before there was even a hint of action on their investigation. And by then, there had already been an ominous straw in the wind. 'Our information was that Patrick Brown was in Denham Town,' said Brennan, 'and there was talk that a detective inspector from a local station was "looking after him". So we weren't all that hopeful.

'Through Trinity's intervention, we managed to persuade the police to pick up Brown's brother and allow us to talk to him. But we got nothing out of him. We stayed on, hoping for a breakthrough, always being promised things which never materialised. In the end, we left after ten days, pretty choked.'

In policing, patience is not only a virtue, it is a necessity. The hunt for Eldon Patrick Brown had to be put on hold, and John Brennan threw his energies into other inquiries. By the beginning of 1992, more than a year after the kidnapping of

Gem, he was beginning to think that this was one file which would have to remain open indefinitely. And then, as so often happens, the breakthrough came about purely by accident.

'I was on early turn at City Road and I was going through the custody records of people arrested overnight. I noticed that an illegal had been picked up with quite a lot of cash on him. He was in the cells so I went to have a chat.

'At first, he tried to make out he was English, and that he hadn't been out of the country. But the Jamaican and US dollars gave the lie to that. From the papers found on him, we had his address and I went round. The woman who answered the door was his baby mother and it turned out I had come across her before in New York. I knew she might be useful so I brought her down to the station for a talk.

'She was quite forthcoming – told me that the guy we had got was a nasty bit of work who used to beat her up and that she would be glad to see the back of him. So, I offered her a deal. "You give me a bit of information that I reckon is tasty. And I will try to make sure your man gets deported."

'She said: "OK, are you interested in Patrick Brown?" And I said: "You bet." She said: "Well, I saw him here in London two days ago, in Shepherd's Bush – and, if you like, I'll give you the phone number." '

Brennan got her to ring the number to check that he was there and then speedily organised an arrest team, with firearms support. 'Our cover story was that we were the Shepherd's Bush robbery squad investigating a blag. We took up positions outside the flat, waited for someone to come out – it was a guy – and then marched him straight back in.

'There was only a middle-aged Jamaican woman inside, Brown's mother, and I said to her: "Is there anyone else here?" She said: "Only Lester, in the back room." I opened the door, and there, sitting on the bed, was Patrick Brown.

'He's a nasty dangerous little man, and arrogant with it. But he stood up quietly, grabbed hold of my hand, and said: "I knew you were gonna get me in the end." It is all part of the legend they build up about you.'

Eldon Patrick Brown, then twenty-five, stood trial at the Old Bailey in December 1992, on charges of abducting, wounding, indecently assaulting and causing grievous bodily harm to Nellie Allen. Once again, Gem made the journey to London to testify. In many ways, it was more of an ordeal than the trial of Fat Pam.

'His lawyer said terrible things about me. That I was a drug smuggler, that I was just as much to blame as the people who had grabbed me. And that I was sleeping with my nephew, Tony. It was real dirty stuff. I was in the witness box for two days and I was nervous all the time.'

But the defence pleas of mitigation did not wash with the jury. And the attempt at character assassination clearly did not impress the judge when he came to sentence Patrick Brown. He was given ten years, the same term as his sister, Fat Pam, had received.

During 1993, Pam was allowed out from jail on home leave for a weekend and indicated that when her sentence was completed, she would be heading for New York, where her husband, Yardie P, and children were living. Gem says she is not frightened: 'I ain't scared, I'm mad. I'm warning her that if she set foot in New York, I'll hunt her down. I'll use the immigration guys and I'll hunt her down and have her deported – to Jamaica, Britain, I don't care where it is. So, she better take heed and stay away.'

Gem claims she is no longer buying and selling jewellery because her injuries make it impossible to get around like the old days. Indeed, she drags her leg painfully and slowly to the door of her eleventh floor apartment to slide back the heavy mortice bolt when a visitor appears. And in the last three years, she has had plenty of time to reflect on the violence which seems to be ingrained in the behaviour of the Jamaican crack criminal. 'I think they grow up with no respect for themselves and no respect for each other. Money is all that concerns them – and once they get a gun, they feel all the power they need to force people to do what they want. They're just plain evil.'

One person who has never re-entered Gem's life since the events of November 1990 is her nephew, Tony. 'He ain't called once to see how I am or to apologise. And it don't bother me if I never see him again.'

Last heard of, the elusive Tony had been deported from the United States to Jamaica. But law enforcers on both sides of the Atlantic have no doubt that they will be hearing from him again. And the likelihood is that his rip-offs will become even more grandiose, if his connections are anything to go by. His erstwhile partner, Steve Moore, is being sought in connection with a scam which left a Colombian importer nursing a deep-seated grudge. He ended up with several suitcases full of fake dollar bills in return for handing over forty kilos of high-grade cocaine. You can make an awful lot of crack with that.

Chapter Fourteen

Mules

'As the plane touched down, my heart was beating so fast, I could hardly breathe. I kept telling myself it would be all right – but my body knew I was lying. I was trembling all over. I've never been so scared in my life. Deep down, I knew I was going to be found out.'

To the first-time smuggler, a drop of Dutch courage seems like a good idea. Winsome had consumed three miniatures of gin and one of whisky on the overnight flight from Kingston. She entered the terminal building at Gatwick in a haze of alcohol and dehydration. But the long walk to passport control began to clear her brain and by the time she had recovered her luggage from the carousel, she was thinking that perhaps her in-flight terrors had been baseless. Three yards from Customs control, she stopped to consider whether she should go through the red or green channel. She had a bottle of rum to declare. As she lowered her gaze from the signs, she found her path barred by a uniformed official. The terrors engulfed her.

'He asked if I had come from Kingston, and when I said "yes", he told me to put my suitcase on a table and open it.

'He took out a small duffel bag – nothing else. Inside the bag was a horseshoe purse and he unzipped it. I knew what was in it – some weed which I had stashed for myself, not

190

much, just enough to build a spliff. He looked at me and said: "Would you please come into this side room, miss?" '

In the room, the Customs officer told her that the marijuana would be confiscated and she would have to pay a £70 fine. Did she have the cash on her? Did she want to phone anyone? But Winsome wasn't really listening. She sensed that a game was being played and that no-one cared a damn about the dope in her purse. They were after higher stakes. Then another official walked into the room.

'He took my handbag and ran his fingers over it carefully. I had the feeling he knew he was going to find something. Then he said: "What's this?" and he took the bag out of the room.'

Winsome says she was never shown what was pulled from the slit lining of her handbag. According to the Customs record, it was a quarter of a kilo of cocaine powder, 90 per cent pure. According to Winsome, Customs valued it at £24,000 on the street, though in court, its value was given as £57,000. (There has been criticism that street values are sometimes fixed with an eye to sentence rather than market prices.)

When the officer returned to the room, her suitcase was re-packed and she was asked to take it to the concourse – in the hope that someone was meeting her. Winsome refused. She told them she felt weak and she needed some food. They said they suspected her of carrying more drugs in her body and that she could not eat anything until she had been examined. The air grew stale in the little room as the day wore on. She felt nauseous and light-headed. She had had a fever in Jamaica after being bitten by mosquitoes and she had not properly recovered. The questioning exhausted her even further.

'They kept on and on asking me if I was a Yardie and who I was involved with. I said: "My mum's from Yard, so's my dad. Is that what you mean by Yardie?" '

Eventually, in the early hours of the morning, a doctor

arrived and carried out an internal examination. She said Winsome's blood pressure was abnormally low and she was probably on the verge of collapse. Having decided that she had not swallowed any drugs, they fed her – and then she was taken away to be formally charged with smuggling cocaine.

Winsome sits in the tiny front room of a council maisonette in Battersea. She wears tinted spectacles and razor-slashed jeans, with dainty gold shoes. She is thirty and has a South London accent. And, as with nearly all drug couriers, it is impossible to decide how much she is holding back and where she has massaged her version of events to present herself as a victim rather than wrongdoer.

'I was in a pretty vulnerable state when they approached me with the proposition. I had just had a miscarriage, I was out of work and mentally, I could not cope. I was under a psychiatrist and I just needed to get away, so when the "opportunity" came up, I didn't think twice about it.'

The 'opportunity' was to get a paid-for holiday in Jamaica, with £500 spending money, in return for bringing back some weed. She knew the person who approached her in London, but she won't reveal any more about him.

Winsome was born in Britain of Jamaican parents, from Montego Bay. They had not returned since emigrating to the UK. Winsome had never been to Jamaica. 'As far as I was concerned, the trip was a holiday and a chance to see my grandfather, and the half-brothers and sisters I had never met before. I accepted the deal to bring back drugs because I could not have afforded to go as an ordinary fare-paying passenger.'

When she arrived at Kingston, she was met at the airport by a man who told her that, shortly before her return, she would be contacted about the arrangements for carrying the weed. She spent five weeks on the island, mainly with her relatives in Montego Bay, and came back to Kingston, where she barely knew her way around, just a few days before the flight home.

'I was given an address to go to and was met by two men. They said the plan had been changed and I was to carry coke not weed. They asked what luggage I had and decided that my handbag was the most suitable item for the purpose. They took it away with them and promised to return it the following day.'

Winsome claims that she felt desperately uneasy when she learned that she would be smuggling cocaine not cannabis. But the ticket had been paid for and she knew she was dealing with people who would be most displeased if she backed out. 'Let's just say these two guys were not the kind of folk you would find in a bank – unless they were robbing it!'

'When they brought the bag back, I picked it up and it felt much heavier. But I knew I shouldn't ask questions, so I took it and said nothing. I had no idea how much powder it was holding.'

She thought of asking if her payment was to be increased, considering that the original agreement had been for marijuana. But she kept her silence. Her only concern was to negotiate the journey safely and hand over the goods in London. She had been given a telephone number to memorise – no incriminating bits of paper – and she was to ring it the moment she got home. She never made the call.

Winsome's suspicion that she was being targeted the moment she stepped off the plane may well be correct. It is routine for sniffer dogs to be sent on board incoming flights from Jamaica and if they pick up the drug scent, there is ample time to do a ticketing check before the guilty passenger arrives at customs control. But there is another possibility – that Customs had been tipped off that she was a 'mule', by the very people who had given her the cocaine. Drug dealers frequently put several couriers on the same flight, using one as the sacrificial lamb.

If three or four kilos reach their destination, the loss of a quarter kilo can be put down as an acceptable business expense.

Another Jamaican drug courier, Gloria, is convinced that she was set up in exactly this way. She was carrying two hundred grammes of cocaine in a condom hidden in her vagina when she arrived at Gatwick.

'They knew I was carrying drugs. No doubt about it. This woman officer just picked me out straight away. She asked to see my ticket, then she searched my luggage. She didn't find anything so they took me into a cubicle and did a body search.

'On the flight over, I was convinced there were other people on board carrying drugs because a guy and a woman were obviously acting as minders. For a time, the man sat right behind me and I could feel him staring at me. When I got up to go to the bathroom – thinking I could flush the condom away – he followed me down the aisle and came up so close I could feel his breath on my neck. I was terrified.'

As with Winsome, the Customs officers asked Gloria to stand on the concourse at Gatwick to try to entrap anyone working with her. 'I never saw the man who'd been on board with me, but the woman came up and asked if everything was all right. Then she walked off. The Customs people made no attempt to stop her – I don't know why.'

Gloria is talking in a visitors room at Cookham Wood prison in Kent. Perhaps muttering would be more accurate because she clings to every word with the tenacity of a patient facing a tooth extraction. Gloria is a tiny, shrunken figure – 'I've lost four stones in this dreadful place' – suffering from clinical depression. She is also very frightened. She probably has good cause to be. She is a higgler who earned a living by buying and selling. Taking clothes and costume jewellery from New York to Kingston and foodstuffs in the other direction. It was a perfect cover for drug smuggling, though to believe her version, she only did it once – and paid the full price.

'I had gone to Kingston for my brother's funeral – he had been killed in a motor bike accident – and this group of people I knew forced me into it. One of them is a very dangerous guy, who carries a gun. He threatened to harm my son if I did not co-operate. I have an eight-year-old called Joshua, who lives there with my cousin when I am away.

'The plan was for me to take the cocaine to my father's house in Birmingham and wait there until it was collected. I don't know who was supposed to pick it up' (a claim I found barely credible).

The day before her flight to London, a man brought the drugs already wrapped in a condom. 'I said I didn't want to do it but they told me I had no choice. They would kill my son. So, I put the condom in my bag and they said: "No, it will be found too easily. You must carry it in your fanny." I was horrified. I had had a woman's operation only four months earlier and I didn't think I could go through with it. But I knew they meant what they said about my son.'

According to Gloria, she was offered no money, merely the price of the ticket. What did her father think about his home being used as a drugs rendezvous? 'I don't know. I have never met my father. He and my mother were living apart in Jamaica when I was born and he left for Britain shortly afterwards. I had never been to Britain before, so I had never seen him.'

It took four hours to entice the above information from Gloria. For the first ninety minutes, she stared blankly at the wall, frequently appearing to be on the verge of speech but rarely surrendering more than a tantalising phrase. Part of the reason for her silence was fear of her drug sponsors. 'They know where my son is, and they have told my cousin they will kill him if I say anything to identify them.' And part was fear of the authorities. This I only discovered when I started to analyse her story and realised that there was something decidedly odd about it. I knew that she had been arrested carrying a British passport. Nothing strange about that – except that she had said she had never been to England before. Neither of her parents was a British citizen, so how could she be?

The question drew the longest pause of all. The answer was barely audible above the ticking of the clock. 'My younger sister was born in England. But she died in Jamaica. I took over her passport and put my photograph in it. I needed it for my work because otherwise, on Jamaican documents, I would have required a visa to enter the United States.'

In other words, she was arrested, charged and convicted in the name of her dead sister. And if she can maintain the pretence throughout her sentence, she will not be liable to deportation afterwards. Some drug couriers are less innocent than others.

Gloria refused to co-operate with the authorities when she was arrested and pleaded not guilty to the charge. She believes that decision determined the length of her sentence – six and a half years. 'For two hundred grammes, it was a lot harsher than I expected. They were punishing me for not admitting the offence.'

Sometimes, though, couriers escape with a lighter sentence than they may have anticipated as part of a deliberate strategy by Customs. By not charging them with every offence for which they are, technically, liable, the Customs case officer retains a measure of leverage over the mule. Under threat of being re-arrested after release, they are sometimes persuaded to supply further information in jail – even, perhaps, to become an informant. A white American cocaine courier in Cookham Wood at the same time as Gloria was being courted in just such a way because US Customs believed they could make use of her inside knowledge. It is a practice which some probation officers and those who work with couriers regard as a form of double jeopardy and, as such, unethical. But, as a Customs officer says, who ever said the drugs business had anything to do with ethics?

As far as Gloria is concerned, it is not the authorities but the dealers whom she blames for her predicament. The long months inside have reinforced her view that she was set up by the people who recruited her in Jamaica.

'I have met other women in here and in Holloway, who have mentioned familiar names – names of people I know from Jamaica – and I keep wondering if we were all working for the same organisation, and were all sacrificed in the same way. It happens in this business.'

Her main preoccupation is to get news of her son. 'I have written letters to my cousin but I have had no reply at all. Joshua does not know what has happened to me. Perhaps it is better that way. I would rather he thought I couldn't see him because I was abroad working.'

Three years after she came out of jail, Winsome is still acutely aware of the shame she brought on her family. She served two and a half years of a four-year sentence, and for the whole period, her father believed that she was out of the country working. He died before she was freed on parole.

'My mum knew the truth and she came to visit me secretly. But she was heartbroken. She was the only one who stood by me. None of my friends contacted me while I was inside. I felt like a leper.'

Though there are a substantial number of Jamaicans imprisoned in Britain for drug smuggling, by far the largest group of foreign couriers in jail are the Nigerians. Until about 1990, they were trafficking principally in heroin but for a number of reasons, West Africa has now become a staging post on the cocaine trail to the UK. One factor is the Commonwealth link, exploiting the traditional trade route between London and capitals like Lagos. But a more persuasive pressure is the endemic corruption in countries such as Nigeria. To find a Customs official or government agent who won't turn a blind eye for a bribe is a rarity and the canny South American exporters have realised that shipping cocaine through West Africa offers more security than bringing it into Western Europe directly. This trend is reflected in the arrest figures. In 1991–92, fifty Nigerian couriers were arrested in Britain, compared to sixty-one from Colombia, the largest producer.

The Nigerians are frequently prepared to take enormous risks. There cannot be a more agonising death than that from a stomach flooded with cocaine, but some Nigerians have been known to swallow as many as a hundred drug-filled condoms. In the space of one month in the autumn of 1992, three Nigerians died while trying to smuggle drugs into the country. One, Lily Ehirobo, became ill during a Sabena Airways flight from Brussels. She was taken first to Ashford hospital in Middlesex, near Heathrow, and then transferred to St Peter's Hospital in Chertsey. Doctors removed from her body 111 small parcels made up of single condoms, coarsely wrapped in cellophane. They contained five hundred ounces of cocaine, much of which had seeped into her stomach. Massive cocaine ingestion causes hyper-stimulation of the nervous system, which leads to cardiac arrest, coma or kidney failure.

One of the other Nigerians who died was having terminal convulsions by the time she reached hospital. Before doctors could even begin treating her, her kidneys had given out and she was declared brain dead. In the same hospital, a British man was fighting for his life after swallowing cocaine-filled condoms in Jamaica. The drug rush sent his heartbeat rocketing from thirty-six beats per minute to more than 200 before his condition stabilised. Unlike the Nigerians, he survived.

The spate of tragedies has been caused by smugglers taking greater risks to avoid detection. Instead of making solid parcels of drugs in two or three condoms, couriers have begun to use alternative methods to cheat airport X-ray machines. An outer coating of carbon paper or charcoal is thought to be effective and one woman wrapped twenty condoms in carbon before ingesting them. But the 'security protection' was rotted by the gastric juices and she died painfully. She was being paid £650 sterling for her trouble.

Aware that the body is an even more sensitive machine than the X-ray, the determined smuggler will take elaborate precautions to try to overcome its natural resistance to carrying foreign objects. Swallowers often prime their gullet by gulping down large grapes smothered in honey first. Oil smeared on a condom or the fingers of a surgical glove acts as an extra lubricant. The trick is also to expel as much air as possible so as to prevent the parcels floating in stomach juices – which are corrosive – rather than passing through the digestive system. Mules will often take pills to block their bowel movements until the journey is over.

For these squalid, life-threatening indignities, the average payment for a Nigerian courier is under £1000, and the average prison term, when caught – six years. And if they manage to evade the Customs checks, there is always the vengeance of the dealers to contend with. Two Nigerian women acting as couriers for a Jamaican Yardie gang in London were suspected of short-changing their employers. They were held prisoner in a flat in Hackney, and had a hot iron pressed to their skin until they fainted. They were then doused with scalding water to bring them round. They are scarred for life.

Yet for all this, there is probably less sympathy for the Nigerians than the Caribbean couriers because they are perceived to be more calculating. Some of the Nigerian men have often financed, or part-financed, the smuggling venture themselves, so they should perhaps be seen as shareholders who have taken a wild gamble and lost, rather than as pathetic victims. Many Nigerian women bring young children with them to Heathrow as a means of gaining sympathy, when they could have made arrangements to have them cared for at home. However it is also true that sometimes they have been forced to turn to smuggling because, at the age of thirty-five or so, their husband has rejected them for a younger, prettier woman, and they have no means of support.

In the arsenal of legislative weapons with which Britain and other Western states have fought their 'war on drugs', draconian sentences against couriers have played only one significant role – to reassure the domestic voter that the defences are being manned. But ratcheting up jail terms has done little or nothing to stem the flow of mules. The concept of deterrence relies on awareness of the penalties and there is precious little evidence that the sanctions imposed by British courts have penetrated the hinterlands of some of the countries from which smugglers come. Most convicted couriers say they believed their supplier when they were told that the worst that could befall them would be confiscation of the drugs and deportation on the next available flight.

As a reporter covering Uxbridge magistrates court pointed out in a letter to *The Guardian*: 'Judges are fond of saying: "The word must go out" – but how is it to go out if people like me have no market for it? Judges may be surprised to know that I do not supply court copy to the *Bogota Times* or the *Lagos Tribune* or the *Karachi Gazette*.'

Chapter Fifteen

Operation Rook

On 12 September 1986, two Jamaican women stepped off a flight from Miami and walked into the transit lounge at Gatwick Airport. There was little to distinguish them from many of the other black passengers except, perhaps, their dresses – a riot of gaudy reds, whites and blues which would brighten even the dullest of autumnal English mornings. Monica Brissett and Beverley Jackson were tired from their eight-hour overnight haul and looking forward to journey's end in under two hours. Their destination was Brussels, a city they knew well. By lunchtime, they planned to be luxuriating in a hot bath at the Hotel Chambord, with a large rum perched on the soap dish.

Although passengers in transit are not subject to anything like the same level of scrutiny as other arrivals, there is still a security check at Gatwick carried out by officials of the British Airports Authority. Beverley strolled through unhindered and turned to speak to her companion. But Monica had been stopped by a BAA official. He was examining a bulging girdle which he had removed from her shoulder-bag. He motioned to a colleague and, after the briefest of conversations, a radio call was put through to Customs. Within thirty minutes, the delights of the Hotel Chambord were already a fast-receding memory. Both women had been arrested for drug smuggling. They were each carrying half a kilo of herbal cannabis.

When Customs officers arrest a courier, they routinely do a ticketing check with the airline. That will throw up a booking reference which enables the ticket's point of sale to be identified. In this case, the inquiry revealed that the tickets had been bought at a travel agent in London – and that two other tickets, Brussels–Kingston, via Gatwick, had been purchased at the same time. The passengers' names were Sandra Andrea Davis and Lorna Brown.

On the following day, 13 September, two Jamaican women were waiting in a transit lounge at Gatwick for their flight to Kingston to be called, when they were approached by Customs officers and asked to come to a nearby interview room. Each woman had about £2000 in cash on her and no convincing explanation as to why she was carrying so much. They were both arrested.

Neither Sandra Davis nor Lorna Brown was prepared to be helpful when interviewed. The question: 'Who are you working for?' elicited no response at all. In many cases, couriers genuinely cannot answer that question because the cleverer traffickers seal off the component parts of their operation for security. On a need-to-know basis, the only information crucial to the courier is how do I hand the stuff over? and how much will I be paid?

In this case, the Customs investigators felt that the four women knew much more than they were admitting. But either from fear or a misplaced sense of loyalty, or a mistaken belief that the boss would honour his pledge to ensure that everything turned out all right if they were arrested, they stayed silent. They were wrong, of course, and no-one came to their rescue. They were charged and committed for trial. Later, a jury convicted them of trafficking and they were all sentenced to between two and three years in jail. But despite their silence, they had provided Customs investigators with a clue, which was to increase in value as time went on. One of the girls had a couple of London telephone numbers written on a piece of paper. Another had a scrap with the name, 'Bird', scrawled on it.

'Bird' was the streetname of Parnell George Perkins, a Jamaican who was known to the police in many parts of North London. His first court appearance was at the age of fourteen before the Tottenham juvenile bench. He was fined £1 for stealing money from an ice-cream van. A year later, he left school and, apart from a brief period of apprenticeship as a tailor's cutter, he appears to have devoted his energies wholeheartedly to crime. His record sheet showed convictions for robbery, living off immoral earnings, criminal deception and possessing controlled drugs. One entry even records his expulsion from the principality of Monaco for 'procuring violence and fighting'.

By the mid-1980s, Customs were taking a strong interest in him because he was suspected of organising the importation of large amounts of cannabis and cocaine into the UK. Hugh Donagher, a senior Customs official who later became the 'star' of the BBC fly-on-the-wall series called *The Duty Men*, remembers Perkins well.

'He was just about the most important Yardie in London. We knew that he went back and forth between London, Jamaica and the States and that posse members from Detroit would travel over to see him. He was also involved in supplying false passports to some of these characters.

'Perkins was based in North London, but he ran a network of dealers south of the river as well. It was a substantial operation.'

According to a reliable Customs informant, the drugs were brought to the UK in a way which cunningly minimised the chances of the couriers being trapped. Perkins knew that the most hazardous stage of any smuggling operation was the point of entry into the UK. In the case of cocaine trafficking, any dealer worth his salt is aware that flights coming from the Caribbean and the States are routinely targeted by Customs.

Some, as we have seen, try to solve the problem by placing a number of couriers on any one flight – hoping that if one gets stopped, the others will slip through. Perkins, though, thought of a better idea. If the drugs were not entering the UK directly from Kingston, or Miami or New York, then the chances of evading Customs attention would be considerably enhanced. And if the couriers, themselves, did not, in any way, fit the typical Customs profiles, then the risk would be reduced even more.

So, here's how the plan worked. Two female couriers would catch a flight from Kingston to London, carrying either cocaine or cannabis in their hand luggage. At some point during the flight, they would conceal the drugs in a body belt worn under their brightly-coloured dress. When the flight landed at Gatwick, they would go to the transit lounge to await an onward connection to Brussels. At roughly the same time, across the other side of London, two white women would be arriving at Heathrow Airport, also bound for Brussels.

Well-groomed, smartly dressed in suits, carrying briefcases and bleeps, they were self-evidently business executives, probably engaged on EC-related matters – or at the very least, high-powered assistants bidden for the day to take notes or interpret. Except that the women were prostitutes and the paper in their briefcases came in bundles of coloured, oblong notes in high denominations. Each courier would be carrying between £2,000 and £3,000 in cash.

Brussels Airport has a highly unusual configuration in which the streams of inward and outward-going passengers are able to mingle before any Customs point is reached. The Perkins plan took full advantage of this. Though the women were strangers to each other, the Jamaicans would be unmistakable in their garish red, white and blue outfits. The white women would make contact and all four would head for the nearest toilet. There, a simple switch would take place: cash for drugs.

The whites would stay around only long enough to catch the next flight to Heathrow. Not fitting the Customs priority profiles, they had few qualms as they approached the arrival hall – even though they would each be carrying a kilo or more of cocaine or cannabis in their body belts. Once they were past the last hurdle, they would take a taxi to Tottenham and deliver their precious haul to Mr Perkins.

Meanwhile, in Brussels, two exuberantly-dressed black women would book in at an expensive hotel, usually the Metropole or the Chambord, and live it up for a few days, before catching a Jamaica-bound flight. Being black, there was a far greater chance of being stopped either in Brussels by the police or by Customs at the airport. But since they were carrying no drugs – only money – there was no evidence to suggest that they were couriers.

As drugs scams go, it was a very successful one. The indictment against Perkins mentioned at least twenty-eight 'large-scale' importations of cannabis via this method. However, it is highly unlikely that the sale of cannabis alone – even large amounts of it – would have generated enough profit to have made such an elaborate and expensive operation viable. And Customs officers believe that perhaps as much as forty kilos of cocaine were also brought in by courier.

Eight couriers were in the team, working in pairs. And to avoid arousing suspicion, the partners would swap around regularly. But habit breeds complacency – even where there is a strong element of danger. And it was a silly mistake by Monica

Brissett, born of over-confidence, which led to the arrests on 12 and 13 September. She simply forgot to put on the body belt during the Kingston-Gatwick flight, and though she could have rectified the omission before landing, she could not be bothered, reckoning that there would be plenty of time on the Gatwick-Brussels leg. She never got the opportunity.

The intelligence which Customs had garnered about Perkins left them in no doubt that he was an important drug trafficker whom they should arrest. But that is still a long way short of having a watertight case to put before a jury. So, a surveillance operation was started to amass evidence which would stick in court. The task was handed to Customs 'R' team and, in keeping with convention, the operation was also given a name beginning with R. Since the man they were targeting was called 'Bird', Operation Rook seemed appropriate. Lesley Allen was the case officer, with a team of twelve working under her.

'The surveillance wasn't easy because it quickly became clear that there were other key members of the organisation, apart from Perkins. We were particularly interested in his common-law wife, Brenda Cambridge, because she bought the airline tickets for the Jamaican girls.

'We tailed her going to travel agents in Hornsey, Tottenham and Wood Green to buy the tickets and later matched the telephone numbers she had given to two of the flats which were used as safe houses.'

Another Jamaican called Audrey Brown, who may have been a girlfriend of Perkins, was also deeply involved in the operation. She lived at Stellar House in Tottenham in a seventeenth-floor flat, from where the drugs were sold. So it was necessary to keep a close watch on her home. Customs also had strong suspicions that Perkins had yet another girlfriend, who may have had a role in the organisation, but they were unable to track her down. There was a high level of interest, too, in Brenda Cambridge's mother, Esmine, who turns out to have been one of the unlikeliest money launderers imaginable.

'Esmine was a short, dumpy Jamaican of sixty, who worked as a hospital cleaner, earning forty pounds a week. And we watched her going into Barclays Bank in Crouch End with carrier bags literally stuffed with money. Forty or fifty thousand pounds at a time! When she was arrested, she admitted paying in one hundred and fifty thousand pounds in cash – it was probably even more than that.'

Parnell Perkins would drive Esmine to the bank himself in one of two cars. Fortunately for the watchers, they were so distinctive – a brand new, crimson Mercedes and a black souped-up Escort XR3i – that the surveillance task was made relatively easy. But there was one aspect of the operation which was fraught with dangers. The address of Parnell Perkins and Brenda Cambridge was 43 Debden House, Gloucester Road, N17. To the uninitiated, that means very little, except perhaps Tottenham. Anyone who knows the area will recognise it immediately as Broadwater Farm.

There is little need here to recount the recent history of Broadwater Farm. Suffice it to say that the riot of 1985, which encompassed the murder of PC Keith Blakelock, and the many, many words written and spoken about the estate since then have made it, justifiably or not, a metaphor for violence on a par with the Falls Road or the West Bank. And since Operation Rook was taking place barely a year after those events and actually while the trial of those charged with the murder was being held at the Old Bailey, it was patently obvious that an ultra-sensitive approach needed to be taken.

Lesley Allen: 'In view of the location, we were liaising very closely with Tottenham police. And if we were ever tempted to forget that we were dealing with Broadwater Farm, there would be a powerful reminder every time we went to the local nick because about the most visible thing there was a huge map of the Farm on the briefing room wall.

'I used to drive discreetly around the estate keeping a watch out for Perkins, and it really was the most eerie place I had ever been to. In the middle of the day, you could see drug deals going down on a number of the blocks. But at that time, nobody was about to risk another riot by going in guns blazing.'

The difficulty of getting close to Perkins was compounded by his reputation as a man who wouldn't hesitate to use violence to protect his interests. As Hugh Donagher put it: 'Anyone who could leave a brand new Mercedes parked on Broadwater Farm without the hub caps being nicked and the stereo ripped out, has to have some clout.' Inevitably, he was high on the police visiting list after the murder of PC Blakelock.

The Rook team were planning to arrest Perkins and his cohorts during the first week of March 1987. They had set that deadline because intelligence from an informant suggested that around 7 or 8 March, Perkins and Brenda Cambridge intended to quit London with the fruits of their enterprise and 'retire' to Jamaica. (In fact, Brenda had already bought the tickets for the journey.)

Inquiries in Jamaica revealed that some of the excess cash had been sunk into property in a fashionable up-country area, outside Kingston. A substantial house in Mickleton Meadow bought for 250,000 Jamaican dollars. Another in St Catherine, bought for 239,000. Both were purchased by Perkins's father, who also attempted to deposit £79,000 in cash in a Jamaican bank. With such a cash flow, it was clear that Parnell Perkins was bringing in large amounts of drugs on a regular basis. So, ideally, the Customs team wanted to make the arrests immediately after an importation. In that way, they would maximise the chances of gathering enough evidence to justify a serious charge.

However, since Perkins wasn't so obliging as to publish a timetable of his intended activities, there was no guarantee that an importation would take place before the deadline for his departure. Reluctantly, the plan was amended and it was decided to try to arrest him in possession of drugs and dealing. Although it appeared to be a second-best option, the Customs squad was buoyed by the thought that, if all went well, this would be the first case in the country to test the provisions of the fledgling Drug Trafficking Offences Act, which became law on 1 January 1987. Assuming Perkins had the kind of resources they suspected, they could look forward to a substantial court order for seizure of assets.

The date fixed for the arrests was 5 March. On the previous Friday, 27 February, Lesley Allen was on her way to Tottenham to make arrangements for the raids with the local police, when, within a few seconds, all of their plans had to be re-thought.

'I got an urgent message at about 1.30 p.m. that our informant had made contact, saying that Perkins would be in possession of cocaine and cannabis later that day. And that we would find drugs at both Debden House (his address) and Stellar House (where Audrey Brown lived – though it turned out that she had taken off back to Jamaica before the net closed in).

'This information put us in a complete panic. We suddenly had to do about ten things at once to get the operation up and running. Given Perkins's track record, we had to organise armed police back-up, especially since we might have to pick him up in the street.

'We had to get a writ of assistance (roughly, the Customs equivalent of a search warrant), which allows you to enter a premises to look for prohibited goods. But above all, we had to organise manpower.'

This was probably the most urgent priority, since the plan called for raids on at least five separate addresses. An emergency call went through to Northcliffe House, the then Customs headquarters in New Fetter Lane, off Fleet Street and the word went out that every available pair of hands was needed. Within minutes, cars were roaring in the direction of Tottenham. By early afternoon, there were nearly sixty police and Customs officers in the area.

Lesley Allen went to Stellar House in High Road, Tottenham because that's where Perkins was: 'Earlier that morning, we had spotted him driving Brenda's XR3 and when we drove past Stellar House, it was parked there. That, at least, was a break for us.

'But observation on the flat at Stellar House wasn't easy. It was on the seventeenth floor and Perkins paid young Jamaican kids to act as lookouts. So, it was considered unsafe to get too close. On the other hand, we had to guard against the possibility that drugs packages might be thrown out of the window, when we went in.

'So, two of us kept a discreet watch. My colleague was an Asian Customs officer, so we looked like a mixed-race couple hanging around. Far less suspicious than two male officers together.'

Up above, the raid team were getting in place. Three members of the Met's PT17 unit led the way, motioning curious residents back into their flats with a peremptory wave of their sub-machine guns, as they clattered up the stairway. Within minutes, Stellar House was sealed off and the order was given to storm number 73.

Perkins was inside with a man called Wayne Barham, a.k.a. 'Fowl', a Jamaican brought over to act as muscle. But as the door burst from its hinges and the raiding party poured through, both men could see that resistance was pointless. And once they had been handcuffed, the reason for Barham's presence

210

became apparent. Perkins was expecting visitors.

Lesley Allen: 'A little while after we had secured the flat and started searching it, there was a ring at the door. The caller was obviously looking to buy drugs but when he saw that the flat was occupied by the fuzz, he came up with a story about an arrangement to collect a suit which was being altered.

'Naturally, we "invited" him in for questioning. But within a few minutes, there was another ring and then another, and before long, the place was beginning to fill up with people. It was like a railway station. And most of the visitors claimed that they had come to buy clothes, or have clothes altered.'

In court, it was part of Perkins's defence that he was a bona fide tailor. But apart from his apprenticeship as a cutter, there was no evidence whatsoever to support his claim. Certainly, the jury did not believe it.

The search of the flat at Stellar House was a terrible anti-climax for the Customs team. Instead of the cocaine they had hoped to find, there was only a kilo of herbal cannabis in the kitchen. Next to it, there were scales and spoons, indicating that dealing was taking place. Nothing more.

'We were chokcd. All that effort – and only some weed to show for it. We reckoned that either the information had been wrong, and he didn't have cocaine in the flat that day. Or, he had had time to flush it down the loo before they broke in.' (They later learned that the day before, there had been at least two kilos of cocaine at Stellar House – showing that in the Customs business, timing is everything.)

But things unexpectedly began to look up when they searched Perkins himself. He was carrying a key ring. Two of the keys fitted the locks on the front door. One was clearly an ignition key for the XR3. But there was another, long key unaccounted for. Then they discovered that all of the flats had lockers belonging to them on the first floor of the building.

'There is always a sense of anticipation on a raid. Partly because the adrenalin is running high. And partly because you are never quite sure what you are going to get – if anything! In this case, we had no idea what might be inside the locker. We certainly didn't know we had hit the jackpot.'

The locker contained two handguns – a Walther PPK 9mm pistol and a JP Sauer automatic pistol, 7.65mm. In a box, there were ten rounds of ammunition for the Walther and seventeen for the JP Sauer. And most intriguingly of all, there was a home-made silencer.

'That silencer had a powerful effect on the court case. It clearly underscored the view that Perkins was a dangerous man and that, in order to protect his operation, he had no compunction about using extreme measures.'

There was no proof that he had ever used the silencer – but such a piece of evidence was a godsend to a prosecution which, otherwise, might have struggled to make its case. Aside from the weaponry, the first-floor locker also hid a small amount of cannabis and a set of scales, which, on subsequent analysis, revealed traces of cocaine. And the cache had one more secret. A sheaf of documents which indicated that Perkins had been illegally obtaining British passports for some of his Jamaican and American associates.

In an ideal world, the raids on Stellar House and Debden House should have taken place at exactly the same time. In a drugs case, any lost moments can be vital for evidence-gathering. But, as we have seen, executing a co-ordinated 'knock' on Broadwater Farm is fraught with problems.

'There was no way we could have gone in with the sirens screaming. It had to be more low key so we decided to park our cars off the estate altogether and walk in. It meant that about five minutes must have elapsed after the Stellar House arrests before we hit 43 Debden House.'

It was probably a critical five minutes. 'Brenda Cambridge was at Debden House and I reckon one of Perkins's watchers had telephoned to tell her what was happening. Unfortunately for us, there was a pathway behind the flats which connected all the back gardens and we believe that Brenda quickly bundled up a load of incriminating material, including drugs, and sent it along this escape route to a friendly neighbour, who either hid it or disposed of it.'

If the scene at Stellar House had been slightly surreal, with hordes of drug buyers queuing to get in, there were more than a few incongruous aspects of the raid on Debden House.

'Brenda had three young children, the cutest kids you could imagine. And while we were conducting this serious inquiry which ended with her going to jail, one of the little girls, about three, was running around with a policeman's helmet on, picking up all sorts of papers, which could have been vital evidence in the case. She was having a whale of a time. It was crazy really.'

The presence of three young children persuaded the Customs team that there were probably no guns hidden in the flat. And they were right. And with no drugs either, it looked at first like another bitter disappointment. But again there were compensations. Brenda insisted that there was no money there, but a search revealed £1,751 in cash in her bedroom, which she said she was keeping for a friend. Elsewhere in the flat there were cash note wrappers from Barclays Bank to the value of £172,000 and several items of expensive jewellery.

And there was an even more interesting find – one which proved to be an important link in the chain connecting Parnell Perkins to a charge of importation. Hidden amongst a stack of video cassettes propped against the VCR was a photo showing him in Jamaica with some of the girls who had been arrested at Gatwick the previous September. Even if the girls had been hard to recognise, their distinctive dresses were unmistakable. The case was looking stronger by the minute. Under questioning, Perkins admitted that he was a drug dealer. But he denied ever importing drugs and claimed no knowledge of the firearms found in the locker at Stellar House.

Brenda Cambridge painted herself as an unemployed mother of three children under the age of four (two of them by Perkins). She said she had two bank accounts and two building society accounts – all with minimal balances. The largest sum of money she had ever handled, so she said, was £4,000 – and that on only one occasion. Her mother, Esmine, was interviewed and said that she was unaware of large deposits in her bank account. She was released on bail.

It was then that the old Customs adage 'follow the money' proved its worth. When the investigators began making inquiries about the bank and building society accounts, they quickly peeled back the layers of deception. They found that Brenda Cambridge held four accounts with Barclays Bank and that Esmine had two joint accounts with the Abbey National Building Society – one held with Brenda, the other with another daughter, Jennifer. Production orders were served, and the financial institutions yielded their secrets.

It emerged that Brenda and Esmine between them had paid in more than a quarter of a million pounds to the accounts, almost exclusively in cash. Both women regularly made cash withdrawals of around £20,000 to keep the wheels of the operation well greased.

The next step was to obtain a High Court restraint order which effectively sequestered the accounts and the red Mercedes car, which Perkins had only recently bought for £20,000, cash down. And Esmine Cambridge was re-arrested and charged with money laundering.

This flurry of activity looked pretty impressive. It certainly

The graves of Jim Brown a.k.a. Lester Lloyd Coke, the founder of the Shower Posse, and his son Jah T. Jim Brown died wanted for murder by the Americans yet he was a community hero in Tivoli Gardens. Jah T was gunned down after a feud with another Posse leader which began at a beach party.

Some of the victims of the outbreak of violence in Kingston which followed Jah T's murder.

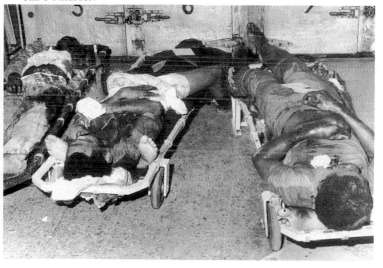

(Right) Detective Sergeant John Brennan, who immured himself in the Yardie world to such an extent that he acquired the street name 'Blondie', with the Jamaican policeman Keith 'Trinity' Gardner who had half his teeth blown away by Rankin Dread. Gardner chased his assailant for half a mile before he escaped.

(Below) Rankin Dread, the 'top rankin' Yardie, is described as one of the most chilling gangsters. Shown here recording a reggae record called 'Fatty Boom Boom' which crept into the charts in the early eighties.

Eldon Patrick Brown, the brother of 'Fat Pam', was tried at the Old Bailey for abducting, wounding, indecently assaulting and causing grievous bodily harm to Nellie Allen. He was given ten years.

(Right) Pam Pinnock or 'Fat Pam' shown loading a gun. Now in prison, she assaulted Nellie Allen in order to take revenge on Nellie's nephew.

(Below) Nellie Allen in her Bronx apartment with the author. She survived a jump from a fourth floor window in a London block of flats after being kidnapped and tortured.

Benji Stanley, aged 14, who was shot dead in Moss Side in January 1993 in a case of mistaken identity.

Bola Adewole, one of two Nigerian drug couriers tortured by Jamaican Yardies in London in 1991. Her injuries were caused by a hot iron pressed to her skin. She was also doused with boiling water. (*Metropolitan Police*)

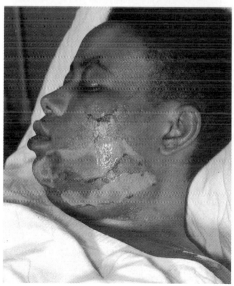

Three of the Jamaican drug couriers employed by Parnell Perkins to bring cannabis and cocaine into the UK. On the left is Sandra Davis and in the middle, Lorna Brown.

Sandra Davis pictured in the Hotel Chambord in Brussels, counting some of the cash she collected in exchange for drugs. Customs officers found this and the photo above at the home of Edris Peters, girlfriend of Parnell Perkins. It is thought that it was held as a form of receipt for the money.

South London gangster, Eddie Richardson (in suit), and Donald Tredwen, photographed by a Customs undercover surveillance team outside Richardson's scrap yard. The car registration number has been obscured by Customs. (*HM Customs*)

Richardson and Tredwen brought South American cocaine from Ecuador into Southampton hidden in a consignment of balsa wood. (*HM Customs*)

(Right) A heavily fortified crack den raided by police in Hackney, East London, in September 1991. The Metropolitan Police have developed special equipment such as hydraulic rams (which other forces, including the Americans, have adopted) to smash their way into such premises. (*Metropolitan Police*)

(Below) The author with Peruvian soldiers. They are on their way to blow up a jungle airstrip used for cocaine trafficking.

helped to build up a circumstantial picture of large-scale drugs importation. The fact remained, though, that Perkins had been caught in possession of a relatively small amount of cannabis. Unless the importation charge could be nailed to him, with no room for escape, he could still hope to get away with a light sentence.

The breakthrough came in the unlikely surroundings of Holloway jail. The four couriers arrested in September had maintained their refusal to co-operate even after Perkins was arrested. And Customs knew they had very little leverage over them. The girls had already been convicted – and, given the appalling deprivation of their backgrounds, most of them considered themselves better off in jail than in Jamaica. For Lorna Brown, it was a chance to begin rebuilding a life scarred by tragedy. She was only twenty-three but had lost six children in a house fire. Her one surviving child had been born when she was only eleven.

Sandra Davis admitted that being in jail was the only time in her life – apart from her few months as a courier – that she had had three meals a day. But it was the brightest and most streetwise of the prisoners, Beverley Jackson, who played the Judas role. She was boiling with resentment at the way they had been abandoned by their patron, Perkins, and was ripe for revenge. So much so that she persuaded the others to make full statements about the operation and to agree to testify in court. *Lesley Allen*: 'We had a good skeleton of a case before the couriers decided to talk. But from then on, we were able to put flesh on the bones. The girls gave us the names of the hotels in Brussels and the dates they were there and we flew over to get evidence at that end.

'We got the immigration cards at the airport confirming arrivals and departures. We interviewed hotel staff who had no trouble recalling the girls because they really lived it up

215

while they were there, drinking at the bar into the early hours, and holding parties.

'And we saw the hotel's telephone records which showed that as soon as the girls arrived, they would put through a call either to Debden House or Stellar House.'

It now became clear that Perkins and Brenda Cambridge – not wishing to trust the Jamaican postal service – used to fly over to Brussels themselves to hand over air tickets for the next importation run. It was probably also a useful way of making sure that there were no problems which might interrupt the smooth flow of the operation.

A Customs team also went over to Jamaica to gather information about Perkins's assets which could be added to the confiscation order for which the prosecution would apply at the trial. There they discovered that the supplier of the drugs was a man named Blacka Douch, who lived in Orange Town. And the go-between was Audrey Brown, late of Stellar House but now back on home soil.

Lesley Allen: 'One of the reasons I remember this case with such satisfaction was the way in which the bits and pieces of evidence gradually fitted together. It was like parts of a mosaic which we had to build up over a period of time. We earned our crust on this one.'

But there was still one piece of the mosaic which had not been found. And it nagged. 'Even before the arrests, we had been told that Perkins had another girlfriend, and we suspected that she played a part in the operation. This was confirmed by the material which we seized after we did the raids. But we had no names and we could not track down this girl.'

And then luck intervened. On 1 April 1987, out of the blue, Customs got a call from the police at Winchmore Hill in North London. Given the sometimes frigid relationship between the two agencies, an April Fool's joke might have been suspected.

But it was a genuine gold nugget of information which helped finally dot the i's and cross the t's of Operation Rook.

The police had been investigating a cheque fraud conspiracy and during the investigation, officers had examined a safe deposit box held at Selfridges in the West End. In the box was £11,000 in cash; jewellery worth £26,000; cash bands to the value of £52,000; an insurance document relating to a Mercedes car; and a Nationwide building society passbook in the joint names of Parnell Perkins and Audrey Brown. Neither of those names meant anything to the detectives but when they ran a check with the National Drugs Intelligence Unit, they learned that Customs had more than a strong interest in both of them.

The safe deposit box had been rented in the joint names of two women, Edris Peters and her sister, Althea Fuller, who both lived in North London. On 7 April, armed with search warrants, Customs officers went to Fuller's home in Edmonton. They found several bundles of cash, totalling £13,100.

Edris Peters lived nearby in Tottenham. In her home, the searchers found ignition keys, a purchase invoice and an insurance cover note for a red Mercedes registered in the name of Parnell George Perkins. And they came across a bundle of letters written to her by Perkins from his remand cell. At last, the mystery of the missing girlfriend had been solved.

Edris Peters also had a copy of a High Court restraint order which she later admitted was the one served on Perkins. This was a strong indication that she knew that her boyfriend was engaged in drug trafficking – and since knowledge has to be proved to obtain an order for confiscation of assets, the investigation team regarded it as another bonus. The evidential mosaic was neatly completed by the discovery in a drawer of photographs of the unmistakable Jamaican couriers, taken in Brussels. Peters and Fuller were charged under the Drug Trafficking Offences Act. Even Brenda Cambridge admitted grudgingly that the Customs squad had mopped up just about everything worth finding – except for one plane ticket.

The trial of Parnell Perkins and five others opened at Southwark Crown Court on 9 November 1987. By that stage, the Customs financial investigation had recovered £140,000. It was alleged that Perkins had made a minimum of £450,000 from the trafficking operation. At the time, it was the largest Jamaican drugs conspiracy prosecuted in Britain.

Despite the high stakes, though, the trial had some of those same elements of farce which enlivened parts of Operation Rook. In everything he did, whether criminal or legal, Perkins was a perfectionist and before the trial even began, he sacked three different counsel for failing to meet his expectations. When the jury were sworn in, they were startled to find that the defendant was representing himself.

Lesley Allen remembers his performance vividly: 'It was quite hilarious. Perkins used to mug up on Archbold (the rulebook of courtroom procedure and precedent) each night, but though he would begin his questioning quite fluently, he would soon become impossible to follow.

'At the same time, he was scrupulous about referring to himself in the third person. So, when he cross-examined the Customs arresting officer, Bob Gray, he would say: "Mr Gray, when Mr Perkins was apprehended, did Mr Perkins say anything?" At times, it was hard to keep a straight face.'

There was a mountain of evidence – much of it involving financial transactions – and the trial dragged on deep into January. The jury was sent out on 21 January 1988 and returned the following day with guilty verdicts on all the defendants. The two principals, Perkins and Brenda Cambridge, got long sentences. Perkins was given ten years for drug trafficking and two years for possession of a firearm. Cambridge – with three young children – was sent down for seven years on the trafficking charge and seven years, to run concurrently, for money laundering. She had the distinction of being the first person to be convicted of laundering under the Drug Trafficking Offences Act. Her mother, Esmine, was given two years – fifteen months of it suspended – and the imported muscle, Wayne Barham, got two years.

Lesley Allen was surprised at the severity of the sentences: 'Considering that we hadn't actually found any cocaine, only cannabis – and not very much of that – we couldn't believe the result we got. But the judge clearly took the view that we had proved a long-term conspiracy. And if there had been any inclination to show leniency, the discovery of the silencer for the pistol knocked that on the head.'

Brenda Cambridge was doubly devastated at the end of the trial. As well as a far longer sentence than she had ever expected, she went to jail with the realisation that her co-conspirator, and father of two of her children, had intended to double-cross her at the very last. He was, indeed, planning to return to Jamaica to live off the proceeds of the operation. But it was Edris Peters he intended to take, not her.

Parnell Perkins also had a surprise in store for the penal authorities – though he had to wait four years to spring it. The terms of his sentence included a provision for another three years to be added to the twelve if he failed to pay the asset confiscation order of £450,000. By early 1992, his journey through the penal system had taken him to Blantyre House prison in Kent. Having served a third of his term, he was allowed out on day release to see the Receiver about the confiscation order. On two occasions, he duly returned to the nick, after pledging to pay what he owed.

In reality, he was doing nothing more than buying a breathing space. On 6 March 1992, he was allowed out a third time from Blantyre House – and was never seen again. Inquiries made in the summer of 1993 strongly suggested that he was living in Jamaica – after all.

Chapter Sixteen

The Masters of the Black Book

When the former Labour Postmaster-General, John Stonehouse, faked his own suicide in 1975 as the first stage in creating a new and secret life for himself in Australia, he took a leaf out of the *Day of the Jackal*. He found a churchyard which contained the grave of a small child who had died of an illness. Posing as a researcher, he obtained a copy of the child's birth certificate at the Central Registry of Births, Marriages and Deaths and, after paying the requisite fee, received by post a passport in the name of someone who had never been abroad and never would. The method has been copied, of course, many times since, provoking periodic pleas for such a glaring loophole to be plugged. But the truth is that a bit of legislative putty in this gap would merely expose the many other points in the system which can, and are, breached with absurd ease.

Junior Adams, a Jamaican, arrived at Gatwick on a flight from Kingston on 26 May 1990, carrying a British visitor's passport which limited him to Code 3 entry. This means that the stay must not exceed six months, the holder is not allowed to work, and has to prove – usually by producing a return ticket at the point of entry – that he or she has no intention of remaining in the UK.

In the event, immigration officials were not satisfied that

Adams was a bona fide visitor and refused him permission to enter. There were no available return flights to Jamaica, so he was allowed to stay temporarily at an address which he had given in East London, on condition that he reported to a police station. To no-one's great surprise, Junior Adams disappeared.

Nine months later, on St Valentine's Day, 14 February 1991, police in south London carried out a raid on a crack house in Streatham. They picked up a clutch of Jamaicans and black British, amongst them, a man who identified himself as Brian Tomlinson. At least, that was the name on the passport he surrendered. But for someone born in Leeds – according to the passport – his English was heavily spiced with patois and his knowledge of West Yorkshire geography non-existent. He kept up the pretence that he was Brian Tomlinson for a couple of hours in a police interview room. Eventually, his resistance evaporated and he conceded that he was Junior Adams from Kingston, Jamaica, and that he was an overstayer.

The police in South London have dealt with so many Jamaican 'illegals' who use their time in the UK to profit from the crack trade that a case like this aroused no more than a momentary flicker of interest. But the information exchange which links the country's forces quickly carried the news to Bristol that someone holding a false passport in the name of Brian Tomlinson had been arrested in London. The Bristol police were intrigued because they were investigating a Jamaican who they suspected of supplying false passports to his compatriots. And amongst the items found on his desk was a card filing system, which contained an entry for Brian Tomlinson. The entry had been scratched out and replaced by the name, Junior Adams.

The man under investigation was Noel Ellis, the co-ordinator of Avon County Council's Race Equality Forum. At the end of the inquiry, he was sentenced to 200 hours' community service for passport deceptions under Section 36 of the 1925 Criminal Justice Act. He had shown that it was quite possible to eliminate one of the stages in the *Jackal* method and still dupe the authorities.

In the Junior Adams case, Ellis went to St Catherine's House, the Central Registry of Births, Marriages and Deaths (formerly to be found at Somerset House), looking for a male born around the year 1960. It did not matter to him whether the subject was alive or dead. He had plenty of names to choose from, of course, and within minutes, he had plumped for a Brian Tomlinson, date of birth, 26.4.61. Tomlinson fitted the bill because he was born in Leeds. Ellis was intending to apply for a passport through the Newport office of the Passport Agency and reckoned that, even if Tomlinson had a passport, he would have made his application through a different office.

It was a calculated gamble which paid off. Newport covered the whole of Wales and the South-West and received between 10,000 and 15,000 passport applications each week, and in 1990, the system was not computerised. In November of that year, it issued a passport in the name of Brian Tomlinson, who stated on the form that he had never before applied for a British passport. Officials were unaware of the fact that on 9 December 1981, a passport had already been issued to a Brian Tomlinson, born on exactly the same day. The issuing office was Leeds, West Yorkshire.

The police tracked down the genuine Tomlinson through the Department of Social Services computer, using his National Insurance number. The white sheet-metal worker was mightily surprised to be told that a black Jamaican sitting in a prison cell in London had documentary 'proof' that he was Tomlinson!

The same police investigation uncovered a passport application in the name of Mark Allen, whose address was given as Rhodesia Road, London SW3. Mark Allen, too, was surprised to be told that he had applied for a passport, since he was then beginning a ten-year-stretch in Wandsworth jail for manslaughter. His trial had been given widespread publicity. He had set fire to his next-door neighbour's house and two elderly women had died. The crime had taken place in Rhodesia Road, SW3.

Fraud is often referred to as a victimless crime – a clever manipulation of paper to make a painless profit. But passport fraud is different. It is a form of theft. To succeed, the perpetrator has to steal someone else's identity. Often, the victim does not even know they have been robbed until, like Brian Tomlinson, they are contacted by the police. Or, like Susan Cole, they suddenly find themselves part of a Customs investigation.

Susan Cole lost her identity to a Nigerian woman who used it for three years as a cover for smuggling cocaine into Britain. The woman, Susan Loveth Udoji, somehow obtained a copy of Susan Cole's birth certificate and used it to obtain a passport, National Insurance number and medical documents – all in the name of Susan Cole. The impersonation was exposed when Customs officers contacted the real Susan Cole's parents to tell them that their daughter had been arrested for smuggling drugs.

'When they told us that our daughter was Nigerian, we thought it was some kind of a joke,' said Susan's father, Richard. Given that his daughter is a platinum blonde from Kent, Susan Loveth Udoji, a black mother of two from Lagos, made an unlikely doppelganger. The stolen identity not only enabled her to remain in Britain but also to claim income support, housing benefit, and legal aid to defend the drug trafficking charge.

For the real Susan Cole, the experience was 'like something out of a film script – unbelievable. Before the court case, I had never met her or heard of her. But she swindled every document I need to prove who I am.

'She has totally taken over my life. If I was to apply for a passport or for credit from banks, I would be refused because, as far as they are concerned, I have already opened accounts in London. I have no idea why she picked on me but she is a liar and a cheat and she has caused me hell.'

The demand for false passports has long been fuelled by international crime and terrorism, and illegal immigration. But the massive growth in drug dealing in recent years has provided an unprecedented impetus. And the passports come from a variety of sources.

Crack is so powerfully addictive that in some cases, addicts have been willing to trade their passports for a few rocks. But, for the Yardies, a more reliable source has been corrupt officials who can deliver the goods in large batches. And over the years, bent civil servants have often been responsible for providing the vital 'black book' – as the old-style British passport is known in Jamaica – for a cash return. A passport is obtained fraudulently in England and sent to Jamaica either by post or with someone who is visiting. For a few pounds, a Jamaican immigration officer will mark it with an entry stamp and the holder is then ready to use it to come to Britain as a bona fide British citizen, apparently returning from a trip to see relatives. If arrested the records will show him to be British even though he may have been in the country for no more than a few weeks.

In Kingston, a man who was wanted for killing a Jamaican policeman and who had been on the run for years, told me that he entered the UK on a false American passport, then returned it so that someone else could use it and was provided with Jamaican documents in its place. This enabled him to slip back into Kingston when he judged the time right. He paid £6,000 for this customised travel service.

In fact, the ghettoes of Kingston are full of people who have entered Britain illegally on false documents. One man who had earned £1,000 a day in Bristol as a crack dealer explained to me how easy it was to change the photograph in a passport. 'You hold a heat gun over the plastic until the adhesive melts, take the old photo out and stick yours in. Once it's stamped, no-one would be able to tell it had been tampered with. Getting false documents to go to Britain or the US is as easy as buying a ticket for a bus.'

But every now and then, a highly organised passport ring is broken, throwing light on the links between passport fraud and organised crime. One of the clearest examples emerged from an investigation by Scotland Yard which showed that hundreds of British documents were being obtained illegally both by the notorious Chinese criminal group, the Triads, and by Jamaican Yardies.

In October 1992, a man called David Lynch was jailed at Southwark Crown Court for three years for conspiracy to obtain passports by deception. Lynch was an examiner at the Passport Office in Petty France and provided at least 100 full British passports for people wanting to leave Hong Kong before the Chinese take-over in 1997. The police believe he was intimidated by the Triads into working for them.

But Lynch was not the only corrupt official at Petty France at that time. The Home Office suspected an executive officer called Vanessa Alexander of working in tandem with him to provide passports, many of which were being channelled to Yardie drug dealers. However, when detectives began investigating, they found to their surprise that Lynch and Alexander had no knowledge of each other. They were both mining their own separate seam, and to great effect.

Alexander was providing passports at the request of someone called Aisha Morgan, who appeared as a co-defendant in the same case. And Morgan was the link with the Yardies. Her

226

Jamaican boyfriend, S.B., charged between £3,000 and £5,000 a time for obtaining passports for drug dealers and couriers, and he submitted about ten applications a week. The profits from this scam went into buying crack cocaine and marijuana, and paying off the mortgages on two houses.

Aisha Morgan would take the completed applications to Petty France in the evenings, when Alexander was on duty and fewer staff were around. Even so, her regular appearances aroused suspicions. On one occasion, another officer on shift recalled Morgan presenting a sheaf of applications which she claimed were for a group of black handicapped children being taken on a foreign trip the following day. When the applications were examined, though, it emerged that they were for black adults in their late teens or early twenties. Suspiciously, all of the birth certificates accompanying the forms were new.

On other occasions, too, Morgan tried a similar ploy. Once, she submitted an application on behalf of a man of forty-six, who she said was resident at a home for the handicapped. In fact, the name belonged to a boy who had died the day after he was born in 1955. The birth certificate had been provided by S.B.

When Vanessa Alexander was arrested in October 1991, the police investigation revealed three Spanish bank accounts in her name, two for sterling deposits and one for pesetas. They held £47,000.

The third defendant in the Alexander prosecution case was a man called Anthony Francis who had worked at the Passport Office for ten and a half years before becoming a telephone systems manager at the Home Office in 1989. Colleagues reported seeing him with large amounts of cash, and he was also spotted regularly in the Passport Office, where he had no reason to be.

He explained that the cash was holiday money because he

distrusted banks. And he said his visits to Petty France were to submit passport applications for friends. It was an account which few found credible and the police began an intensive surveillance operation on him, beginning with a search of his office which turned up fifteen passport applications in his desk, some new passports, and a number of building society pass books and cheque books, including one for an account in Spain.

Francis had taken precautions against a detailed log of his phone calls being recorded by 'barring' them from the Home Office system. But with the help of a technical manager, the detectives were able to surmount this obstacle. When they discovered a high number of calls to Vanessa Alexander, at both her home and office numbers, they knew that Francis had a key role in the passport fraud.

Two plain clothes officers were assigned to tail Francis. They found that he paid regular visits to the Passport Office in Petty France, going in by the public entrance like any visitor. But, after waiting a while in a queue, he would suddenly dart through a security door marked 'Staff Only', re-emerging a short while later holding a brown manila envelope in one hand. His route would then take him across Victoria Street and into Horseferry Road, where he had a regular rendezvous at 'Just Joe's' cafe with RC, the client for whom he was obtaining the passports.

Later in the day, the surveillance team followed Francis to a pub called 'Adam and Eve' close to the Passport Office, where his assignation was with Vanessa Alexander. He sat opposite her with a black attaché case placed on the table between them. No words were exchanged as he took out an A4-sized envelope, which she put in her bag without glancing at it. Francis then handed over what looked to the watchers like bank notes. Alexander tucked them into her purse. It was a routine which went like clockwork until the participants were arrested.

Francis was picked up at 7 a.m. on Tuesday, 29 October

1991 and his house in Maidstone searched thoroughly. In the front room downstairs, a briefcase contained several British passport applications, several passports, both black and the newer burgundy version, birth certificates, photographs and two bundles of notes to the value of £1,550.

In another room, there were sixty-seven British visitor's passports – part of a batch of a hundred issued to the 'late duty' officer at Petty France from July 1989 onwards. One was in the name of Dr Ian Malcolm Aird, of 4 Clarendon Road, Cliftonville, Kent. According to the date, it was submitted on 27 February 1991. It was signed in the name of Aird, and counter-signed. But there were a number of discrepancies concerning this application. When contacted, Aird revealed that he had submitted his application form, together with his birth certificate, not in 1991 but in July 1989. When he went to Petty France to collect the passport, he was told that the birth certificate could not be found. Indeed, it never turned up.

Aird also confirmed that he was not a doctor and that he had not lived at 4 Clarendon Road, Cliftonville since he was six years old. When shown the signature in Section Ten of the passport found at Francis's home, Aird said that it was a forgery. Close to the application form was a passport in the name of Dr Ian Malcolm Aird, bearing a photo of Anthony Francis. Along with it was the original birth certificate which Aird had not seen since he submitted his application. The passport was issued between 4 March and 13 March 1991. The name of the issuing examiner was Vanessa Alexander. When she was subsequently arrested, a search of her home turned up documents relating to a Spanish bank account in the name of Ian Malcolm Aird. The missing birth certificate had been put to profitable use.

Another application form found at Francis's house was in the name of David Kwang, of 175 Fountain Road, London SW17 – date of birth, 11.10.51. The counter-signatory, Susan

White, was shown as a nurse working at St George's Hospital, Tooting. In this case, the address at Fountain Road does not exist and no-one called Susan White ever worked at St George's Hospital. And for good measure, there is no trace of a David Kwang born in England in 1951.

Anthony Francis was clearly kept very busy submitting false passport applications, and some of those who stood to gain from his efforts had serious form as criminals. One of the scraps of paper recovered from his office desk carried the name, Robert Calvin Mason, date of birth, 13.10.60. Mason was jailed for six years in 1989 for drug trafficking. Why he should need a passport in Maidstone prison when his earliest possible release date was more than two years away, is a mystery – unless he was planning an escape.

The other name which the Francis investigation unearthed had an even more impressive pedigree – and, coincidentally, knew quite a bit about jail escapes. Amongst the items found at Francis's home was a 1989 diary. One page contained a passport number, 5323377, and a four-figure number.

The latter code was a telephone extension at the archive section of the Passport Office at Hayes in Middlesex. When the police checked it out, they learned that the holder of passport number, 5323377, was the celebrated Great Train robber, Charlie Wilson, who spent only a year inside before breaking out of Winson Green prison in Birmingham and fleeing to the south of France.

By the time he was in need of the services of Anthony Francis, Wilson was firmly ensconced on Spain's 'Costa Del Crime'. But before Francis had even come to trial, the requirement for another false passport became academic. Charlie Wilson was shot to death by a lone gunman on a motor bike. It was widely assumed that a drugs dispute was the motive.

Chapter Seventeen

Manchester Dis-United

'I now look on the period when criminals used a knife or a good kicking to enforce their will as the good old days. Here in Manchester, the tool of the trade is the gun. That's how you resolve disputes – with firepower. The gun is an everyday currency. You can hire it and return it. Just like a library book. Except there are more suppliers of guns in these parts than libraries.' – a senior detective with the Greater Manchester police.

Reporters like an identifiable front line. In London, the junkies of violence used to make the short hop to Railton Road in Brixton or Hackney's Sandringham Road and imagine they were in Belfast or Beirut. Flak-jacketed prose conveyed an ever-present thrill of danger. But crack has changed the topography of crime in the capital. The front line is wherever the drug is being sold. And wherever that is, there is a risk of death or injury. When a police officer gets murdered in gentrified Clapham, it's clear the old certainties have vanished. So, in the early nineties, it was almost reassuring to know that only an inter-city ride away, there was a battlezone which still conformed to all the war clichés: Moss Side.

'This is the notorious Quinney Crescent,' said the taxi driver as we drove at speed through the Alexandra Park estate in Moss Side. 'You wouldn't catch me coming down here at night. They throw lumps of concrete at you. You've got the Pepperhill mob over there and the Gooch Close gang on the other side. These kids wear body armour you know. And this is the front line between them.'

In the gloom of a January afternoon, England's 'Bronx' didn't look much like its New York namesake. The Moss Side Leisure and Shopping Precinct was boarded up and almost deserted. The occasional mountain bike flashed down one of the pathways which cuts into the estate – a complex of two-storey homes, with their satellite dishes jutting out like surveillance cameras. Another soulless monument to post-war planning, sure – hardly the nightmare ghetto summoned up by the tabloid feature writers.

But though crime comparisons between Britain and the United States are sometimes fanciful and often unhelpful, Moss Side stands on its own and is, perhaps, the only place in the UK where drug dealing has followed an American model.

In Los Angeles, for example, a network of tough street gangs, such as the Crips and the Bloods, existed well before crack arrived on the scene. They had an organised structure which drew its strength from tightly-knit ethnic loyalties. Nothing moved in the territory they controlled without the gangs getting their cut and putting their stamp on it. When drug dealing became the fastest route to a quick buck, the gangs had the organisation in place to exploit the new opportunities.

Manchester has had a reputation for drugs since the 1960s if not earlier but most of the dealers traded in weed – cannabis. The market was carried out openly in two principal locations in Moss Side – outside a parade of shops on Moss Lane East known as The Front or at the Moss Side shopping precinct. There were, of course, consumers of hard drugs too. And if you were a heroin addict, you would almost certainly buy it from someone who was also a user but paid for his habit by supplying a bit on the side. This was the pattern in satellite towns like Rochdale and Oldham, as well.

But, from about 1987, the police noticed a change in the drugs profile. In amongst the weed sellers of Moss Side, there began to appear a new type of dealer who was using the market place to hawk heroin and who was a businessman not a user. As word spread, the Moss Side shopping precinct became a magnet for heroin addicts firstly from all over the city, then Greater Manchester, then eventually the entire region, stretching from the Midlands up to Cumbria. By the time the police mounted a major undercover operation, codenamed Corkscrew, in 1989, Moss Side had become a heroin bazaar where the traders were raking in a fortune.

As detectives watched and filmed through video cameras, they were astonished at the amount of drugs activity they were recording. And it is true that the surveillance pictures make riveting viewing. On the face of it, the scene is one of everyday normality. Mothers push buggies, small boys kick a football about, women are steering shopping trolleys in and out of the supermarket. But at the same time, youths in baseball caps and expensive trainers are flashing hither and thither carrying small plastic bags to the buyers who are parked in the car park. They conduct their negotiations through half-opened driver-side windows.

At the edges of the frame, two black men, one with a mountain bike, stand at either side of the car park as lookouts. They show their usefulness when a police van cruises into shot. By the time it has drawn to a halt, the dealers have miraculously melted into the surrounding estate, leaving no trace of their existence. Thirty minutes later, life has returned to 'normal' and the dealing is running at full pitch again. It looks like the trading floor of the old Stock Exchange transplanted to the open air.

'These guys,' says a drugs squad detective, 'are good at their job. They put a hell of a lot of effort into what they do. They're prepared to negotiate hard, to barter. If this was legit, they would make excellent businessmen.'

The hustlers sell their wares from sealed plastic bags containing 15lb of heroin. In 1989–90, the street price was around £80 per gramme and the average sale was a 'quarter' – in theory, a quarter of a gramme though, in practice, more like a hundred milligrammes. If the dealer controlling a particular pitch bought his kilo for £25,000 wholesale, he would expect to realise three times that when it had been parcelled out and sold.

Operation Corkscrew was primarily aimed at heroin trafficking. Cocaine was not perceived as a significant problem in Moss Side at that time – though one of those arrested had some rocks of crack on him. In all, there were some twelve successful prosecutions. Two of the principal heroin dealers in Manchester were amongst those convicted. The sentences were stiff – between seven and ten years. But like many drugs initiatives, this merely displaced the problem to another area – and gave the police a much bigger headache. The jailing of two of the big boys left a void which inevitably meant that the market place would expand. After Corkscrew, it was obvious that open-air trading in such a public place as the shopping precinct – while having commercial advantages – was a security nightmare. And the fact that the police had video surveillance demonstrated the need for counter measures. The answer was to switch the operation to Gooch Close, where one of the notorious Moss Side gangs exerted an iron grip on the territory.

Detective Sergeant Tony Brett, of the drugs squad, later earned a commendation from the Chief Constable for his undercover work in the area. 'The move to Gooch Close was significant because it involved the established gangs for the first time. These people had grown up with each other. They were fiercely loyal and they had no qualms about using violence to protect their plot.

'Within the Alexandra Park estate, they had created a "sterile" area which was cut off from the main arterial road and was unsafe for outsiders to enter. They had broken into most of the derelict properties and taken them over for their own use as stash houses, where they hid weapons and drugs.'

Within this zone, there were points at which drugs could be sold with relative impunity. Organised groups of spotters – schoolkids on their bikes – were paid to watch out for the cops. If the 'meatwagons' dared to penetrate the inner sanctum, it was usually fruitless because the dealers had long since dispersed into the estate through the ratrun of walkways.

And the involvement of the gangs gave the crime problem a heightened sense of urgency. As in the United States, the vast profits at stake imbued the turf battles of old with a new viciousness. As the Gooch Close gang and Pepperhill Mob battled for supremacy, the casualties mounted. In a single April weekend, a man was shot dead and two others badly injured. At the junction of Sedgeborough Road and Flaxpool Close, seventeen-year-old Carl Stapleton was hacked to death with a machete. Darren Samuels died at the age of nineteen – shot by three men in a pie shop. Eggy Williams was gunned down outside the Pepperhill pub.

In an insidious copy of American gang violence, Anthony Richards was shot in the eye in a drive-by attack. He was just twelve. Another drive-by shooting left the owner of a Fiat Strada fighting for his life when he was picked off at traffic lights on the corner of Moss Lane West and Alexandra Road. On one night, a man was beaten and stabbed in Pepperhill Walk, and an hour later, a Gooch Close member was shot in the face outside a house in Upper Lloyd Street. Many of these were tit-for-tat assaults. And in one remarkable sequence of attack and counter-attack, over a five-week period, leading up to a murder in April 1991, the crazy spiral of violence went out of control.

It began with an attack by a Gooch Close member on a youth from the rival Dodington gang which shares the embattled Alexandra Park estate. This was followed by the theft of a car outside a shebeen, and a fight in which one Dodington member lost part of an ear.

Then a car was set on fire in retaliation, and a firearm discharged in Gooch Close. Thirty minutes later, the Pepperhill pub was attacked and a gang member slashed with a machete. Two weeks later, a Gooch Close man was stabbed in the city centre by a Dodington rival.

Now the stakes were being raised and on the day after, the Pepperhill pub was attacked again, with a 9mm handgun being fired at a group fleeing for safety. Within twenty-four hours, a Dodington man was shot by a gunman on a motor cycle. Later the same day, a Gooch Close member was macheted.

That evening, two Gooch Close youths were caught by a Dodington group, who poured fluid on them and set them alight. During the next week, the Dodingtons increased the pressure by shooting at two rivals driving a Golf GTi and by machete and gun attacks. The orgy culminated with the fatal shooting of a Gooch Close member.

And against this background of frenetic violence, the drug dealing was becoming much more organised.

Tony Brett: 'There was clearly a structure at work here. Certain gang members would dominate the dealing at certain times of the day and at certain places. And when they handed over to someone else, it was almost like a change of shift.

'Much more care was being taken now about hiding the

drugs in nearby properties so that unless the dealers were arrested at the point of sale, they would be clean. And, for the first time, we were seeing Vodaphones used as a regular tool of the trade.'

The police information came from an elaborate operation, codenamed China. Undercover officers, men and women, posed as buyers. Video cameras, installed in a concealed observation post, recorded the transactions. Over a five-week period during 1991, thirty-seven drug deals were filmed. Thirty-six were for heroin and only one was for crack. A video extract shows a dealer waiting to be approached by punters with his stash of drugs hidden under a stone in a nearby garden. At the top left of the frame, another dealer is touting for business. A short while later, these same youths and others stone a police van which has strayed too close to their turf.

In August 1991, forty unmarked vehicles poured into Alexandra Park at dawn, carrying 200 Greater Manchester police officers. They arrested twenty-three people and seized drugs and a quantity of weapons, including a loaded handgun and a crossbow. The majority of those arrested were aged between eighteen and twenty-four. Some were earning as much as £3,000 a week. Nine months later, they paid for their enterprise with jail terms ranging from three to seven and a half years. But once again, it was little more than a temporary setback to a drug culture so stubbornly rooted and so adaptable. And the police found themselves planning yet another operation.

Detective Sergeant Tony Brett: 'As we interviewed drug addicts and inspected their diaries, we were coming across more and more Vodaphone numbers and streetnames. And it became clear that the Voda was now the greatest single asset to the dealers. In fact, it was dictating the pattern of dealing.'

The dealers who had survived Operations Corkscrew and

China had learned an invaluable lesson. That there were more secure ways of taking money off the punters than standing out in the open where they could be photographed by long lenses. The mobile phone gave them the flexibility to decide where and when the transaction should take place. And put them, rather than the buyer, in the driving seat.

Tony Brett: 'If a buyer had the Vodaphone number of a dealer, he would go to a public phone box and put a call through. If the dealer didn't know the caller and suspected a set-up, he could refuse to sell or he could make an arrangement which would give him the advantage.

'He might name a time to meet and then get there ten minutes earlier to check out if it was a trap. Or he might have something more elaborate in mind. In one transaction which we monitored, a punter put through a call to a guy who was in a bookmaker's placing a bet. He was the dealer but he was too clever to do the trade face to face. He then initiated a series of calls which led to a young man handing over some crack in a disused railway tunnel, six miles from where the original call had been placed.

'The intermediate calls were part of a system of cut-outs which protected the identity of the boss. And the guy who was actually carrying the rocks had no idea who he was working for. This is a practice which the crack gangs in the States have developed and it has proved very effective.'

The Vodaphone also offered the dealer greater protection against the police. 'If a dealer says to a punter: "I'll meet you at the usual place", how the hell do you know where that is? You can end up chasing shadows.

'Of course, this whole system depends on making sure that there are plenty of public phone boxes which are working. And, do you know, when we ran a check, we found that there wasn't a single call box in Moss Side which was out of order. That's the power of drug dealing!'

Based on their experience with Operation China, the drugs squad assumed that heroin was still the overwhelming preference of the drug-taking fraternity. But the evidence gathered in 1992–93 during the new operation, codenamed Miracle, surprised them.

'One of the undercover buyers said that more and more people were asking for "one plus one". And that meant a quarter gramme of heroin in a plastic bag plus a rock of crack. As a drug squad officer with years of experience, I couldn't get my head round this, because I hadn't come across poly-drug dealing – at least not on any kind of regular basis.

'During Operation Miracle, we monitored thirteen Vodaphone drug networks. Only three dealt solely in heroin. One in crack. And nine offered both heroin and crack.'

For the first time, Manchester, like many cities in the United States before it, was coming to terms with the fact that two of the most powerfully destructive drugs – far from being mutually exclusive – were highly compatible. The rush of exhilaration induced by crack is followed by a headlong swoop into paranoia as the central nervous system begs to be stimulated again. But an injection or snort of heroin – the strongest-known analgesic – allows the crack user to float down gently from his high on a cloud of euphoria. For the dealers, it was a match made in heaven.

The progress of crack in taking its place as the street drug of choice can be measured in the statistics of Operations China and Miracle. In 1991, out of thirty-seven purchases made by police undercover buyers, only one was for crack. By 1993, the police bought drugs on eighty-five occasions over several weeks. Fifty-two of the transactions were for heroin. Thirty-three for crack. But the impact of crack could be assessed by more than mere figures. The dealers, again following the pattern established in the United States, were changing their methods.

Heroin is, to an extent, self-limiting. An addict, who is mainlining or chasing the dragon, will fall into a stupor for several hours, perhaps even most of the day, under the influence of the drug. Even if he is a heavy user, it may be physically impossible to spend more than a few hundred pounds a week on his habit. A crack addict is afflicted with a similarly voracious craving which has to be appeased, certainly. But a rock offers such an abbreviated high that it has to be followed by another and another. A crack user can easily burn £1,000 in one all-night binge.

To respond to the demand, the dealers realised they had to offer rather more than a nine-to-five service. Being unavailable in the middle of the night could cost money, so some found an ingenious way of guaranteeing round-the-clock attention. They called it 'taxing'. They allowed users to get into debt, sometimes running up bills of several hundred pounds which they had no hope of meeting. The dealers then offered the hapless addicts a proposition. 'I'll wipe the slate clean, if you run my Vodaphone for me during the night from your home, take all the incoming calls and arrange delivery.'

It was an offer which those few who refused bitterly regretted. They were badly beaten up. It was, in a way, almost as if the Vodaphone had an independent existence of its own, separate from the person who had originally bought or leased it. And, indeed, after the police made arrests during Operation Miracle, they discovered that some of the Vodas had been passed along the line and were still being used. 'It is the system which is important,' says Tony Brett, 'not the individual dealer.'

Manchester has had a steep learning curve during the drugs operations of the early nineties and the force feels there are more lessons to be absorbed – from the United States. In 1992, two GMP officers flew to Florida to see how the law enforcement agencies there were responding to the crack explosion. One was Inspector Danny McGrory

McGrory: 'After Operation Miracle, we wanted to try to look ahead – to anticipate what the next development might be. We had already been confronted with dealers wearing hoods and scarves across their faces to hide their identity, and we wondered whether they might decide to forsake the street altogether and set up fortress – like drug dens such as they have in the US.

'But the question is: how far do we mirror the United States? In Miami, for example, the street gangs don't get involved in organised drug dealing so we have a different kind of a problem here in Manchester.'

There is also a big difference in the heroin markets in the two countries. The purity level in the States has traditionally been lower and when high-grade cocaine began pouring into the country from South America and became available cheaply, many heroin users eagerly transferred their allegiance to coke, or became poly users. Since many of these addicts were black, it enabled crack, when it arrived, to penetrate swiftly into the ghettoes. In the UK, heroin has traditionally been a white drug and the market has been far more stable. It explains why the arrival of crack in a city like Manchester has been slower than some predicted. But crack has arrived now and because it has taken root in a city which already has an organised gang structure, many believe that the potential for violence is greater than anywhere else in Britain.

In April 1993, the head of the Greater Manchester Police drug squad, Detective Superintendent David Brennan, drove up the M6 to Preston to make a presentation to the thirteenth national drugs conference organised by the Association of Chief Police Officers. This was the same forum addressed so memorably four years earlier by Robert Stutman, of the DEA, and Brennan's speech demonstrated the transformation in police awareness which the arrival in the UK of Jamaican crack criminals had wrought in the intervening period.

Here was a drugs chief willing to compare his own city with the US and to admit that a criminal phenomenon which many said would never establish itself in Britain was a fact of life. Brennan talked about the Crips and the Bloods of Los Angeles and how the Jamaican posses had spread crack dealing and gun trafficking to wide swathes of the United States. He then gave a remarkably candid analysis of the gang structure in Manchester.

'In Moss Side, there are two rival gangs – in Gooch Close and Dodington Close (the latter having replaced and absorbed the remnants of the Pepperhill mob who were decimated by police drugs arrests). Each has around thirty identified members. The average age of the Dodington is eighteen. The Gooch average is about twenty.

'But about two miles from Moss Side, just north of the city centre is the Cheetham Hill gang, whose numbers are considerably larger. About sixty members have been identified, with an average age of twenty-six.

'Apart from the fact that Moss Side's gangs are weakened by division, Cheetham Hill have always been stronger and more sophisticated, and they are organised almost on military lines. They are beginning to wear standard "uniforms", of boiler suits and balaclavas and they are almost militarily precise when it comes to achieving their objectives. The Moss Side gangs distinguish themselves by different coloured bandannas.

'And there are the Salford Lads who tend to be involved more in the supply of the "clean" drugs such as Ecstasy and amphetamines to the rave scene in the city centre (as against the dirty ones like cocaine, crack and heroin). There is also a tendency to become increasingly involved in the supply of weapons. The Salford Lads number around forty and their average age is twenty-six.'

Pointing out that it is often said that Britain is five-to-seven years behind the Americans, Brennan explained why there was cause for fearing that, without a resolute response, Manchester was about to stumble down the US path.

'We know that a significant number of Jamaican criminals regularly visit Britain under assumed names and false passports. And some are living here illegally – not just in London but in northern cities too.

'We have good reason to believe that there are strong ties between some of our gang members in Moss Side and Jamaican criminals, both in Kingston and London . . . cash proceeds from drugs dealing in Manchester regularly find their way to families still living in Jamaica. That leads me conveniently on to the subject of guns and their availability and use in Moss Side.'

Chapter Eighteen

No Mercy

Denise Stanley was in the bathroom washing her hair when she heard the shots. This being Moss Side, she wasted little time on it. 'Some bugger's got it tonight, I thought – and then slammed the window shut. Shots were a regular occurrence at that time.' That time was January, 1993 – Saturday, 2 January, to be bleakly precise. It was around 8.30 p.m. and Denise had not long left her friend's house at the top of Cadogan Street to return to her own home, number sixteen. Cadogan Street is one of those time-capsule Manchester streets fresh from a Lowry painting. Neat, red-brick terraces, two up, two down, stretching straight as an arrow. As usual, Denise's front door was ajar.

She came downstairs, turbaned in a towel, and plugged in the hair dryer at the wallpoint in the front room. She didn't have long. Benji was going baby-sitting for a neighbour at 9 p.m. and he had asked for a flask and some sandwiches. The dryer's motor had barely gathered momentum when the voice of her good friend and neighbour, Maxine, filtered through the hallway. 'Denise, I thought you should know, there's been some trouble at the shop and Benji's name has been called.'

The finger which pressed the off switch on the dryer was

already trembling. 'I felt ice cold in my stomach. I wrapped the towel tight round my head and ran up the road as fast as I could in my slippers.'

Great Western Street is no more than 200 yards away. Turn left and you are walking in the shadow cast by the Kippax Street stand of Manchester City Football Club. To the right is the dual carriageway which divides the area from Alexandra Park. As Denise neared the corner of Cadogan and Great Western, she could see bars of blue light spinning across the fascia of Alvino's Pattie and Dumplin Shop. Yards of yellow tape created a cordon sanitaire within which men in white boiler suits were scooping shards of glass into black plastic bin liners. There were police cars parked at crazy angles across the road. No ambulance.

Denise was halted as she ducked under the tape. A policeman said: 'I'm sorry, you can't go in there.' Denise said: 'I am looking for my son, Benji.' The policeman replied: 'He's run off. Look, there's his bike.' A mountain bike was propped against a low brick wall.

Denise was beginning to unravel: 'I was shouting, screaming, over and over: "Where's Benji?" and the policeman said very politely: "Would you come and sit in the back of this patrol car, please?" Then a policewoman came out of the shop and said: "I have got to take you to Greenheys Lane police station." She wouldn't tell me anything else, not a thing.'

The station sergeant told her that two people had been shot at the shop. One was seriously injured, one was not. No names. No elaboration. Like an incantation, she murmured over and over: 'Please let it not be Benji.' They put her in an interview room and brought her a coffee but she couldn't drink it. The tension knot in her stomach was the size of a grapefruit. At twenty minutes to ten, a WPC opened the door and stood half in and half out of the room. 'She just looked at me without saying anything and I said: "It's Benji, isn't it?" Then, I just kicked off.'

She freely admits to going berserk. The WPC tried to comfort her but Denise thrust away her proffered arm with such violence that the woman toppled against a metal filing cabinet. 'I threw the coffee at her, I was bawling and shouting. I was completely out of control. And then, as it all got released, I suddenly felt weak and I fainted.'

The first familiar faces she saw were Junior, her former husband, and her other adopted son, Nicky, at Manchester Royal Infirmary. They were just emerging from the room where Benji's corpse still lay. Before the door closed, Denise caught a glimpse of a naked foot.

'They've killed our boy,' she said. 'I know,' said Junior blankly. 'I've known since nine twenty. Nicky and I had to identify the body.'

The outburst of grief at the police station and the two rides in the back of the panda car had drained her of emotion. She was now calm to the point of numbness. 'I went up to the surgeon and asked him if he was with Benji when he died. He didn't reply directly – but he said that Benji hadn't felt anything. I said: "Did he ask for me?" There was no response.'

The surgeon had been rather more forthcoming with Junior. 'He said he was sorry to have to tell me that Benji had just died on the operating table. He said the boy was pretty messed up when they opened him up, a piece of his heart and a lung had been shot away. He didn't stand a chance.' The time of death was put at two minutes past nine.

Benji Stanley was two months past his fourteenth birthday. All the photographs of him show a face of transparent openness. Handsome half-caste features exuding impudent fun. A face that girls couldn't resist. At Ellen Wilkinson High in Belle

246

Vue, many of the girls fancied him, and the boys admired him. At six foot one and a half, he had a natural advantage at basketball but it was supplemented by a graceful athleticism. He was also a good swimmer and a star at dance and drama. Academically, he struggled at English but was more than competent in science and maths.

His height made him noticeable whatever he was doing. And, despite his popularity, he carried with him the double stigmata of being a half-caste and a Moss Side boy. Sometimes, says Denise, it made people pick on him.

'He loved to wear a baseball cap to school. He thought it made him look cool. But his class teacher said: "You can get that off. You're not from Gooch Close." As far as some people are concerned, if you come from Moss Side, you're a gangster.'

Benji also liked to wear a signet ring set with a black onyx stone. The same teacher told him she was going to call the fire brigade to cut it off. It was too flash. But Junior says that was Benji all over – style personified.

'He lived in the bathroom that kid. First in, best dressed. I always thought he'd become a dancer – or a male model. He had done a fashion show once at carnival and got lots of cheers. He could carry that sort of public display off easily. He loved himself and he loved life.'

On the day that he died, Benji had been into town looking for a jacket to buy with his Christmas money. But he found nothing which would quite suit his fastidious taste. It didn't matter. There was always next weekend.

Before he went off for that night's baby-sitting, he went round to see his friend, Neville 'Tito' Gunning, and play some records. Tito persuaded him to come to Alvino's while he bought some take-away. Benji was reluctant because he felt that the owner didn't like half-castes. But he didn't want to let his friend down. The two boys took their bikes. Benji was wearing his favourite bottle-green baseball cap.

There was only one other customer in Alvino's when they got there – another teenager. He was waiting for his dumplings to be fried, and they took their place in the queue behind him. The boys were bantering with each other and never even heard the car pull up suddenly right outside the plate glass frontage.

As the doors opened, a thunderous blast of ragga spilled onto the pavement. But the boys only looked out when a shadow fell across the floor. A stocky black man wearing army-style combat gear, his features masked by a balaclava, faced them. He was cradling a pump-action shotgun. The glass imploded under the weight of the first shot which caught Benji in the leg. He gasped as blood seeped through his baggy denims but the gunman had already pressed forward and aimed again through the doorway.

Without the glass to slow its passage, the bullet tore into Benji's upper thigh and side, hurling him to the floor in its ferocity. It may have been enough to kill the boy but the assassin was taking no chances. Picking his way through the broken glass, he stood over Benji, pointed his lethal weapon down at the chest and fired a third time. At that range, it was nothing less than an execution.

An experienced CID officer, Detective Chief Superintendent Ron Astles, took charge of the murder inquiry. As head of Greater Manchester Police's southern crime area, he had investigated a number of drug-related shootings – they had been running at almost one a day since August – and his first thought was that this was yet another.

'Benji was not known to the police,' he told an interviewer in a news report shown on television the following day, 'but the possibility that the killing stems from recent drugs-related incidents cannot be eliminated.'

Despite the caution with which he had chosen his words,

Denise Stanley was apoplectic when she saw the report. 'Benji never had anything to do with drugs. A kid once asked him if he wanted a "draw" and he got very angry. Even though I smoke a lot, he never even showed any interest in fags. Sometimes, being a protective mum, I would search his room when he was out – but I never once found a thing.

'So, when I saw Astles on the box saying that, I went wild. I rang up the incident room and shouted: "Get me the chief pig!" I gave him a real earful when they put him on. "That's my baby you're talking about." It was such a ding-dong that he put the phone down on me in the end. But he sent round an officer to the house to sort it out. And, I must say, that later, when I met Mr Astles face-to-face, he was very decent to us.'

At his first news conference, Mr Astles said: 'I am aware that some witnesses are reluctant to become involved. Let me assure these people that we are well able to offer them protection. This incident has got to be the catalyst that persuades the public to come forward and give us the information we need.'

He was thinking in particular about a woman who had telephoned the police anonymously little more than an hour after Benji's murder. She began to give them potentially crucial details and then rang off. According to Mr Astles, she had provided sufficient information to suggest that she knew the personalities involved. 'We have been steered in the direction of possible suspects,' was how he put it to the press. 'But I appeal to her to ring again. I will meet her anywhere, any time.'

Despite the frequency with which sudden and violent death has come to Moss Side, the circumstances of Benji Stanley's murder, and the age of the victim, provoked widespread media coverage – and a frenzy of speculation about possible motives. In this atmosphere, people seemed willing to believe almost anything, however banal or fanciful. It was suggested that a dispute over a mountain bike might have prompted the shooting.

Benji had recently lent his new bike, bought as a birthday present, to Tito and it had been stolen. Newspapers reported that when Benji's stepfather, Junior, approached the people responsible, he was told: 'Fuck off, or someone will get shot.'

A tabloid newspaper carried a claim by Tito Gunning's younger brother that Benji's death had been foretold by a fortune teller, who predicted that 'your best friends will soon be going to your funeral'. Benji was said to have laughed it off. Then it was revealed that Junior Stanley had convictions for drug dealing and that the murder may have been connected to his past – a case of the sins of the father being visited on the son. Junior had actually served sixteen months of a two-year sentence for supplying heroin, though he says he was an addict and not a dealer. 'As it happens, the WPC who was looking after Denise on the night of the murder, was the one who had arrested me on the heroin charge. So the police knew all about that side of things from the word go. They had actually warned me that the media would probably resurrect a TV interview I had done a couple of years before about drugs.

'Mind you, I was still gutted when all this came up in the papers. And I reckon that some of the cops thought – and maybe still do – that because of my past, I knew more about the murder than I was letting on.'

The direction which the inquiry took in the days and weeks after the murder is the subject of bitter controversy. The police maintain that, for a Moss Side shooting, they received a higher than usual amount of information from the public, at least seventy calls in the first week – and that they followed up every lead assiduously. But others suggested that the investigation was proceeding on tramlines because detectives were trying to prove that the murder was linked to the internecine gang warfare within Moss Side. The main proponent of this view is a woman called Brenda Brownlow who believes she knows what the motive for the shooting was.

Three days after the murder, Brenda was at home watching the television news when a picture of Benji Stanley was flashed onto the screen. She almost dropped her tea cup in amazement. The likeness to her own son, Winston, was staggering. 'The similarity to one of Winston's school photos was so strong, they could have been brothers.'

Winston Brownlow moves in bad, dangerous circles. He is a member of the Dodington gang and not long after Benji's death, he was arrested and charged with attempted murder. His mother had no illusions about the number of people who might wish to see her son dead. It wasn't the sort of suspicion she could confront him with – and, in any case, she knew that he had gone to ground because the police were looking for him. 'But my mother's instinct told me that I was right. Benji's murder was a case of mistaken identity.'

She rang the police incident room and shared her suspicions. 'To their credit, they came round straight away to interview me. But they didn't believe me. They thought it was a trick or a diversion, to somehow take the pressure off Winston – to make out that he was in fear of his life. They told me it could not have been a case of mistaken identity. They knew that for a fact.' The chief reason why the police were intensely sceptical of the 'wrong victim' theory was the circumstances of the murder. The final, fatal shot was fired into Benji from a range of four or five feet. At that distance, surely the killer must have known whether he had got the right target?

Nevertheless, officers made every effort to track down the fugitive Winston Brownlow. Initially, they had no success but then it transpired that he had been arrested in connection with an attempted murder and was being held on remand in Walton jail, Liverpool. A member of the Benji Stanley inquiry team went to Liverpool to interview Winston and later told a colleague that he needed a stiff whisky when he met him, 'the resemblance to Benji was so great'. But otherwise, the visit proved abortive. Winston, true gang member that he was, refused to grass – even on his sworn enemies. 'If I've got a problem,' he said, 'I'll deal with it myself.'

Brenda Brownlow decided to go and see Denise Stanley. The two women had known each other before Brenda had moved out of Moss Side. She thought Denise deserved to be told why her son had met such a pointless death. For Denise, it was almost a comfort after all the unanswered questions.

'It must have taken a lot of guts to come to see me. Imagine any mother being in that position. And she was scared about Junior's reaction. But after I spoke to Brenda, it began to make some kind of sense at last.

'Winston was into guns and drugs, that whole scene, and even though he was twenty-one, you've got to remember that Benji was very tall for fourteen and with the cap on and the sort of clothes they all dress in round here, he would have looked very similar to Winston.'

The police prefer to begin with facts and then proceed to theories rather than the other way round, and the inquiry concentrated on the painstaking task of gathering evidence. Forensic scientists were very interested in the spent cartridges found on the shop floor. They contained chunks of shrapnel which dispersed on impact to cause terrible injuries. It was a refinement which had been used in the United States but very rarely seen in the UK – only three times before, in fact. It led the ballistics experts to surmise that the gun had probably originated in the US, though it almost certainly underwent several crude alterations before being fired at Benji Stanley. There was a spurt of hope when a similar gun was recovered in a pub in Manchester but it was tested in the lab and the cartridges failed to match the ones found in Alvino's. The murder weapon has never been found.

Considerable effort was spent in trying to track down the car used in the attack, a silver-grey, upmarket Rover. And towards the end of January, it was found abandoned in Leavenshulme, about two miles away from the scene of the killing. To nobody's surprise, it turned out to have been stolen – in Sheffield – and fitted with false number plates. Further inquiries established that the car had been stolen by members of a Moss Side gang but sold on to their rivals from the north of the city, Cheetham Hill. For Denise Stanley, this was a true breakthrough.

'I think at the beginning, the police were convinced the murder had been done by a Moss Side gang and they couldn't be shifted from that. Now, the evidence pointed strongly to Cheetham Hill. It was a move in the right direction.'

Despite nearly 700 door-to-door inquiries, a number of arrests and files full of statements, no-one had been charged. In May, Denise decided to take a break from the strain and anxiety by spending a few days with her sister-in-law in Belgium. The day before she left, she got a phone call.

'It was one of the officers dealing with the case and he said it was a good thing I was going to be abroad for several days because there was about to be a major development and it would be better if I was out of range of the media when it happened. I can't tell you how excited I was. I thought this was it.'

Two days later, in a series of dawn raids, fourteen people were arrested in Cheetham Hill. The media reported that the police were acting in connection with the Benji Stanley inquiry. Denise returned from Belgium expecting to hear that charges had already been laid. She was given the bad news.

'The police were pretty sure they had picked up the right

people. They were gang members, with violent records, who had been feuding with the Dodington on Moss Side. But there was no damn evidence, not even witness evidence from the night of the shooting.'

In theory, there were four eye witnesses to the murder, because there were four people in the shop at the time, apart from Benji. One was Tito Gunning, who was sprayed with shotgun pellets when Benji was shot. He told police that he had been too petrified even to look up while the attack was going on. 'I just closed my eyes,' he said to his mother.

The other teenage customer had dived over the counter to take cover and said that he kept his head down until the gunman had disappeared. Of the two staff serving in the shop, one said he was out the back, making dough. And the other had just gone to fetch some made-up dumplings from him when the shooting broke out. None of those in the shop could supply even the sketchiest description of the murderer.

Denise was furious. 'I saw one of the shop staff and I mashed him up for not telling the police what he knew. I realised what was behind it. People are just too scared to talk.' She had expected this to be the biggest obstacle from the very beginning. Her own, typically, direct answer had been to place a school photograph of Benji in the shattered window of Alvino's, with a note handwritten in biro, saying: 'Please find my son's murderer.' But even this plea failed to penetrate the wall of silence.

Brenda Brownlow is not at all surprised. She remembers only too well what happened when she was a witness to a gang killing in Moss Side in October 1991. The victim, Darren Samuels, had been in her home only moments before his death. He was a friend of her son.

'Darren left the house a few minutes before me. I didn't know he had gone down to the shopping precinct. I was just outside the pie shop when I heard these crashing sounds – like someone was smashing the place up. Then three boys burst out and rushed off on mountain bikes and a youth came running out after them saying: "They've shot Darren. They've shot him." '

Darren died in her arms. He was nineteen and left a baby aged four and a half months. Brenda was brave enough to tell the police what she knew and on the strength of that, two men were charged with murder. But she hadn't actually seen the trigger pulled. A teenage girl, who was in the shop waiting to be served, had. The girl had far less resolve, though, than Brenda, and after receiving threats, went into hiding rather than expose herself to the risks of standing in open court. She later took a drugs overdose. Despite Brenda's evidence, the two defendants were cleared on the direction of the judge.

'I learned my lesson from that. I was supposed to have my identity protected when I gave evidence but the press and radio carried my address. That's why I decided to get out of Moss Side altogether. Whatever the police say about protecting witnesses, it's a joke.'

As the year wore on, with no signs of progress, Junior Stanley decided to make use of his own contacts to do some sleuthing. It was partly prompted by anger at innuendos that he knew more about the murder than he was letting on.

'I come from Alexandra Park and I grew up with the gangs before they became so violent, but the idea that I would protect any of them over Benji's murder is complete crap. So, I tried to discover what people were saying on the street.' He thought it best not to tell the police what he was doing.

It was a hazardous enterprise. Even someone who knows the territory is taking an almighty risk asking sensitive questions around Gooch Close and Dodington Close. Junior approached a couple of girls he used to hang about with and asked them to help set up a meeting with some of the Dodington crew – 'for old times' sake'. It took a little while but eventually, he got his clandestine face-to-face. 'They assured me that no-one from Dodington was involved in Benji's murder. They said folks in Moss Side knew who did it – it was Cheetham Hill people. But nobody would talk to the police.'

Two days before Christmas 1993, almost a year after the murder, an inquest recorded a verdict of unlawful killing on Benji Stanley. The coroner made an emotional plea to those shielding the murderer to come forward. 'There are people who know and it is just horrific that they can stay quiet and allow this to happen to an innocent young man,' he said.

For the police, the murder file remains open. They know that someone can finger the killer if they choose – and though it is an increasingly long shot, they have not abandoned all hope. One of the officers on the case said bitterly: 'I've got six years to my retirement, and I want to put away the bastards who did this before I go.' As to what happened on the night of 2 January, the best assumption from the evidence detectives have pulled together is that Benji was the victim not only of mistaken identity but freak timing. The silver Rover was cruising Moss Side looking for Winston Brownlow, and picking streets at random.

It was Benji's fatal misfortune to emerge from an alleyway on his bike just as the saloon was passing along Great Western Street. Whether the people inside knew Brownlow well or were carrying out the hit on commission is not clear but the decision was taken there and then that they had found the target. As Benji parked his bike and went into Alvino's with Tito, the Rover made a U-turn. The rest is history.

Benji Stanley is buried in Southern cemetery on Princess Road, the road that leads to the airport. He was placed in his coffin wearing a blue baseball cap. There were 860 mourners at the funeral – two-thirds of them were girls who wept throughout the service. A few fainted.

Denise goes to the graveside three times a week to tend the flowers. She smiles ruefully when she recalls that, while her son was alive, her biggest fear was that one day an irate father would knock on her door and say that Benji had got his daughter pregnant. Now, despite the valiant neighbourliness of many Moss Side people, 'good, decent people who don't deserve the labels which get stuck on this area', she just wants to get away, start afresh.

The council offered her a home in Old Trafford and she was all set to accept when the item came on the television news. Eighteen-year-old Andrea Mairs was standing in her bedroom in an Old Trafford council house, when a gun battle erupted in the street outside. A stray bullet from a semi-automatic crashed through the window and struck her in the chest, less than an inch from her heart.

Those who know about these things say that with Moss Side sewn up, a new piece of drugs turf is being colonised. And after Old Trafford, where next?

Chapter Nineteen

The South American Connection

The rock star, Sting, once said that cocaine was 'God's way of telling you, you've got too much money.' For some of Britain's most experienced criminals it was clearly God's way of announcing that there was an easier life than vaulting over bank counters with a sawn-off shotgun, knowing that the Flying Squad might be in wait around the corner.

The coke game has many players in it. The Jamaicans have largely cornered the market in crack but the couriers arriving from Miami, New York or Lagos bring in only a fraction of the cocaine powder which is shipped to Britain every year. In the main, the South American cartels are reluctant to deal with the violent and unpredictable Yardies, so they have looked for more reliable business partners. Enter the old-time blaggers ripe for a new little earner. Men like Eddie Richardson, who was jailed in the 1960s as part of a notorious South London torture gang, with his brother, Charlie, only to re-emerge in the late 1980s as a big-time drugs dealer. And with the transformation of Eddie came the first concrete evidence that the Colombian moguls were ready to place their own representatives in Britain to oversee the cocaine sales drive.

The case which first demonstrated the new alliance at work was called Operation Revolution. On 8 March 1989, at

Southampton docks, Customs officers seized two tonnes of herbal cannabis and 153 kilos of cocaine – at that time, the largest cocaine haul directly targeted on the United Kingdom. Within twenty-four hours, Eddie Richardson, a Colombian called Antonio de Abreu Teixeira, and six other men were in custody, and an elaborate world-wide drugs conspiracy had been scuppered.

The case began in 1987 when Customs got wind that a man with a long track record in smuggling, a South London car dealer, Donald Tredwen, was active again. A surveillance team was put together, including police officers from the South-East Regional Crime Squad, to monitor his movements twenty-four hours a day. And with a character like Tredwen that was not easy.

'He's a kind of Arthur Daley figure,' said one of the Customs officers involved. 'Very cunning, very slippery. Knew all the tricks and took elaborate precautions against being watched. We knew he was a radio freak and that he might be listening to our frequency so when we followed him by car, we had to maintain complete radio silence.

'And following him, in any case, was damn hard. He would shoot off all over the place, double back on his tracks, stop suddenly – anything which would show up a pursuit car. Once, it paid off, because a couple of regional crime squad guys were tailing him down a country lane when he stopped around a corner and just accosted them, accused them of following him. We had to "burn" the car, in other words, take it off the operation. And the two cops had to be replaced as well.'

Despite his precautionary measures, Tredwen did not succeed in pursuing his business unobserved. The number of times his car was spotted in pub car parks around Crawley in Sussex, and one pub in particular, The Parson's Pig, began a chain of inquiries which eventually established that he was meeting contacts who worked at Gatwick Airport.

And in South London, it wasn't long before an interesting face made its appearance – long-time crook, Eddie Richardson, who was sticking to the script written for all Cockney villains by running a scrap metal yard. Surveillance photos showed him and Tredwen holding frequent meetings, sometimes in unusual locations. Once, they were filmed, both crammed into a BT phone box – which might just have been explicable except that it was right outside Tredwen's office.

The Gatwick connection led the Customs team to suspect that an airport rip-off was in the making. One of Tredwen's car park contacts was identified as Robert Ritchie, a baggage supervisor working for a cargo handling company based at the airport. He, too, was placed under surveillance, though, in the short term, it yielded nothing of value. But over a period of many months, it began to become clear that a significant drugs importation was being planned at Gatwick and that the source was Thailand. For a car dealer, Donald Tredwen had expansive horizons and had made eight visits to Bangkok between September 1986 and May 1988. The most significant took place in January 1987 when he was staying at the Nipa Lodge Hotel. A later check of the hotel records showed that Tredwen put a call through to a London number identified as the premises of a firm called KWP Metal. It was the company name of Richardson's scrapyard.

On 7 January, Richardson visited the Thai Bank in London and asked to transfer £11,000 to Tredwen in Bangkok. The bank's rules, however, permitted a maximum of £5,000 only – and on the following day, that amount was wired to Thailand. Tredwen was in Bangkok again in November and December 1987 and made further telephone calls to England. Those calls resulted in thirteen transfers of cash from the Thai Bank in London to its counterpart in Bangkok. And Tredwen was not the only visitor to the Thai capital. In June and again in September 1987, Richardson was there. He, too, called London and not because he was homesick.

By the spring of 1988, Customs were certain that the Thai connection had been established to smuggle a large amount of cannabis into England. An informant in Bangkok had discovered that the plan was to pass off 300 kilos of the drug as a consignment of magazines which would be airfreighted to Gatwick. Six parcels of magazines were to be presented for Customs inspection in Bangkok. After they had been stamped and passed through, the labels would be removed and gummed onto an identical set of parcels, containing the cannabis. In the export warehouse, these parcels could be swapped for the genuine magazines and stored in an area reserved for goods which needed no further checks.

The drugs would be sent on a flight arriving at Gatwick at a time when the rip-off team was on shift and able to remove the haul before it was submitted for Customs inspection. 10 June 1988 was chosen for the delivery date. Customs officers, armed with their inside knowledge, made plans to intercept the shipment as it was unloaded at Gatwick. But chance scuppered the plan. At the last minute, it was discovered that the 10 June flight from Bangkok had less cargo space than expected and the shipment had to be delayed for a week. Five days later, a sniffer dog on a routine sweep of the warehouse became agitated when it nosed the consignment of parcels. They were opened and the cannabis was found.

Thai officials had not been taken into the confidence of their British counterparts – for security reasons – so they knew nothing of the plan to allow the drugs to travel to Gatwick. The cannabis, worth £900,000 at street level in Britain, was seized. And a chance to make arrests disappeared.

In September 1988, the conspirators tried again, with an

261

even bigger cannabis consignment – but this time by sea. Four and a half tons of the drug, with a street value of nearly fourteen million pounds, was loaded at Bangkok aboard a freighter called *The Frankfurt Express* bound for Southampton. The cannabis was hidden in a consignment of plastic flowers. On this occasion, the smugglers were frustrated at the British end. Whilst artificial flowers, made from silk, might be economic to import, plastic ones, worth only a few pence each, almost certainly would not be. And Customs officials at Southampton became even more suspicious when they checked the given weight of the load with its actual weight. Once again, the gang had failed. But though the evidence against them was mounting, it was not yet conclusive enough to justify arrests.

Surveillance was intensified on the key conspirators. And in November 1988, it bore fruit when Eddie Richardson was observed meeting three foreign men at the Craven Gardens Hotel in Bayswater. Four days later, Richardson, accompanied by Tredwen, returned to the hotel, collected the three foreigners and drove them to a house in a new development at Surrey Docks. The house, which belonged to Richardson's daughter, was the venue for further meetings between the group over the following week. During that period, the three foreigners were identified as South Americans. One was Antonio de Abreu Teixeira, a Colombian businessman. The other two, called Alarcon and Garcia, had both Colombian and Venezuelan passports and their nationality was never established beyond all doubt.

On 28 November, Alarcon and Garcia flew back to Venezuela, leaving Teixeira in London. Customs put a tail on him and it quickly produced the goods. 'After Tredwen, who took every precaution possible, Teixeira was a godsend to us,' said one of the surveillance team. 'He clearly didn't know his way around London so we had no problems keeping track of him.

'And on the second day we were assigned to him, he went into a print office in Fleet Street to send a fax. When he had left, we had to decide whether to risk questioning the staff or not. After all, it could have been a bent outfit working with Teixeira. But because he clearly didn't know London and it appeared that he had just come across the fax office by chance, we reckoned it was worth gambling on the staff's co-operation.'

The gamble paid off. The fax had gone to an office in Quito, the capital of Ecuador. It contained details of amounts of money received from Ed (a reference to Richardson), Don (Tredwen) and Edon (both men). There were dates on which the money had been handed over. They tallied with the dates of the meetings at Surrey Docks. And the amount of cash was staggering – nearly half a million pounds. Teixeira's fax also referred to arrangements for a couple to fly to England from Quito via Frankfurt – but with no names or dates. The couple were Alarcon's wife, Maria, and a man called Troya. On 30 November, Teixeira went to the Craven Gardens Hotel to meet them.

Five days later, the pair flew back to Quito. A Customs surveillance team at Gatwick noted that they were carrying no luggage. Checks established that they had both had suitcases when they arrived. Those suitcases contained forty-four kilos of high-grade cocaine – none of which was ever recovered. The cases had been removed from the aircraft's hold by baggage handlers working for Ritchie's rip-off team and spirited away without passing through any Customs checks.

The economics of the deal showed that this unique tie-up between the South American cartels and the London criminal underworld was playing for huge stakes. At roughly £26,000 a kilo, Richardson and Tredwen would have paid out more than a million pounds for the consignment of forty-four kilos. Teixeira and his two associates, who bought the drugs from the 'factory' in Quito, would have made a mark-up of at least 300 per cent. So would Ed and Don when they sold the drugs on. And that profit was intended to finance an operation which would have poured an unprecedented single amount of cocaine into the British market.

Over the next few months, the Customs surveillance teams were kept very busy. Richardson was observed, on several occasions, handing over plastic bags containing wads of notes, to the South Americans. When he was eventually arrested, the police found a bag on the floor of his Volvo, with almost £19,000 in cash in it. Throughout December 1988, Teixeira paid regular visits to banks in London where, on average, he paid in £20,000 in sterling each time and remitted that amount in dollars to accounts in South America. He used a company which he had purchased, Globe Overseas, as the remitter. This frenzy of financial activity peaked on 4 January 1989, when, on a single day, he visited ten foreign banks and the Trustees Savings Bank. Four days later, he was back at the Fleet Street print office to send another fax to Quito. In the weeks which followed, Richardson and Tredwen had a spate of regular meetings and were then seen meeting Teixeira several times. It seemed to the Customs squad that another, even larger, importation of drugs was imminent.

The breakthrough came when Alarcon returned to London in January. Customs tailed him to a West End hotel where he checked in. With the agreement of the management, officers searched his room and discovered a shipping document, a bill of lading for a vessel called the *Silver Happiness*. They photocopied it and replaced it. Inquiries in Ecuador confirmed that the *Silver Happiness* was bound for Europe in February, carrying a consignment of balsa wood. The ship's destination was Le Havre in France but its cargo was to be transferred to a ferry and taken to Portsmouth. A drugs liaison officer in South

America established that the ship would almost certainly be carrying drugs.

The container of wood was duly loaded at Quito on 15 February and the *Silver Happiness* set sail on the 16th. Its progress was carefully monitored until it arrived in Le Havre on 7 March. While it was at sea, the Customs team had to perform a sensitive diplomatic task to make sure that all their patient detective work was not undone at the last moment. The team leader was Hugh Donagher.

'It was a potential problem for us that the vessel was arriving in France because, coming from South America, it would be in the high risk category for drug smuggling and the French authorities could be expected to check it thoroughly. If they discovered the contraband, there would then be the legal and technical problem of having the stuff seized in one country while all the documentary evidence of the conspiracy was in another.

'It could have been a nightmare. So, I went over to see the French Customs to persuade them not to intercept the drugs at Le Havre. Fortunately, we had pretty good relations with them and they were very amenable.' With one hazard overcome, Hugh Donagher travelled back to Le Havre on 7 March to ride shotgun as the container with the balsa wood was transferred to a cross-channel ferry, *The Viking Valiant* bound for Portsmouth.

'I watched that consignment like a hawk, I can tell you, on the way over. There was no way we were going to let anything go wrong at the last moment. But everything went smoothly right into Portsmouth.' At Portsmouth, the container was hoisted aboard a transporter and driven down the coast to Southampton docks. It was the final journey.

If there had been any doubts about the information which had led to the Customs operation, they were dispelled when the container was opened. X-rays showed that what appeared to be piles of solid balsa were actually wooden shells with hollowed-out centres, into which the packages of drugs, wrapped in plastic, had been inserted. It took Customs officers the best part of a day to excavate the booty. When they had finished, there were 154 separate bundles stacked on the floor of the warehouse. They contained two tonnes of cannabis and 153.8 kilos of cocaine, worth some £43 million if it had reached the streets. Some of the cocaine was marked, Calidad, indicating that the source was the rapidly growing Cali cartel from Colombia.

Within twenty-four hours, all the principal conspirators had been arrested. When Teixeira was picked up, his telephone pager was displaying a message from Richardson asking him to call. Twenty thousand pounds in cash was found at Teixeira's house in Blackheath and photocopies of the bill of lading for the *Silver Happiness* in his BMW. Tredwen's only comment to Customs officers when they arrested him was: 'I knew it was you.' Richardson, like the old pro he was, elected to say nothing after he was cautioned. Following the arrests, the Customs authorities in Quito were asked to search the offices which had been the administrative headquarters of the businessmen, Alarcon and Garcia. They found some of the faxes which Teixeira had sent from London and bills of lading referring to balsa wood. They also discovered a key to a cellar in which was stored six parcels of cocaine and a heat-sealing machine for securing plastic bags. This was where the drugs had been prepared for transportation. For Customs, both ends of the trafficking operation had been neatly tied up.

The twenty-five-year jail sentence imposed on Eddie Richardson in the summer of 1990 will rule him out of drug smuggling for the foreseeable future though there are plenty of other criminal 'faces' like him who are now plugged into the cocaine network.

'Richardson brought a kind of stature to the operation,' says Hugh Donagher. 'He was introduced to the South Americans as one of the main criminal capos in England, a guy who could provide muscle to protect the London end of things and, at the same time, help to raise money on the strength of his name and reputation. Richardson was never especially bright – but people like him can be very useful.'

Richardson and Tredwen, using their long-established criminal contacts, clearly had a number of ready buyers for the drugs they were bringing in. But one of the most surprising aspects of the cocaine story is that no-one – neither police nor Customs, nor any other so called 'expert' – has more than the haziest idea what happens to large imports between arriving at port or airport and sale on the street. A senior Customs official argues that this is the most pressing problem facing law enforcement in the drugs field. 'I was taking a seminar recently and amongst the group, I had six police superintendents with responsibilities for drugs squads. I asked them about the profile of the middle level dealers, the people who would buy cocaine from someone like Richardson in amounts of ten or perhaps twenty kilos.

'I said: "Who are they? And who do they sell the gear on to further down the chain?" And the supers admitted frankly that they did not have a clue. It's frightening.'

In case this should be interpreted as yet another cheap shot in the war between Customs and police, it is patently obvious that the police side, too, where it is prepared to be candid, concedes ignorance. A Chief Inspector from the Metropolitan police, who has done extensive research, says that after large shipments of cocaine come into the country, they usually disappear rapidly into a 'black hole'.

'It would be very risky to keep large consignments of coke hanging around intact – and, in any case, the market is so buoyant that there is no need to. So, the gear is parcelled out into ten or twenty kilo amounts very quickly, and it may go to fifteen different distributors.

'They, in turn, will divide it up and so it goes on, along the line, until it appears either as powder on a silver spoon in some Hampstead pad or as rocks in Brixton. I reckon there may be as many as ten different levels between importation and street use. But if you start your search for intelligence from the top and work down, you very soon run into a brick wall. That's why it makes sense to concentrate on the street dealers and work upwards.'

The problem is that the majority of the street dealers are black and any policy which concentrates on arrests at that level lends itself to censure on grounds of racism. Viv Reid, director of the Newham Drug Advice Project, says crack brings out the worst instincts in policing.

'To most police officers, a rock of crack might as well be a lump of coal. It symbolises blackness. It creates an instant image of a young black male out on the street selling. But it takes no account of the involvement of the organised white criminal class in drug dealing.

'They are the ones who control the cocaine trade. And that is the wider picture which the police tend to ignore. The Yardies run an undisciplined cottage industry. They are not the big boys.'

That view is widely shared and it is perfectly true that most of the big-time drug smugglers in Britain's jails are white. But some black commentators seem to take a perverse satisfaction in suggesting that black traffickers do not have the level of organisation or sophistication to join the premier league. The fact is that some do. Wendell Daniels, for example, is a

Jamaican who began his drugs career by importing substantial quantities of cannabis and then turned to the more lucrative crack, in the 1980s. In December 1991, after the police had enlisted the aid of an informant, Daniels was arrested in London.

As detectives moved in on him on the street, he threw away two plastic bags which contained seven grammes of cocaine. His 'safe' house was also raided and the police recovered 480 grammes of crack, in levels of purity ranging from 90 per cent to 97 per cent; 717 grammes of cocaine powder; and 675 grammes of cannabis. A Metropolitan police forensic scientist was asked to estimate how many rocks of crack Daniels could have made from the cocaine seized. The expert suggested that 4,000 was a realistic figure. At a rough street price of £25 per rock, the haul would have netted £100,000.

When his assets were traced, it was discovered that Daniels had bought eleven properties – private houses and businesses – nearly all of them for cash. The total cost of the properties, some of them in Jamaica, was £653,000. He had also made cash deposits of more than £130,000. But Daniels was astute enough not to draw attention to himself by flaunting his wealth. He drove around in a 1979 van worth about £200 – even though he owned a number of brand-new vehicles, including a BMW and a £17,000 Volvo which had been paid for in cash by a third party on his behalf. Daniels adopted the same arms-length approach with his property acquisitions in order to dupe the Inland Revenue. In the end, though, the details of his money-laundering and trafficking were painstakingly recorded and he was brought to trial and convicted. His assets, in Britain and Jamaica, were calculated as £1,012,152. These had been accrued during a six-year period in which he had declared his total income as £58,980.

Another Jamaican, Derek Gregory, also took the well-worn,

gold-plated route from cannabis to cocaine trafficking into Britain. In 1989, he was deported from the UK after serving two years for smuggling cannabis. In 1994, he was jailed at Bristol Crown Court for 25 years for organising the largest-ever importation.of drugs in passenger luggage. The jury heard that more than 100lb of Bolivian cocaine had been hidden inside packages designed to look like gifts, which were carried in four suitcases passing through Stansted Airport in Essex. The cocaine had a street value of £29 million.

A Customs investigation showed that Gregory had made a single deposit of £250,000 in 1991 to open seven bank accounts in Zurich which operated in four different currencies. He was known to have visited drug locations in South America, Africa, India and Europe, as he developed an elaborate smuggling network. Although there was a dispute about how much money Gregory had made from his activities, the judge passed an asset confiscation order of £313,830.

The examples of Wendell Daniels, Derek Gregory, and the mastermind of Operation Rook, Parnell Perkins, prove that many assertions about the differences between white crooks and black crooks are simplistic and misleading. It is frequently said that the Caribbean drug hustlers are vulnerable because their operation is out in the open on the street. Whereas the white villain like Eddie Richardson will follow the time-honoured precept of 'fronting' his ill-gotten gains in the form of a business – even if it is merely an unprepossessing scrapyard.

The fact is though that some of the 'ragamuffin' Jamaican dealers on the street corners of Brixton, or St Pauls or Moss Side, may be worth a substantial amount of money and are using their down-at-heel appearance as a ploy to avoid attracting attention. In some cases, it has been highly successful.

For all their differences, Eddie Richardson and crack dealers like Sammy Lewis, in Harlesden, were prospecting in the same cocaine goldfield. But by forging direct links with the South American producers, the white blaggers-turned-traffickers were a jump ahead. Some of them had even travelled out to the source countries, Bolivia, Peru and Colombia, in the early 1980s to try to set up deals. But by the end of the decade, as Operation Revolution showed, the trend was being reversed. The Venezuelan passport-holder, Teixeira, was sent to London to make sure that the money from Richardson and Co found its way back to the cartel. Now, many others, Peruvians, Colombians and Venezuelans, are established here performing a similar role.

Operation Revolution, though a success, allowed British Customs an ominous foretaste of the future. Both in Britain and the United States, policy-makers and academics had contended that drug traffickers would deal in one commodity only. It was the basis for arguing that those handling 'soft' drugs should be treated differently from dealers in 'hard' drugs. And it helps explain why the Americans under-estimated the Jamaican posses when they appeared to be engaged in selling marijuana only.

The lesson from Operation Revolution was that the same organisation was prepared to import both cannabis and cocaine and would finance smuggling operations from various source countries so that all of its eggs would not be left in one basket. It was also an unmistakable signal from South America that for the rest of this century and into the next, the cartels intend to remain firmly in control.

Chapter Twenty

Beginning and End

When the most wanted drug trafficker in the world, Pablo Escobar, died in a hail of bullets in December 1993, President Bill Clinton sent a telegram to the Colombian leader, Cesar Gaviria, congratulating him on having brought Escobar 'to justice'. It was a phrase entirely in keeping with the US approach to the cocaine problem ever since Presidents Reagan and Bush declared their 'war on drugs', both at home and abroad.

Fighting a pointless war with martial rhetoric and open-ended subsidies to corrupt regimes is a time-honoured American practice, of course. But in the case of cocaine, it has seemed all along like a spectacular folly. If Republican presidents, in particular, ought to know anything, it is that Wall Street is right when it insists that you can't buck the market. And when you consider the product in question, at source, no amount of moral outrage from Washington or London holds water.

There are many places, literal and metaphorical, from which to observe the 'cocaine trail' but few better vantage points than the road which leaves La Paz, the capital of Bolivia, for the region known as Las Yungas. In a matter of one hundred kilometres, you exchange the cool, painfully thin air of the altiplano – where walking even fifty yards leaves a buzzing in the ears and a knot of nausea in the stomach – for the sub-tropical heat of the valley floor. A crazy switchback of tarmac which hurls the traveller more than three thousand metres down the mountainside into a coca-growing fastness.

Assuming you survive the journey – and the occasional roadside wreaths and primitive shrines are testimony to those who have not – you can get your first lesson in narco economics by just looking around. Stretching up towards a cobalt-blue sky, terrace after terrace of stubby bushes carrying the Huanaco leaf – known to botanists as erythroxylum coca. The proportion of cocaine to other alkaloids in this strain of leaf is the highest in South America. In 1985, before the Americans began the first of two intensive and controversial anti-cocaine operations in the Andean countries, the peasant farmers, the *campesinos*, could get $360 for every hundred pounds of leaves they sold. With the right chemicals, the end product of this trade would be one pound of cocaine hydrochloride. Retail price in the UK: £30,000.

At a roadside stall selling banana and papaya juice and bags of dried coca leaves for 2,000 pesos a bag – about seventy pence – a buccaneering businessman called Jorge Petit enlightened me about this mysterious product, coca.

Petit came to Las Yungas nearly forty years ago from his native Germany and when I met him, he was ranching 360,000 acres of land. He was clearly wealthy. Two days earlier, I had been entertained on his spacious motor launch on Lake Titicaca, where the Incas once built their temples. He clearly knew about the many ways in which cocaine corruption had spread its tentacles throughout his adopted country and told me of an acquaintance who had recently returned from Japan having successfully negotiated to take over a car-dealing franchise. Not because he had fallen in love with their vehicles but because he urgently needed a front for laundering grubby narco dollars.

'Frankly,' Mr Petit confided, 'there are parts of this land where the drugs mafia carries far more weight than the military or the police. The civil guards go on patrol with 1942 carbines and a dozen cartridges between six of them. They are up against people with M16 assault rifles and M6 machine guns. And whatever the brave words of politicians, nothing speaks louder in Bolivia than money.'

Indeed, it is said that in the mid-eighties, one of the country's most powerful cocaine barons offered to pay off the entire national debt in return for immunity from prosecution. And as Jorge Petit explained, the raw material which made such overweening ambition realisable was within touching distance of us: 'The coca bush has no rival. You plant in January and with very little effort, the first crop arrives in November. Even a moderate coca-growing area will yield three crops a year. In Chapare province, they are getting five crops.

'By contrast, if you planted coffee (which is what the Western-backed aid projects have been attempting to persuade the *campesinos* to do) you would have to wait three years for the first crop – and expect to break your back just harvesting that. So, tell me where the incentive is to plant anything but coca?'

Two days after leaving Las Yungas, I travelled in a twelve-seater twin Otter aircraft over the snow-tipped spines of the Andes to the town of Tingo Maria in Peru. Tingo Maria is the Tombstone, Arizona of Peru. These are the badlands where life is far, far cheaper than cocaine. Shortly before, nineteen men working on a crop eradication project funded by the US Drug Enforcement Administration were machine-gunned to death near here, their bodies left by the roadside for days as a terrible warning.

The upper Huallaga Valley is Peru's chief contribution to

Western society – coca production on a gargantuan scale. It is also a key staging post on the cocaine trail. And from the air, the expression takes on a literal meaning as you look down on the infamous jungle highway which runs along the edge of the eastern Andes. The road belongs indisputably to the narco gangsters in their four-wheel drives. (The car dealers in Tingo Maria outsell those in Lima on the strength of their patronage.) As the Otter dips down towards the town, you can see that it is little more than a dusty clearing in the jungle. What semblance of law exists here is administered by the Guardia Civil, who, like their counterparts in Bolivia, are woefully ill-equipped and undermanned. But the fight against the traffickers is mainly borne by the army's elite Condor squads, and I am here to accompany one on an operation to find and destroy a clandestine landing strip deep in the jungle.

A thirty-minute ride by Bell helicopter from Tingo Maria is a revelation. The vegetation is so dense that, from the ground, it would be quite impossible to detect anything at all. From the air, though, it becomes apparent that the words 'landing strip' hardly do justice to some of the concrete runways which have been hewn from the jungle. Some are a thousand or twelve hundred metres long, with lighting, for night arrivals, which would not disgrace an international airport.

Two weeks before, a military surveillance mission overflying a section of territory further north spotted a formidable complex of buildings sheltering beneath the jungle canopy. At ground level, the soldiers uncovered a fully automatic coca-processing plant powered by an eighty kilowatt generator. It was newly installed and hadn't begun operating. At full capacity, chemists working around the clock would have been able to churn out two tons of cocaine paste every week. Beside the laboratory was an armoury containing revolvers, rifles, machine-guns, grenades and anti-tank rockets. Fortunately for the Condor squad, the site was deserted. In different circumstances it could have been a suicide mission.

In half an hour, we spot fifteen covert landing strips and the commander decides to demonstrate how the army deals with them. It has to be said that it is not an impressive display. Forget smart bombs and laser-guided rocket technology, this is destruction by hand and it is agonisingly slow. For three hours, the soldiers take turns to smash the top surface of the runway with pickaxes so that they can dig craters in it. Eventually, three holes each about four feet deep have been gouged from the rough-hewn concrete. The holes are stuffed with sticks of dynamite which are packed around with loose stones. Then, a moment bordering on farce. Having laid the charges and fixed the fuses, the captain overseeing the work detail suddenly becomes aware that he has nothing with which to light them. Oaths are exchanged and eyeballs roll heavenwards. The Condor commander – a bulky figure, sweating in his army fatigues, who has a reputation for demanding sexual favours from his smooth-faced, teenage bodyguards – looks thunderous. The tension is palpable. Fortunately, a cigarette lighter is found and we beat a hasty retreat.

As the Bell's rotor blades power us skywards, we get a bird's eye view of the explosions. A violent geyser of chippings marks each spot where the dynamite has bitten out chunks of the strip. We wheel away towards Tingo Maria, leaving funnels of grey smoke lingering in the breezeless air. It looks spectacular. In reality, it is a gnat's bite. The traffickers will have the runway in full working order again within forty-eight hours. The cocaine production line won't register the hiccup at all.

Across the Equator, in the port of Guayaquil on the Pacific coast of Ecuador, I learn of recent aid from Britain which has helped supply the anti-narcotics police with two Land Rovers and eight Zodiac patrol boats. The boats will attempt to intercept the shipments of cocaine paste and precursor chemicals which are dispatched along the network of jungle waterways to be processed into hydrochloride powder in the production plants dotted throughout the Amazon basin. But however much they intercept, it won't be enough.

After three weeks trailing the precious cargo northwards, I am running out of continent. But no understanding of the profile of this drug would be complete without passing a few tense days in Colombia. This, after all, is where Cocaine Inc. has its corporate headquarters – and the bloody boardroom rivalry between the cartels of Medellin and Cali makes even the fratricide of the Five Families in the United States look like a minor tiff. But that rivalry has been a godsend to agencies like the US Drug Enforcement Administration. Informants from both sides have leaked valuable intelligence on the other, paving the way for arrests and seizures of cocaine bound for the US and Europe. Ironically, Escobar's death may well be a setback. He was the greatest single obstacle to a rapprochement between the cartels. Now, there are signs that without his presence, the divisions may be healed in the unending pursuit of narco profits.

In London, Manchester, New York or Miami, even in Kingston – wherever I have investigated the crack trade – it is usually difficult, often impossible, to track the route along which the cocaine has travelled before it reaches the streets in rock form. In Colombia, it is sometimes easier to make the connection. Here, I was told about an ambitious dealer from Cali called Mario Villabona who, in the mid-1980s, worked on a strategy to extend the cartel's reach into the United States beyond its base in Miami. Harassment by the DEA in Florida had made it advisable to scout for new territory but there were economic as well as geographic considerations. The US market was glutted with Colombian cocaine and the price was falling.

The cartels needed to find new customers and Villabona was the first to spot the enormous potential of the black ghettoes. He moved to Los Angeles and forged an alliance with the notorious street gangs which already controlled the distribution of drugs like PCP (a hallucinogen often known as Angel Dust).

Very soon, Villabona was importing a ton of cocaine into Los Angeles every month and dozens of 'rock' houses, where the drug was converted into smokeable form for $25 a hit, appeared all over south central LA. And southern California was just the beginning. One of the street gangs, the Crips, was beginning to expand its operations beyond the West Coast and had made contact with an enterprising black American called Rayful Edmund III. Edmund, from Washington, had set himself the goal of building the most powerful drugs operation in the capital and the key was buying the powder in bulk for conversion to crack.

By 1988, Edmund had realised his ambition, on the strength of Cali cocaine supplied by Villabona. In just one month, Edmund imported 750 kilos of cocaine from Los Angeles at $17,500 a kilo. Despite the vast cost, his profit, when it was converted and sold as phials of crack, was spectacular – and Edmund was only twenty-three!

He prospered until April 1989, when a highway patrol officer stopped a van containing 500 kilos of cocaine, stamped with a scorpion, the trademark of the Cali cartel. The van was traced to Edmund and not long after his arrest, Villabona was picked up in a 'sting' operation. But by then, he was expendable. The Cali cartel was on its way to domination of the US market.

Much of my time in Colombia has been spent anxiously checking the body count. Twenty-five murders in Medellin in one weekend. 'Routine,' says a policeman. Of more alarming interest to me, another journalist has been killed in Cali. 'That makes twenty-two in the last ten years,' says the cop. 'Bad country for *periodistas*!' But if cocaine is an evil child, this is its womb. Where better to watch its delivery into the world?

The northernmost tip of Colombia is the Guajira peninsula. It is a desolate chunk of territory which juts into the Caribbean Sea like an outstretched arm. At its narrowest point, the Guajira tapers to some thirty miles across – a featureless piece of rock which has left civilisation far behind and is inhabited by Indians and smugglers. Its flat expanse is the perfect launch pad – for a billion pound delivery service which connects this remote corner of South America with the Caribbean islands and ultimately, the United States and Europe.

I wanted to know exactly how the cocaine run worked. And for that, I went to an American who has worked for a US government agency in the Caribbean, Mexico and South Florida since 1982. He spoke slowly in an Alabama drawl, pulling fitfully on slim cheroots. His eyes were wary from a decade spent standing guard at America's back door. And the price of his information was complete anonymity. So we will call him Ray.

'The Guajira is like one big landing strip. It is so remote that the police rarely penetrate, certainly not as far as the coast. So the smugglers, the *contrabandistas*, have a free run. Once the cocaine powder has been taken to a designated airfield, the pilots take over.

'These guys are mainly Americans who live either in the Caribbean or the southern United States. In the early days, the best of them were Vietnam vets. You know the type. Unable to readjust to civilian life. Away from the job market too long. That old Nam adrenalin still rushing through the veins and needing regular shots of adventure.

'But most of the pilots now are younger, just mercenaries really, looking for an easy dollar. And it's pretty good dough.

Thirty thousand bucks plus expenses per run. Not bad for four or five hours' effort!'

So here's how it works. Chuck or Cliff or whatever his name is brings in his Cessna 210 to an agreed airstrip. He is really little more than a glorified, if well-paid, taxi driver. Following the longitude and latitude directions and arriving when he's instructed – invariably at night. He sleeps under the plane and rises at dawn to supervise the loading of the cargo and the refuelling. The Cessna is fitted with an extended bladder fuel tank which will easily carry it the 450 miles to the islands of the western Caribbean. An average payload will be between 900 and 1100 pounds of cocaine. Assuming all goes smoothly, the flying time should be about four hours. If the pilot intends to land his cargo, he will fly solo. But increasingly, the cocaine is dropped from the air, so a second person known as a 'kicker' is needed to throw the bundles out from the tail of the plane.

Ray again: 'We know from the wash-ups around the south coast of Haiti and the Dominican Republic, the hundreds of islands east of Puerto Rico and even off the Bahamas and the Florida Keys that the favoured method tends to be the air drop.

'The coke comes in bundles of twenty to thirty kilos. Each one is heavily wrapped in plastic and burlap to make them buoyant in water. And they will be picked up by fishing boats or forty-foot pleasure craft.'

Bundles of plastic and burlap hurled down into the vastness of the ocean may seem a perilously haphazard method of delivering such valuable cargo. But the traffickers have enlisted technology to ensure that the rate of loss is kept to acceptable levels.

'These boats carry a great device called a GPS – stands for Global Positioning Satellite. It is about the size of a tape recorder. It costs no more than a thousand dollars and it is perfectly legal. It is a navigational aid which feeds off some twenty-five military-launched satellites around the globe. And, boy, is it something. Your pick-up point may be no bigger than a pin-head but this baby will home in on the exact longitude and latitude, no sweat.'

Who knows how much cocaine powder leaves the Guajira peninsula every week? Before the US market became saturated, it must have been at least 500 kilos, maybe more. With such a blizzard pouring northwards, the snow fluttering down over the Caribbean leaves behind an ugly slush in the form of addiction, corruption and murder. It is the Medellin curse which has already weakened governments throughout South America. The cartel would like to do the same to the fragile economies of the Caribbean.

But even the Colombians are wary of getting too closely involved with the Jamaicans. They have had too many bad experiences. Ray again: 'We had a recent case where the Medellin Mafia contracted to ship four hundred kilos of cocaine to the New York market – with Jamaica to be used as the trans-shipment point. I say "contracted" but there ain't no bits of paper in these transactions. No estimates or receipts. Just "thieves' honour".

'The four hundred ki arrived by air drop near Montego Bay and the deal was that the local boys would stash it for a few days while the Colombians negotiated with their buyers in the States over the sale price. In return, the Jamaicans were to get five kilos to keep.

'But, of course, they got greedy with all this lovely powder in their hands, and they decided to hold onto seventy-five. Now, if anyone else had ripped the Medellin off to the tune of seventy-five ki, there would have been mayhem. Blood all over the place. But the cartel are businessmen and they know that even their level of violence don't scare the Jamaicans.

'So they just put this one down to experience and backed

away. And the "missing" coke? That was split into one and two kilo amounts and body carried to the US and Britain. It must have all ended up as crack. Someone made a hell of a profit there for doing damn all.'

The unpredictability and violence of the Jamaican underworld explains why the Colombian cartels have preferred, wherever possible, to control the cocaine distribution into the United States themselves. But when the limitless dollar potential of the drug first became apparent, the Jamaicans were sitting on two assets which suggested that no-one was going to be able to prevent them grabbing a slice of the action.

Firstly, the island's geographical position, midway between Colombia and the beckoning market of South Florida made it a natural trans-shipment point. And secondly, a number of Jamaican dealers had already developed successful operations smuggling marijuana into the United States. With the stash houses, the routes and the customer base firmly established, it was relatively easy to start pushing cocaine along the same pipeline.

Ironically, it was the US government which provided the impetus for the invasion of its own territory by the new and much more corrosive drug. The arrival in power in Jamaica of Edward Seaga in 1980 led to much closer ties with the Americans and in the early eighties, generous aid from Washington paid for a big drug eradication programme. All over Jamaica, the fields of ganja, which had virtually kept the economy afloat as a major cash crop in the 1970s (and, incidentally, which paid for many of the US-made weapons imported to give muscle to the political gangs), came under attack from chemical sprays. The drug and crime agencies in the US sat back and congratulated themselves on a devastating strike against the traffickers. But with their obsession about marijuana and heroin, they utterly failed to anticipate that another drug posed a far more dangerous threat to the society they were seeking to protect.

There are two principal gateways which the United States is desperately fighting to defend against the drug traffickers. One is the land border with Mexico. The other is the waters off the Florida Keys.

Some 70 per cent of the cocaine entering the US now comes through Mexico. It's known as 'The Jump' – getting the contraband across the border. Perhaps half a dozen trafficking groups act as conduits for the drug, but the most powerful is a cartel based in Sinaloa state on the Pacific coast. It operates from Central America to California as a distribution agent for the Colombian Mafia. The scale of its ambition can be measured by the construction of a 1500-foot tunnel, complete with air conditioning, to ferry cocaine between Tijuana and Otay Mesa in California. Another tunnel – also discovered – came out near Douglas, Arizona.

The alleged head of the cartel, Joaquin Guzman Locra, nicknamed El Chapo (The Short One) was captured in the summer of 1993 after a shootout with rival traffickers in which a Roman Catholic Cardinal and five others were killed. The Mexican cocaine barons may not yet be as addicted to violence as their Colombian mentors – but they are learning fast.

At sea, there is also a vicious struggle for supremacy going on, with cocaine as the prize. The battleground is the Florida Keys, a necklace of tiny islands curling southwestward from the tip of the Florida peninsula. The narrow creeks and channels, thick with mangrove roots, have absorbed the scent of generations of treachery and intrigue. Elizabethan buccaneers, the colonial privateers of the nineteenth century, French pirates and Confederate gun-runners and Second World War German U-Boats have all left their imprint here. Somehow, it seems appropriate that the tradition is being maintained in the stealthy confrontations between smugglers and law enforcers.

In the blackness of a spring night – at one o'clock in the morning – a Marine Patrol of the Metro-Dade County Police is barrelling along the shoreline, heading for Cesar's Creek in the Keys. There is good intelligence that something big is going down, that a large consignment of cocaine is on its way. There are three boats in the patrol. Two are Magnums – light-draft nineteen-footers, which ride low in the water as sleek as sharks. The third is a Bertram, a twenty-eight-foot custom cruiser, with a square well dock and step-down forward cabin, topped by a flying bridge.

On board one of the Magnums, Mike Krutulis, one of the boaters – as the police refer to themselves – is stashing a shoulder weapon into a large nylon bag. It is a Ruger Mini 14, a powerful semi-automatic. But it won't frighten too many of the 'enemy'.

Mike: 'The dopers have the real firepower. We've confiscated fifty-calibre machine guns, grenade launchers, Uzis and M16s. These guys are playing for high stakes and they sure know it. Thank God, they are far more likely to use the weapons on other dopers than against the cops.'

His colleague, Bobby Hegg, grimaces, and explains why: 'Fact is they ain't scared of us. Why should they be? With the kind of money they got, they can jump a million dollar bail without thinking about it. They're in and out while we're still writing the O and I report.

'They're like tourists you know. You bust them carrying a coupla mil in uncut coke and they figure they'll spend the night in Miami – only in jail instead of the Hilton. Next morning, they're on their way back to the islands.'

The South Florida press dubbed one South American

trafficker the 'Snow Queen'. The court set bail of two and a half million dollars when she was captured. The bond was raised within two hours. And the same day she was on a flight to Bogota. In the same way, boats which cost a six figure sum to buy, are sacrificed with few regrets.

Mike Krutulis: 'It's called cutting your risks. When a doper boat takes off to make a delivery, it faces two main hazards. Once coming in. If we nail them, they're going to lose millions in dope. And once going out. If they try to take the cash out by sea, they risk losing it if we catch them.

'So if they think there's the slightest chance of being intercepted, they will run the boat aground, tear the guts out of her, let her sink, and head for the woods. Forfeiting the boat? Well, it's just a business expense.'

Any other business, though, would find it impossible to sustain the losses inflicted on the cocaine traffickers. In one night, a joint American-Bahamian interdiction operation, called Blue Lightning, netted drugs worth eighty-eight million dollars. In one night. There is no evidence, though, of any of the cartels having to call in the receivers as a result!

The Magnum is cruising a deep-water channel called Cutter Bank, when off in the distance, the crew spot what appears to be a large family cruiser flashing its spotlight around. It gives all the appearance of being lost. It could be vacationers, trying to avoid the treacherous inshore sandbars and mangrove entanglements. But the cops are suspicious. They stop briefly to pick up a Customs agent, which is obligatory if an international arrest is likely. Then they head for the cruiser. As they close in, Hegg raises a hand-held spotlight above the windshield and reads off the name plank, fastened to the hull: US Coast Guard Reserve. Three men wearing Coast Guard uniforms are standing at the rail.

Now, Krutulis and Hegg are straining at the leash to get

aboard. After all, the men of the Coast Guard Reserve are chosen for their familiarity with local waters. How could they get so hopelessly lost on Biscayne Bay?

'Where are you headed?' calls out Krutulis. The reply comes in a heavy Spanish accent. It is sufficiently vague to prompt further questions. The responses become still vaguer and the cruiser – a Custom 26 Formula – is ordered to stand by for boarding. The search doesn't take long. In the hold, the boaters uncover a stash of uncut cocaine. The three crew members – one of whom actually is a member of the Coast Guard Reserve – are arrested. Their boat is led off to the National Park anchorage. 'Score one for Metro,' says Bobby Hegg.

Could this be the 'something big' which had been rumoured? 'Doubt it. More than likely it was greedy amateurs looking to make a couple of bucks. Pros would never have gotten lost like that, then flashed their lights around until they attracted every cop on Biscayne Bay.'

Suddenly, the radio crackles with urgency. A Customs cutter has intercepted what appears to be a doper boat. The patrol gets close enough to shout instructions through a bullhorn. 'Heave-to and prepare for boarding.' The response is brief and to the point: a burst of automatic weapon fire, and the angry whine of an engine being gunned to full speed. There is little doubt that this is the one the law enforcement agents have all been waiting for. The doper tries to run for it, churning through the island channels at full speed. It is heading for the ebony expanse of ocean which represents its best chance of escape. But the more powerful patrol craft are closing fast on its boiling wake like a shoal of piranhas. They drive their prey one way, then the other. The doper twists and turns, its fantail cleaving the water at twenty-two knots. But it can't shake off the pursuers.

In a final gamble, the smugglers run their boat ashore on a

sand spit and take off into the night. Up and down the bay, lights flare as police, Customs, and coastguard vessels converge on the scene. An armed search party goes off in pursuit of the traffickers while the wreck of their boat is examined. It doesn't take long to find the contraband – the hold is a nest of waterproof bundles, each package containing two kilos of uncut Colombian cocaine. The haul is carefully transferred to police boats and taken back to Key Biscayne. When investigators have finished weighing and testing the packages, they are amazed. It amounts to 874 pounds of cocaine powder – the largest seizure ever made off the coast of Florida.

There is a postscript though, which puts the whole US anti-trafficking programme into context. Not long after first light, the two men who fled from the doper boat are captured. The isolated key where they ran aground has too few hiding places. One admits to being Puerto Rican, the other is a Cuban exile. And under interrogation, back in Miami, they reveal the unpalatable truth – that they have been acting as a decoy to allow a much larger shipment to be landed safely further up the coast.

An investigation by detectives confirms the story. A fishing boat carrying nearly a ton of Cali cocaine has brought its cargo ashore while the marine picket has been distracted by the action off Cesar's Creek. The rusting hulk of the boat is discovered where it has been run aground. Its contents are already on their way through one of the many arteries which send the cocaine flowing across the States. For the cartel, the sacrifice of 874 pounds of cocaine and an expensive boat – total value, perhaps three quarters of a million dollars – is an acceptable part of the balance sheet. The wider objective has been achieved. And, for the Americans, what is the price of what they call 'interdiction'?

Since Presidents Reagan and Bush declared their jihad on drugs in the eighties, the Pentagon's anti-drugs budget, alone, has exceeded a billion dollars. Air Force E-3 radar planes, US Navy Aegis cruisers, and the expensive hardware and technology of the Customs and coastguard have all been pitted against the traffickers. And the impact on the availability of cocaine in the US has been minimal. No wonder then that, finally, in 1993, the penny dropped and the National Security Council, in a classified report, conceded what many critics had argued for years – that the US is losing the war against the cartels. In an unprecedented admission of failure, the NSC admitted that world-record seizures of cocaine had had virtually no impact on the price or purity of the drug at street level, or on the number of cocaine-related hospital emergencies.

President Clinton's response was to scale down the anti-smuggling patrols in both the Caribbean Sea and the Gulf of Mexico, and Congress chipped in by slashing the budget for the US-funded joint operations in Peru, Bolivia and Guatemala. When the NSC report was leaked to the *Washington Post*, an unnamed State Department official said: 'We're facing a real disaster in South America.' The coca leaf at the beginning of the trail will flourish for a long time yet.

Epilogue

In December 1993, in Kingston, Jamaica, a man called Tony Brown explained to me why we in Britain should be apprehensive about the threat from the traffic in crack cocaine. Tony Brown knows a thing or two about crime. He was once a gunman for the People's National Party. When he killed a police officer in 1980, he became Jamaica's 'Most Wanted' man and fled the country, first to Cuba, then to the United States.

According to well-placed US sources, Tony Brown became a drug trafficker in the late eighties and they believe that he is part of a New York-based group responsible for shipping cocaine via couriers to England for conversion to crack. By his own admission, Tony Brown slipped into London on a false passport in 1989 when the heat got too fierce in New York. It is a trend which he says is going to accelerate.

'For Jamaicans, the American crack market is broken now. Many people are in jail, others have been deported, and the price of coke is not high enough to make it worth the risk any more. It is finished. The best shot is Europe. It is the only undeveloped area. It is still expanding – and everybody wants a piece of the cake. Over the next two or three years, you will see more Jamaican dealers coming to England because it is safer for them there. The police don't carry guns and the sentences are not as tough as in the US.'

All the signs are that he is right. Crack no longer holds the same potent appeal for American addicts as it did a decade ago, and the really big profits are to be made on this side of the Atlantic. At the same time, US prosecution policy has chilled the environment for crack dealers.

In cities like New York, successful pro-active strategies have been put in place to take the big operators out of circulation. The first stage is to target the smaller fry – usually the street dealers – and carry out arrests. But this is merely a means to an end, the aim being to persuade them to turn state's evidence and help trap those higher up the line. The key inducement is the well-established practice of plea bargaining – in which judges will offer big discounts on sentences for those willing to plead guilty and testify against others in the same organisation.

For those who refuse to cooperate, the penalties are harsh. US law treats crack differently from other drugs – including powdered cocaine. If you're caught in possession of just five grammes of crack, there is a minimum mandatory sentence of five years. If you are carrying a gun or have a prior narcotics conviction, the sentence is automatically doubled. The result is that there are people in US jails serving thirty or thirty-five year terms for offences which, in Britain, might attract a sentence of five or seven years. Inevitably, a disproportionate number of these offenders are black and it has been argued, with some justification, that America's draconian legislation against crack dealing is tainted with racism.

In the United States, the crack epidemic, which some say is on the wane, lasted for about a decade. Most patterns of drug behaviour tend to cross the Atlantic after a time lag of perhaps five to seven years. By that calculation, we in Britain are less than halfway through the crack cycle and have almost certainly not yet hit the bottom of the trough. With more and more crime connected to the drug trade, it is a bleak prospect.

This prognosis partly explains why this book was written. It may seem bizarre to use an epilogue to justify the preceding 90,000-odd words. But we live in an age of political correctness in which certain subjects have been declared unequivocally off-limits. One of these is black crime. And anyone who strays knowingly onto this territory prepared to challenge the received wisdom of liberal orthodoxy can expect to be subjected to a bombardment of abuse and scorn.

Even before the hardback version of this book appeared, I was warned that to write or broadcast about the Yardies is racist, that it helps criminalise black people in general and Jamaicans in particular. If you want to write about drugs, I was told, write about white traffickers, who sit smugly at the top of the pyramid. Or better still, write about corrupt cops who supply some of the street dealers with the crack which enables them to make a living.

That may or may not be true but it ignores the extraordinary level of violence frequently used by the Yardie criminals – and the way in which their methods have been imitated by many of the black British youngsters with whom they come into contact. That callous shootings and stabbings should be a routine feature of crack deals worth a miserable few hundred pounds, or a response to an imagined slight suffered at a dancehall, is itself a phenomenon worth exploring. Which explains why this book has more than its fair share of brutality and nastiness.

Blinkered self-righteousness masquerading as liberal concern is the stock-in-trade of the politically correct and one of the penalties of mounting a defence is that you are forced to state the obvious. After all, it should hardly be necessary to make the point that writing about the Yardies is no more an attack on Jamaicans than writing about the IRA stigmatises all

Irish people. Or, for that matter, investigating the Mafia casts a slur on every Italian.

Prejudice is in the eye of the beholder and those looking for it will find confirmation where they choose. But to raise the banner of racism in order to block fair reportage and analysis is, itself, disturbing, not to say, dangerous.

It is more than revealing that a few black commentators have recently dared to say in print that crime committed by black people against black people – usually related to drugs – has been growing with little or no discussion because of the argument over racism. And when I appeared on a phone-in programme on the Brixton-based radio station, Choice FM, to defend my thesis, a small number of callers (admittedly less than a quarter of those who were ringing to verbally lynch me) agreed that it was time to speak of such things.

The blunt truth, uncomfortable or not, is that Yardie crime finds a disproportionate number of its victims amongst the black community. Not to talk about it does a disservice to those struggling to live decent lives amidst fear and intimidation.

Ironically, this myopia towards the black victims of drugs crime is far more acute in Britain than it is in the United States, the home of political correctness. Where are the black civic leaders, members of parliament or opinion-formers who are prepared to make a public stand in this country and denounce those who terrorise their communities?

By contrast, consider the stance taken in recent years by one of the doyens of black awareness and self-pride in the United States – the Reverend Jesse Jackson. Amongst the rhetorical fireworks which Jackson tosses from pulpits and platforms all over the States is one especially manufactured for a black ghetto audience. He will ask, 'How many of you know a brother who has been shot by the Ku Klux Klan?' Invariably, no response. 'How many of you know a brother who has been shot by a white cop?' Another negative reaction. Finally, 'How many of you know a brother who has been shot by a brother?' At last, the jackpot button has been pushed and a growl of recognition pulses through the church hall or community centre, growing in intensity until Jackson halts it with the admonition, 'We have to deal with the enemy within.' Just so.

But, as we have seen, sensitivity about race cannot be disentangled from the crack story. In August 1993, Scotland Yard launched a new initiative to fill the void left by the disbandment earlier in the year of the Crack Intelligence Co-Ordinating Unit (a decision fiercely opposed by a number of officers).

At one stage, the new outfit was going to be called the Caribbean Crime Desk – until senior officers became horrified at the implications. Instead, it was adorned with the rather unwieldy title, The Drugs Related Violence Intelligence Unit. Although it keeps a watch on a wide range of criminals, a significant number of its targets are Jamaican Yardies and their black British neophytes. And over the last eighteen months, the new unit has been kept very busy indeed.

A flavour of this activity was given at a press briefing held at Scotland Yard at the end of June 1994 to counter suggestions that the Met was 'going soft' on drugs crime. The scene was set by Commander John Grieve, the Met's Director of Intelligence, a man whose earthy straightforwardness is a refreshing contrast to some of the vapid management-speak which often emanates from the top echelons at Scotland Yard.

It was Grieve who used the phrase 'thinking the unthinkable', in relation to the debate on legalising drugs, thus setting in motion a number of hares which are still running. And in reviewing the first year of the new intelligence unit, Grieve's description of the drugs market as 'violent, treacherous, paranoid and unstable' remains the most candid and accurate assessment of the murky world which this book has explored.

Grieve and his deputy, Detective Chief Superintendent Roy Clark, made it clear that halfway through 1994 the violence associated with drugs, especially crack, was taking a heavy toll on the capital. In one 39-day period, the Met logged 470 firearms incidents. On average, the police were dealing with two shootings every day and they estimated that several hundred crack dealers had access to firearms – which in practice often means automatic weapons including even machine guns.

It is no surprise then, though shocking nonetheless, that between the beginning of 1993 and the summer of 1994, there were thirteen murders and thirty-two attempted murders directly linked to the trade in crack cocaine in London.

And whereas in 1991, at the time of the arrest of Sammy Lewis, number seven area of the Met, North-West London, was topping the league for crack seizures, by 1994, the epicentre had shifted to four area, with Brixton, Clapham and Peckham within its boundaries. The number of firearms recovered in this area was also higher than any other part of London.

So, given the scale of the problem, have the law enforcers succeeded in keeping their heads above water? The approach of the new unit, in keeping with the current fashion in policing, is intelligence-based. To the uninitiated, its offices on the fourth floor of Scotland Yard could be the home of the DVLC or the Inland Revenue. All that's visible is a series of desks and computer terminals. There are only seven staff, some of them civilian employees. And their role is to collect and disseminate information.

But that information is the lifeblood of the operation. Streetnames, names of baby mothers, scars and birthmarks, car registrations, criminal activity in cities as far apart as Houston and Toronto, Dallas and Manchester – all this is amongst the million separate items of intelligence stored on database. Some of it may lead directly to arrests on the streets of London via one of the field intelligence officers who liaise between the unit and the five area drug squads. Other information may be passed on to Customs or Immigration, both of which have representatives in the unit.

According to John Grieve and Roy Clark, the unit's success can be measured in the twenty per cent increase in the number of drug dealers arrested in the first quarter of 1994, compared to the same period a year earlier. But the sceptics haven't been assuaged. 'You can use statistics to prove anything,' complained one officer. 'If the unit is so effective, how is it that a Yardie who's wanted for a number of serious shootings in Canada has been wandering unmolested around South-East London for at least six weeks? Intelligence is one thing but if the real hard nuts are not being taken off the streets, you have to wonder whether it is being applied effectively.'

To that extent, critics say that the initiative has duplicated some of the faults of the Crack Intelligence Co-Ordinating Unit. Strong on analysis, weak on enforcement. However, the adoption of a multi-agency approach, involving customs and immigration officers as well as police, deserves to be applauded as a step forward. And perhaps if there is one word which offers a signpost to salvation as crack takes a grip of so many communities, it is 'co-operation'.

In London's King's Cross, for example, the police, two local authorities, a neighbourhood association and a cluster of health agencies formed a ground-breaking alliance to cleanse one of the seediest corners of the capital. The area around the mainline rail station had long been a haunt of prostitutes but in the late eighties dealers in crack and heroin had begun to colonise the territory.

In late 1991 and 1992, the police carried out two operations, codenamed Welwyn 1 and 2, in which they arrested 174 dealers. All but a handful were convicted, many receiving jail terms of between two and seven years. But the law is not much of a deterrent when the pickings are rich enough, and for every one dealer banged up, there were five others queuing for his pitch.

At the peak of drugs activity in King's Cross, there were dealers clearing £2,000 a day without breaking into a sweat – £60,000 a month tax-free. A lot of this profit came from 'skanking' or cheating the customer. Half of the wraps supposedly containing crack consisted of chalk or even shards of glass wrapped in cling film.

Some of the dealers used prostitutes to store their supplies of crack, others preferred to keep the precious merchandise closer to hand. Police surveillance officers video-recorded a man who was known to be HIV-positive, removing rocks of crack from his anus and placing them in his mouth (which the police were unable to search under the Police and Criminal Evidence Act). From his mouth, they would be passed on to the customer.

By late 1992, nearly a quarter of all the crack seizures in London were being made at King's Cross. And that indicated that the special features of the area – the high number of prostitutes and vagrants, the many premises which stayed open into the early hours or all night, and the fact that law-abiding residents had all but given up on it – needed to be tackled.

In January 1993, Welwyn 3 was launched, but only after the police had joined forces with Camden and Islington councils and local residents and tenants associations to plan a strategy. During the year, 136 people were arrested, most for drug dealing and possession but others for soliciting. Eighty-five people were cautioned for kerb crawling. In March, a 24-hour fast-food shop next to the mainline station was raided. It yielded a substantial haul of stolen property which had come from local burglaries, as well as 22,000 new disposable syringes and a large number of drug kits, containing spoons, lemons, matches and other paraphernalia.

In tandem with the policing, the two local authorities began a campaign to break the 24-hour cycle of activity which made the area a magnet for crime. Late night opening licences were successfully opposed, extra street lighting installed, cleaning rosters adjusted so that rubbish no longer piled up at certain spots. Government departments such as Environment and the Home Office were sounded out about providing funds for longer-term renewal projects.

By the middle of 1994, when the chair of the King's Cross Neighbourhood Association talked of the area having been 'reclaimed from despair' it was not mere rhetoric. Something significant was actually happening. A few miles away, a similar transformation was taking place at the Mozart estate in Kilburn, a low-rise sixties development, once dubbed 'Crack City'. Here, too, a partnership between police and planners brought rewards – an arrest operation was reinforced by design changes which began to eliminate the stairwells and intimidating walkways where the drug dealer had been king.

If this was a fictional morality tale, it would end on such a note of optimism. But the script is being written by people for whom the word 'community' means nothing more than a group of like-minded entrepreneurs with semi-automatics and unfulfilled greed. Those who obstruct them may pay an awful price.

In March 1994, two police constables, Simon Carrol and Jim Seymour, were carrying out a routine licence check on a motorcycle in Brixton when the pillion passenger opened fire with a 9mm pistol. Carrol was shot in the thigh, Seymour in the back. They both survived.

Five months earlier, their colleague, PC Patrick Dunne, was

not so fortunate when he went to answer a call for assistance in Cato Road, Clapham. At the exact moment that he stepped out into the front garden, a gang of men was emerging from a house across the street, having murdered one of the occupants, William Danso. Dunne's yellow fluorescent jacket, illuminated by a nearby street lamp, made him an easy target. After shooting the policeman, the men 'ran off laughing' according to witnesses.

Unfortunately, it was a murder waiting to happen and the image of an unarmed community bobby riding his bike into a grudge shoot-out may be the douche of cold water which British law enforcement has needed. For one officer, Detective Constable Yozzer Hughes, with whom this book began, the murder of Patrick Dunne provoked an understandable reaction. 'There but for the grace of God.'

Index

A selection of non-fiction from Headline

THE DRACULA SYNDROME	Richard Monaco & William Burt	£5.99 ☐
DEADLY JEALOUSY	Martin Fido	£5.99 ☐
WHITE COLLAR KILLERS	Frank Jones	£4.99 ☐
THE MURDER YEARBOOK 1994	Brian Lane	£5.99 ☐
THE PLAYFAIR CRICKET ANNUAL	Bill Frindall	£3.99 ☐
ROD STEWART	Stafford Hildred & Tim Ewbank	£5.99 ☐
THE JACK THE RIPPER A–Z	Paul Begg, Martin Fido & Keith Skinner	£7.99 ☐
THE *DAILY EXPRESS* HOW TO WIN ON THE HORSES	Danny Hall	£4.99 ☐
COUPLE SEXUAL AWARENESS	Barry & Emily McCarthy	£5.99 ☐
GRAPEVINE: THE COMPLETE WINEBUYERS HANDBOOK	Anthony Rose & Tim Atkins	£5.99 ☐
ROBERT LOUIS STEVENSON: DREAMS OF EXILE	Ian Bell	£7.99 ☐

All Headline books are available at your local bookshop or newsagent, or can be ordered direct from the publisher. Just tick the titles you want and fill in the form below. Prices and availability subject to change without notice.

Headline Book Publishing, Cash Sales Department, Bookpoint, 39 Milton Park, Abingdon, OXON, OX14 4TD, UK. If you have a credit card you may order by telephone – 0235 400400.

Please enclose a cheque or postal order made payable to Bookpoint Ltd to the value of the cover price and allow the following for postage and packing:
UK & BFPO: £1.00 for the first book, 50p for the second book and 30p for each additional book ordered up to a maximum charge of £3.00.
OVERSEAS & EIRE: £2.00 for the first book, £1.00 for the second book and 50p for each additional book.

Name ....

Address ....

....

....

If you would prefer to pay by credit card, please complete:
Please debit my Visa/Access/Diner's Card/American Express (delete as applicable) card no:

Signature .... Expiry Date ....